renewe
author

Gl
Li
n

# THE MYSTERY OF THE
# PARSEE LAWYER

# THE MYSTERY OF THE PARSEE LAWYER

*Arthur Conan Doyle, George Edalji and the Case of the Foreigner in the English Village*

Shrabani Basu

BLOOMSBURY PUBLISHING

LONDON · OXFORD · NEW YORK · NEW DELHI · SYDNEY

BLOOMSBURY PUBLISHING
Bloomsbury Publishing Plc
50 Bedford Square, London, WC1B 3DP, UK
29 Earlsfort Terrace, Dublin 2, Ireland

BLOOMSBURY, BLOOMSBURY PUBLISHING and the Diana logo are
trademarks of Bloomsbury Publishing Plc

First published in Great Britain 2021

A catalogue record for this book is available from the British Library

ISBN: HB: 978-1-5266-1528-2; TPB: 978-1-5266-1530-5; EBOOK: 978-1-5266-1529-9

2 4 6 8 10 9 7 5 3 1

Typeset by Newgen KnowledgeWorks Pvt. Ltd., Chennai, India
Printed and bound in Great Britain by CPI Group (UK) Ltd, Croydon CR0 4YY

To find out more about our authors and books visit www.bloomsbury.com
and sign up for our newsletters

For my late father,
Chitta Ranjan Basu

# Contents

CONTENTS

But look at these lonely houses, each in its own fields, filled for the most part with poor ignorant folk who know little of the law. Think of the deeds of hellish cruelty, the hidden wickedness which may go on, year in, year out, in such places, and none the wiser.

Sherlock Holmes in *The Adventure of the Copper Beeches* (1892)

The police should get rid of the notion that anyone whose name they were unable to spell or pronounce is a foreigner, or that foreigners are most likely to commit such ferocious crimes.

George Edalji, September 1912, in the *Daily Mail*

I am an English woman, and I feel that there is among many people a prejudice against those who are not English, and I cannot help feeling that it is owing to that prejudice that my son has been falsely accused.

Charlotte Edalji to Sir George Lewis, 25 January 1904

Map of Great Wyrley and the surrounding areas, showing
the crime locations

# *Dramatis Personae*

Sir Arthur Conan Doyle – author, creator of the Sherlock Holmes
    mysteries
Jean Leckie – Sir Arthur's second wife

## The Edalji household
Shapurji Edalji – Vicar of Great Wyrley
Charlotte Edalji – the vicar's wife
George Edalji – eldest son of the vicar
Horace Edalji – second son of the vicar
Maud Edalji – daughter of the vicar
Elizabeth Foster – maid
Dora Earp – maid

## The Staffordshire police
Captain Hon. G. A. Anson – chief constable
Sergeant Upton
Inspector Campbell
Sergeant Robinson

## Village locals
Royden Sharp
Fred Brookes
Fred Wynne
Wilfred Greatorex
Harry Green
Frank Arrowsmith
R. Beaumont

## Campaigners

Justice Roger Dawson Yelverton, retired Chief Justice of the
    Bahamas
Sir George Lewis, leading criminal lawyer
Henry Labouchère, MP

## Author's Note

In keeping with the period of the book, I have used the old spellings for city names (Bombay instead of Mumbai, Cawnpore instead of Kanpur etc.).

Parsee can also be spelt as 'Parsi'. I have chosen to use the old spelling.

'Hindoo' was used generically by the British to describe all Indians, and not necessarily those persons who practised the Hindu religion.

Warning: animals are hurt in this story

# Introduction

The train pulling out of Birmingham New Street at 12.12 p.m. was not very crowded: a middle-aged couple, a young Japanese girl anxious to know if it would stop at Walsall, a group of young boys in their teens. The train was going to Rugeley, a small town in Staffordshire, an hour away. To the other passengers, busy on their phones, there was nothing remarkable about the train which would go past eight small stations in the Midlands. I was trying to trace the journey that would have been made by George Edalji, first as a schoolboy, then as an adult, on the same branch line over a hundred years ago.

George lived with his Indian father and English mother in the small village of Great Wyrley. His father, Shapurji Edalji, was the Vicar of Great Wyrley. George's mother, Charlotte Stoneham, had taken the daring step of marrying an Indian man at a time when interracial marriages were frowned upon. Shapurji, a Parsee from India who had converted to Christianity, had become the first South Asian to be appointed a vicar in Britain in 1876. George was born the same year. I was heading to St Mark's Church and the Old Vicarage, once the home of the Edalji family.

The rain slashed against my window as the train chugged through the semi-industrial town of Walsall, passing behind the backs of houses, car-repair workshops, garages, tyre shops and small industrial units. Soon we were out in open fields with sheep and horses standing patiently in the rain, as if watching the train go by. Once there were mines and collieries on this land. Shafts rumbled through the night bringing up coal from the depths. Boys as young as twelve would go down the pits following in the footsteps of their fathers and grandfathers. Horses and pit ponies were the mainstay of the area, pulling the cartloads of coal to the canals and railway wagons for transport to the industrial centres in the north. Sheep dotted the countryside, then, as they did now.

I was passing through a region that had provided the most sensational crime and subsequent trial in Edwardian Britain. The branch line running between Walsall, Bloxwich, Landywood, Cannock, Hednesford and Rugeley was the link to a series of brutal animal mutilations committed over a century ago. Every village had a connection with the story. Beneath the normality of my present commute, I felt I was entering what would have been the heart of darkness.

Looking out of the train window in June 1903, George would have seen two horses lying savagely attacked in the fields, their entrails hanging out. It would be on the platform at Wyrley and Cheslyn Hay station on that fateful day in August 1903 that he would be told that the inspector wanted to see him.

The arrest and trial of George Edalji for the alleged mutilation of a horse and the threat to kill a policeman attracted huge media attention. The dark-skinned prisoner, son of a 'Hindoo vicar' provided fodder for scribes to focus on the 'mysterious Orient'. George was sentenced to seven years' penal servitude. He was released three years later on parole.

However, he still remained convicted of the crime and was disbarred from working as a solicitor. It was then that he wrote to Sir Arthur Conan Doyle to help him clear his name. The creator of Sherlock Holmes swung into action. He took upon himself to be the conscience of the nation, and set out to point out in detail why the case against George Edalji was racially motivated, and that there had been a gross miscarriage of justice. He compared it to the 'squalid Dreyfus affair' in France, which revealed anti-Semitism at the heart of French society, saying there were parallels in both cases. In France, the miscarriage of justice happened with a Jew; in England it happened to a Parsee. His articles in the *Daily Telegraph* in January 1907 led to the case attracting international publicity. Conan Doyle had insisted that the articles be non-copyright so they could be used by other papers. Sold for a penny at street kerbs, the story was widely read, so much so that in Conan Doyle's own words: 'England soon rang with the wrongs of George Edalji.'[1] Eminent authors like J. M. Barrie and George Bernard Shaw backed George Edalji and lauded Conan Doyle's efforts to clear him of blame.

Letters of support poured in from around the world. Even Jawaharlal Nehru, an eighteen-year-old student at Harrow School at the time, read with interest the reports about Conan Doyle and George Edalji and wrote to his father, Motilal Nehru: 'I suppose you have heard about the Edalji case and the new phase it has taken here. Whole pages are devoted to it in some of the papers and you know what a page of a newspaper is here. The poor chap must have been quite innocent and I am sure he was convicted simply and solely because he was an Indian.'[2]

Conan Doyle's campaign eventually led to a pardon for George and the formation of the Court of Criminal Appeal in Britain.

I had always been fascinated by the case of George Edalji, and Arthur Conan Doyle's involvement in it. I had read about George briefly in books about Asians in Britain, but always wanted to know more. I wanted to know how Shapurji arrived in Britain, what made him convert to Christianity and how he became the first Asian vicar of a small village in the coal-mining area of Staffordshire. As they were the only mixed-race family in the area, I wanted to know about the racism the Edaljis suffered and how it had all impacted on George's trial. Conan Doyle had compared it to the Dreyfus affair, but unlike that famous case, captured in history and literature by Emile Zola's letter titled 'J'Accuse', and the subject of books and films, few today have heard of the Edalji affair. The story of the Indian man targeted for his race and religion in England was soon buried and forgotten, just another casualty of Empire.

I often thought about the family at the vicarage even as I worked on another book set in Victorian Britain.[3] It was the true story of Queen Victoria and her Indian servant, Abdul Karim, who quickly became a firm favourite and caused a storm in the royal court. She gave him land and titles. He introduced her to curries and taught her Urdu. The lonely widowed queen lived the last years of her life in an Indian dream with the handsome turbaned youth by her side. It was more than the establishment could take. Victoria's household and family closed ranks against Karim and conspired to defame him. Unable to destroy him while the Queen was alive, they swooped on him within hours of her funeral, and burnt all the letters that Victoria had written to him (often several in a single day). He was unceremoniously asked to return to India, and every attempt was made to erase him from history. Though their circumstances were completely different (Abdul worked in the royal palaces, and George lived in a mining village), and their personalities were a world apart, there was one parallel between George and Abdul. Both were victims of racism in a society that was ready to believe the worst of a foreigner.

At the time I was writing, Julian Barnes published *Arthur & George*, a fictional account of the Edalji story. It was shortlisted for the Man Booker Prize and I felt there was no point in trying to write anything more on the subject. Yet, every time I watched a repeat of a Sherlock Holmes drama on television, I would think of George Edalji and Arthur Conan Doyle. There is nothing quite like the calling of an unsolved mystery, a dark crime set in the English countryside over a hundred years ago.

In 2015 a small article in *The Times* newspaper caught my attention. It said that a collection of letters written by Arthur Conan Doyle dealing with the George Edalji case were to be auctioned. These were letters written by Conan Doyle to Chief Constable G. A. Anson, head of the Staffordshire police. The correspondence had never been published. It was a sign. There was hope of new material. I called up Bonhams auctioneers to look at the letters and made my way to their offices in Kensington. As I held the letters written in Conan Doyle's neat handwriting from Undershaw, his house in Surrey, and from hotels across Europe, I could feel the obsession he had had with the case. Here was Conan Doyle wearing the deerstalker of his fictional detective, trying to solve the only mystery that he ever investigated himself. It coincided with a period in his life when he was coping with grief and emotional turmoil. His wife, Louise, had passed away and he was going to marry the love of his life, Jean Leckie. There was guilt about having loved Jean for nine years while his wife was ill and dying. In a way, the case of George Edalji lifted Conan Doyle from his melancholy.

'In 1906 my wife passed away after the long illness which she had borne with such exemplary patience,' he wrote later. '... For some time after these days of darkness I was unable to settle to work, until the Edalji case came suddenly to turn my energies into an entirely unexpected channel.'[4]

Conan Doyle threw himself into the investigation, travelling to Staffordshire to meet the Edaljis and revisit the scene of the crime. His correspondence with Anson was combative. The chief constable was scornful of the famous crime writer trying to do the work of the police. Conan Doyle was convinced that the police evidence had been shoddy and that Anson was a racist. Anson's personal notes revealed his character.

I must have been lost in the letters when the staff at Bonhams reminded me – as politely as possible – that they were not a library. I felt a sense of panic as I saw all the other unopened boxes that I had not had time to look at. What if they went into the hands of a private collector, and I never saw them again. I had come so close to George Edalji. But luck was on my side. The papers were bought by Portsmouth Library, and few months later I was able to make an appointment to see them.

Within the boxes lay a story, not just of the trial of George Edalji and the investigation by Arthur Conan Doyle; it was a story that went back to when George was just a young schoolboy in Great Wyrley, targeted for being the son of an Indian. Page after page of hate-filled anonymous letters lay in the boxes, directed at the family in the vicarage.

From Enoch Powell's 'rivers of blood' speech to Theresa May's 'hostile environment', immigrants and outsiders have always been identified as the villains of society. British tabloids cranked up the public fear of thousands of potential migrants arriving on British shores during the 2016 Brexit referendum campaign, creating a toxic atmosphere. The Windrush scandal of 2018 saw the systematic detention and deportation of numerous black British citizens from the UK, many of whom had arrived as children from the Caribbean and lived in the UK all their lives. The leaked report into the Windrush scandal in Britain, published in 2020, concluded that the Home Office was 'institutionally racist', but the line was later deleted from the published report. Facts are still being rewired to hide an uncomfortable truth.

In 2016, the British prime minister, David Cameron, authorised Labour MP David Lammy to look into discrimination against black and ethnic minorities in the criminal justice system. The report, published in 2017, was severely critical. The Lammy report concluded that ethnic minorities still faced a bias, 'including overt discrimination' in parts of the justice system.[5] Even worse, where overt racial prejudice was declining, it was being replaced by problems of covert and unconscious bias, which was on the rise.

Black people made up 3 per cent of the population in England and Wales, but were 12 per cent of the prison population. Young black people were nine times more likely to be locked up in England and Wales than their white peers, according to the Ministry of Justice analysis.

In May 2020, as the world reeled under the coronavirus pandemic, the killing of George Floyd in the US city of Minneapolis brought 'Black Lives Matter' protesters on to the streets. The videos of the eight minutes of brutality led to a volcanic outpouring of rage and frustration. In the English city of Bristol, where slaves from Africa were historically shackled and shipped to work in the US, protesters dragged down the statue of the seventeenth-century slave trader Edward Colston and threw it in the harbour. Colston had been responsible for transporting 84,000 men, women and children from Africa to the Americas between 1672 and 1689. It was from the docks of Bristol that the slaves from West Africa were branded with the letters 'RAC' (Royal African Company), and herded on to ships for America. As many as 19,000 slaves died on the treacherous six-week voyage, their bodies cast into the sea to be devoured by sharks. The historical chain of oppression and exploitation that joined the dots between countries and continents over centuries was highlighted once again. With Colston lying in the same waters from where his slave ships had sailed, there were demands for other statues glorifying Empire and imperial power to be torn down. However, as the statues toppled, the culture clash began. 'Defenders of statues' arrived in London with swastikas tattooed on their chests to allegedly preserve British history.

The events of over a hundred years ago in Great Wyrley could have been taking place in the present. Miscarriages of justice in Britain have happened before – the Guildford Four, the Birmingham Six – to name a couple. Prejudice, doctored evidence and decisions made on circumstantial evidence have also occurred in the recent past. In 1998, the Macpherson Report into the murder of black teenager

Stephen Lawrence revealed there was institutional racism in the police force. In 1903, George Edalji was virtually sentenced before he had even walked into the dock.

~~~

The train pulled up at Landywood, waking me up from my reverie. The small station was nothing more than a bare platform directly connected to the road. St Mark's Church was a mile away. My Pakistani cab driver was curious as to why I wanted to go there. 'Are you going for a funeral?' he asked me, wondering why an Asian woman wanted to head to the church in the middle of a weekday. As we passed a curry house, I asked him if there were any Asians in the area. 'No,' he said. 'It's all white. The only Asian faces you'll see here are the taxi drivers.'

It would have been the same for the Edalji family all those years ago. Taking the service from the pulpit of the church, Shapurji Edalji would have looked down at a sea of white faces. As I stood outside the red door of St Mark's Church in Great Wyrley, I could visualise Shapurji in his priest's robes, greeting his parishioners after Sunday service. He remained Vicar of Great Wyrley for forty-two years. It was here that he died in 1918, months before the Great War ended. The last years of his life, he would have watched the young men of the village go out to fight in the trenches, many never to return. He never gave up the campaign to clear George's name.

I walked in the drizzle in the church grounds, searching for Shapurji's name among the gravestones. Finally, I found it. It was at the far end of the churchyard, in a corner under the trees; a humble grave without any large headstone. A plaque on the grave said: 'Sacred to the Memory of Reverend Shapurji Edalji, 42 years Vicar of this Parish. Died 23rd May 1918, Aged 76 years.' No other family member was buried near him. George had never returned to live in the village after his arrest.

The vicarage was just behind the church. I walked to the house where George had been born. His bedroom was on the first floor. He would have looked out from there over the churchyard and fields for twenty-nine years of his life. Next door were the church hall and the schoolroom, venues for many of the meetings held by his father, to rally support for his cause.

The church was preparing for Easter service a few days away, and the usual notices were up. I was reminded of a photograph of the young Edalji family standing outside the vicarage taken just before Easter in 1892. Shapurji is wearing a dark overcoat over his clergyman's robes; his wife Charlotte is standing beside him in a long checked dress, with a shawl around her shoulders and a small hat on her head. They are surrounded by their three children: sixteen-year-old George, wearing a jacket and a cap, standing next to his younger sister Maud, ten, who is perched on the steps. Next to Shapurji stands his second son, Horace, thirteen, dressed in the same style as George. They look happy, if a bit awkward, like any well-turned-out Victorian family of the day. But the dark clouds had already begun to descend on the Edaljis of Great Wyrley. The following decades would only get worse.

A few months after my visit, I found myself in the secure room of the National Archives in Kew, going through the Home Office files on the George Edalji case. Among the numerous documents in a box, was a small white envelope. Written on it were the words: 'Horse skin'. I gingerly opened the envelope. Inside was a strip of horse hide, the chestnut hairs perfectly preserved. It felt almost surreal. Once, a pony with this beautiful rich colouring would have pranced around the fields of the Great Wyrley Colliery. When it was attacked on that fateful August night, it would change the life of George Edalji for ever. I looked again at the piece of hide that lay in front of me. This is where it all began.

## *Prologue*

### Great Wyrley, 1903

The sound of a horse neighing loudly in pain and distress rang out over the deserted fields of Great Wyrley Colliery. It was a wild and windy night with the rain beating down in heavy squalls. A pony with a beautiful chestnut coat limped around the field in agitation. His stomach had been ripped open and a portion of his gut was hanging out. Someone had crept up in the dead of night, grasped the animal and slashed its stomach, leaving it in agony. Almost as silently as the assailant had come, he left again.

It was at 5.45 a.m. on 18 August that young Henry Garrett, on his way to work at the colliery, saw the wounded pony in the field, still alive at the time. Garrett saw it walk into the shed. It was collapsing quickly. He did not follow it in, but raised the alarm immediately. The police soon appeared on the scene. By 8.30 a.m. the veterinary surgeon, Mr Lewis, reached the spot. The wounds had been inflicted in the last six hours, he said, placing the attack between well past midnight and early morning. The pony was shot to put it out of its misery. Police removed a section of the hide near the gash and took it away for examination, and soon the little mining village of Great Wyrley was in turmoil. The news of the horse mutilation spread rapidly. The incident was not a one-off. For months, the village and surrounding areas had been living in terror as horses and cows were slashed at night.

The first of the killings had happened on 1 February 1903. A two-year-old colt was killed in Cheslyn Hay. Its stomach had been slashed. Within months there occurred another attack: a second horse was killed on 10 April.

With deadly intent, the killer struck again. In the month of May, a cow was mutilated. This was followed by the killing of a sheep and a horse. The police seemed to be making no headway in the case. The villagers felt under siege. Farmers locked their cattle at night and women and children were told not to walk alone after dark. The police patrolled the empty streets. It felt as if a curfew had been declared in the village.

And yet the killings continued. On 6 June, two cows belonging to Captain Harrison were killed. On 29 June, a horse belonging to Blewitt and Company was killed and another mutilated. In every case the animal seemed to have been attacked in the same way, and with a similar instrument. Newspapers covered the story of the 'Wyrley Ripper', the man who crept out on full moon nights to fields where horses and cattle were peacefully grazing, and slashed them with a sharp blade, leaving them to die a torturous death.

The summer of terror continued. Hundreds of pounds' worth of livestock was lost and farmers were in despair. Rumours were spreading around the village. Names of likely killers were whispered in shops and ale houses. No one felt safe. The Staffordshire police received anonymous letters saying there was a gang at work. The letters named members of the gang. They mentioned the name of George Edalji. The police urgently needed to make an arrest. A newspaper described Great Wyrley as the 'Village of Fear'.[1]

## London, 1903

In his first-floor office on Paternoster Square in the shadow of St Paul's Cathedral, London's top literary agent, Alexander Pollock Watt, adjusted his glasses and reread the telegram he had just been handed. A broad smile spread across his face. The elderly Scotsman banged on his desk in delight and let out a chuckle. The reason for his merriment was the sentence: 'Very well, ACD.'

Watt was a formidable force in literary circles, the first agent to work professionally on commission, charging his authors 15 per cent to negotiate deals for them. Many of the famous writers of the nineteenth century – H. G. Wells, Lewis Carroll, Wilkie Collins and Rudyard Kipling – had walked through his door. He was used to receiving letters from his clients either discussing forthcoming books, or thanking him for having one published. The shelves of his office were lined with signed and dedicated first editions that he had helped to publish. But not all authors are created equal.

Conan Doyle was one of Watt's most commercially successful authors. His fictional detective, Sherlock Holmes, had collected fans on both sides of the Atlantic, racking up a considerable fortune for both agent and author. The public, it seemed, could not get enough of the pipe-smoking, opium-addicted, dry-humoured detective, who could deduce at least twenty facts about a person within minutes of meeting him. They believed Holmes was real, they wrote to him to solve their problems, they walked around Marylebone looking for 221b Baker Street. Some claimed to have seen Dr Watson.

Yet, the global success of Holmes had begun to irk Conan Doyle. When a delivery of shirts he had ordered arrived marked to 'Sherlock Holmes', it was the last straw. Fed up of having his life hijacked by the character he had created, the author decided to end it all. To the shock of his fans, he killed off Holmes in 1893, sending his hero over the Reichenbach Falls in Switzerland along with his arch-rival Moriarty in *The Adventure of the Last Problem*. He wanted instead to focus on writing historical novels. But his readers would not have it. As his fans protested in disbelief and clamoured for more – it was said that City of London clerks donned black armbands to mourn their favourite detective's death – Conan Doyle was forced to bring Holmes back for another adventure. He published *The Hound of the Baskervilles* in 1902. He cleverly set it in 1889, before the fatal incident at the falls, keeping the Holmes timeline faultless.

It was an instant bestseller. American publishers were hungry for more. Fifty thousand copies of the *Strand Magazine*, where the mystery was published, sold in the first ten days in the United States. In the spring of 1903 he received an offer from American publishers. If he could bring Sherlock Holmes to life in some way, explaining the event at the Reichenbach Falls, they were prepared to pay $5,000 a story for six short stories or more. In Britain, his publisher, George Newnes of the *Strand Magazine*, would match that figure. It was a tempting offer, and Watt urged Conan Doyle to consider it positively. As the letters demanding the return of Holmes continued, Conan Doyle sent his brief telegram to Watt accepting the inevitable. Sherlock Holmes was alive and would return.

To the delight of readers, Conan Doyle penned the first of the thirteen stories that would bring Holmes back for more adventures. With characteristic verve, he wove the story to cover the missing years. In *The Adventure of the Empty House*, Holmes reappeared from the dead and told a stunned Watson that he had not died when he plunged down the Reichenbach Falls. Instead, the detective had saved himself. As he had watched Moriarty plunge to his death, Holmes had had an idea: he would pretend to be dead and use the time to track down Moriarty's partners in crime. Only Holmes's brother, Mycroft, knew the secret. With that, Holmes and Watson were back in action, as was Conan Doyle.

His readers around the world were ecstatic. The queues at railway bookstalls to buy copies of the *Strand Magazine* resembled the last day of the sales. 'It was as we suspected,' declared the *Westminster Gazette*. 'The fall over the cliff did not kill Holmes. In fact he never fell at all. He climbed up the other side of the cliff to escape his enemies, and churlishly left poor Watson in ignorance. We call this mean. All the same, who can complain?'

Sherlock Holmes had returned and that was all that mattered. Conan Doyle celebrated his comeback. Elite London clubs like the Athenaeum toasted his success. The champagne flowed freely and he was invited to join the Crimes Club.

The book was published in 1903, the same year that the quiet, hitherto unremarkable life of George Edalji would change for ever.

They arrested him on the morning of 18 August.

George Edalji had been on his way to work as usual, wearing a light three-piece check suit and a smart straw boater. He was waiting to catch the 8.45 train to Birmingham, when a local police constable came up to him and said he was wanted at Cannock police station. Inspector Campbell had asked to see him. He asked what it was about. The policeman said he did not know. Somewhere on the platform George heard a man say that a horse had been killed. He told the constable that he had important work in his office and would call on the inspector later. The constable asked him if he could not take a holiday for a day. He shook his head and turned his face away. Later, they said he had been smiling. He said he had smiled at something else.

That morning the police called at his house in the village of Wyrley and interviewed his father, the Reverend Shapurji Edalji, and his mother, Charlotte. They removed a coat, a waistcoat and a pair of shoes.

Then they called at George's office in Birmingham. The coat had bloodstains they told him, the shoes were muddy. Could he see the coat, he asked. No, they said. They had left it at the police station as they 'could not carry it so far'. They described the coat and asked him if he had worn it the night before. He said he had not. It was an old coat that he used only in the house and in the grounds. They told him they had found horse hairs on it. He said he may have picked them up while leaning on a fence. 'You must let me have your pistol,' the inspector demanded. 'I have no pistol,' he replied.[2] 'What's that? That's a pistol, isn't it?' said the sergeant pointing to a large railway-carriage door-key that was lying on his desk. Afterwards they said they were 'only joking'. Soon after, they arrested him on the charge of mutilating and killing a horse in Great Wyrley in fields half a mile from the vicarage. He denied the charge, saying he had not left the house that night.

On the way to the police station at Birmingham, the detective said: 'I know you very well, and you don't look like one who would do this sort of thing.'

He replied, 'I did not, but I am not surprised at this, as I had had warning.' By afternoon he was in a cold, white-tiled cell in the lock-up in Steelhouse Lane, where members of the notorious Birmingham gang the Peaky Blinders would soon be imprisoned. He, George Edward Thompson Edalji, twenty-eight, a solicitor of Newhall Street, Birmingham, the son of an Indian vicar and an English mother, was a prisoner of His Majesty's government.

In his book-lined study in Undershaw in the Surrey town of Haslemere, Arthur Conan Doyle was going through the morning papers. It was a fine day and the fir trees on his estate were glistening in the August sunlight. An item in the papers caught his eye. It said the son of the Vicar of Great Wyrley had been arrested on the charge of cattle-maiming. The vicar, said the newspaper, was a Parsee. Conan Doyle was intrigued.

# PART I

I

# A Baptism in Bombay

It had been a long journey for Shapurji Edalji from his birthplace in the bustling city of Bombay on the shores of the Arabian Sea to the small mining town of Great Wyrley in England. He was born into a traditional Parsee family in 1841.[1] Hymns from the Avesta, the sacred texts of the Parsees, were sung before his birth to ensure his mother would have an easy delivery and a healthy child. A lamp was lit when he entered the world and was kept burning for three days to ward off evil, while mother and child were in confinement.

His father was Doralji Edalji, a moderately wealthy merchant who interacted frequently with Europeans, but was firmly rooted in his Parsee religion and culture. At the age of nine, little Shapurji was formally initiated into the faith with the Navjote ceremony. A white shirt and a sacred thread were put on him and he was blessed by the priests. The family house in Colaba in Bombay was a busy place. Doralji was an active member of the Parsee community and Nawroz (Parsee New Year) would be celebrated with a joyful feast with his family and friends.

The Parsees were Zoroastrians who had arrived on Indian shores from Iran between the eighth and tenth centuries AD, fleeing from the persecution of the Arab conquerors. The name 'Parsee' was given to them as they had come from Persia. Followers of the Iranian prophet Zoroaster, their supreme deity was Ahura Mazda, the Wise Lord. They were keen traders and businessmen and settled in the port areas of Surat, Karachi[2] and Bombay on the west coast of India on the Arabian Sea. Over the centuries they adapted to the region, learnt the local language, Gujarati, and lived as a close-knit community. They followed their holy scriptures, the Avesta, worshipped in their fire temples and left their dead on the Tower of Silence. The Parsee merchant elite worked closely with the British, gradually imbibing Western cultural sensibilities.

The canny Parsee businessmen in Bombay had profited from the opium trade run by the East India Company, running ships laden with opium from India to Canton. The British found it easy to work with the westernised Parsees and allowed them to join the trade. By the mid nineteenth century, the Parsees had also started trading in cotton and other commodities, setting up the first of the textile factories in Bombay.

The Portuguese territory of *Bom Bahia* (Bombay), the seven islands that made up the city of Bombay, passed into British hands in May 1662 after King Charles II married Catherine of Braganza, daughter of King John IV of Portugal, and received it as part of her dowry. Charles II agreed to transfer control of Bombay to the East India Company and soon it became their base. The Portuguese had already established trading centres in western India and churches had been built in many areas in Bombay. By the time Shapurji was three years old, Bombay had transformed into a major seaport. It was a melting pot of religions and cultures: Parsees, Gujarati and Marathi Hindus lived side by side with Baghdadi Jews and Ismaili Muslims. Their combined energy made Bombay a thriving business and cultural centre. In 1924, the port city would build its most recognisable structure – the Gateway of India – to commemorate the visit of King George V and Queen Mary in 1911. The imposing Gateway on the Apollo Bunder would be the symbolic entrance point to Bombay for the viceroys as their ships docked in the harbour. When Shapurji lived in Bombay, Apollo Bunder was just a port area, with horse carriages lined up to take passengers home as they walked onshore from the sailing boats and dhows.[3]

Doralji was a pragmatist. Knowing the value of a Western education, he sent his son to Elphinstone College in Bombay, the leading institution of the day. The imposing building was designed by James Trubshawe and funded by a leading Parsee citizen of Bombay, Sir Cowasji Jehangir. The aim was to create a class of Indians educated in the English language, who could be easily absorbed into the civil service and help tackle the heaving files of the East India Company's administration.

Many of the students at Elphinstone College were Parsees. Educated Parsees would play a leading role in industry, science and politics in the nineteenth and twentieth centuries. Britain's first Asian MP, elected in 1892, was a Parsee – Dadabhai Naoroji – an alumnus of the same prestigious college that Shapurji would attend. He would be followed by another, Mancherjee Bhownaggree, born in Bombay in 1851, who would serve as Conservative MP for Bethnal Green from 1895 to 1906. The third British MP of Indian origin would also be a Bombay-born Parsee, Shapurji Saklatvala, who would win a seat for the Communist Party of Great Britain in 1922. Naoroji – who earned the name of the Grand Old Man of India – was one of the founders of the Indian National Congress in 1885 along with Sir Dinshaw Edulji Wacha, a classmate of Shapurji. Parsee women, too, were westernised and educated. Cornelia Sorabji became the first woman to study law at Oxford in 1892.

Doralji hoped that Shapurji – receiving the best education in Bombay – would eventually join the legal profession or the family business. When he sent his son to Elphinstone College, he would never have imagined that he would choose a totally different path.

The trouble started in June 1856 when a few Parsee students at Elphinstone College declared that they had been born into a 'false religion'. Four students wrote to the local Scottish Missionary Society that they wished to be baptised and admitted into the 'Visible Church of Christ'. The letter caused a storm. The families of the students accused the staff of converting their children and laid siege to the Mission House in Ambroli, which was headed by Rev. John Wilson, a powerful figure in Bombay.

Wilson was no ordinary missionary. In 1828, at the age of twenty-four he had been sent out to India by the Scottish Missionary Society to spread the gospel in the East. He was an Orientalist with a keen understanding of Hinduism, Islam, Buddhism and Zoroastrianism. Within six months of landing in Bombay he had mastered the Marathi language and delivered his first sermon. Wilson wanted to cast his net wide – from orthodox Brahmins to westernised Parsees. Unlike missionaries before him who had preached in English, Wilson took the word of Christ to the people in their own language, using Marathi, Gujarati, Hindi, and even Persian, Arabic and Sanskrit to preach.

Wilson was already fifty-two years old at the time of the trouble and considered himself an old India hand. He had clearly succeeded in his mission.[4] Elphinstone College had become a ripe recruiting ground for Christian converts.

On the morning of Monday, 16 June, the four Parsee students – Behramji Eersasji (eighteen), Darasha Rattonji (seventeen), Bhikaiji Ardaserji (seventeen) and Nassarwanji Babjobji (nineteen) – arrived at the Mission House with some clothes and books. A legal agent prepared a document which they signed. 'These Parsees came here today, and expressed their determination to make a public profession of Christianity ...'[5]

As the Parsee families rushed to the Mission House, Wilson called in British and Indian armed guards to hold them back. For three days the stand-off continued. At length they managed to persuade three of the students to return to their homes. Only Behramji remained firm. Three months later he was admitted into the Church, on 31 August 1856.

The conversion of Behramji had a deep influence on fifteen-year-old Shapurji Edalji. The teachings of the Christian faith seemed to confirm to him that everything he had believed in the past was pagan. His attraction to Christianity had put a strain on his relations with his father. When Doralji found him with a copy of the Bible, he took it away from him. But Shapurji was determined to get his hands on Christian texts. He bought Bishop Home's *Sermons* from a Borah Muslim convert. So obsessed was he, that he cut the book into small pieces so that he could smuggle it home and read it in portions without being noticed. He found a kindred soul in his Muslim friend, Sayyad Hussain, a student from a well-to-do and highly educated family, and soon the two were fervently discussing the teachings of Christ. Sayyad and Shapurji became members of the 'Juvelien Improvement Library', where they could borrow several Christian publications. There was one particular book that would have a deep influence on Shapurji: Dr Wilson's *Sermon to the Parsis*. He had it reissued six times, keeping it for ten days on each occasion, devouring the content. Soon the native committee of Elphinstone College noticed his reading habits. Offended by the Parsee youth who was repeatedly borrowing Christian books, they excluded him from the library.

Barred from accessing his texts, a distressed Shapurji visited Wilson at the mission on 17 and 24 June and confided in him. Wilson presented him with a copy of his *Sermons*, the book that had led to his exclusion. Next Shapurji requested a pocket *Testament*. Along with his friend Sayyad, he attended the services of the Scottish missionary. On 15 October he presented himself at the Free Church Mission House and asked to be baptised. Wilson readily took him in.

Doralji was not going to let his son leave so easily. Shapurji's brother went to the Mission House and pretended to be sympathetic to Christianity. He promised to give Shapurji complete freedom to follow his preferred faith if he returned home. However, Shapurji soon discovered that his brother had lied. Once back home, he was kept in virtual imprisonment for nearly a month. In desperation he wrote to Wilson, describing the condition he was being kept in. Then, defying his family, he daringly escaped from his home in Colaba and made his way secretly to Wilson's house. Finding the teenager at his door, the priest took him in once again.

Along with his other sons and relatives, Doralji battered the doors of the Mission House for weeks on end, asking Shapurji to return home. However the young boy stood his ground. He had rejected his Parsee faith, the sacred thread that had been put on him as a boy and the hymns that he had heard sung from his childhood. Doralji eventually gave in. Sayyad Hussain's family also relented and he and Shapurji enrolled in the college division of the Free General Assembly's institution, part of the Scottish Mission.

The friends were baptised together on 8 February 1857 at the Free Church Mission House at Ambroli in Bombay before a congregation of Indians and Europeans. Today, the grey stone Ambroli Church stands dwarfed by high-rise apartments on all sides. Just over a mile from Chowpatty Beach and Marine Drive, a favoured spot for city dwellers to savour the famous street food and enjoy the sea breeze, it was here that Shapurji would take the step that would change his life. Standing nervously before the congregation, he declared: 'I feel that I am a sinner, a great sinner in the sight of God. Sin has debased and defiled my soul. It has produced in me unruly passions, tormenting anxieties, a terrified conscience, a wounded spirit.' Referring to his fire-worshipping Parsee faith, Shapurji said: 'I found that by worshipping fire, the sun, the moon, the stars, the sea, my own soul ... all the animals both aquatic and terrene, the caves, etc etc etc, I could not be saved.'

Even at this early stage, there was an evangelist spirit in Shapurji's speech: 'I recommend you, my Parsee friends, as indeed many have done before, to take the Bible into your hands ... I speak this to the Zoroastrians ... So do you repent and come forward, and boldly but humbly confess the name of Jesus, the only saviour ...'[6]

And with that the fifteen-year-old received the baptism and was admitted to the visible Church of Christ, his 'Saviour and Redeemer'.

Estranged from his parents and relatives, Shapurji threw himself into the work of Christ. In 1864 he was admitted to the Free Kirk College in Bombay. He began his missionary work among the Warli tribes of North Maharashtra, working in remote areas. His health suffered in the searing heat and with the unfamiliar diet, but he remained committed. He embarked on a project to produce a Gujarati and English Dictionary to make the English language more accessible to his countrymen. Influenced by Raja Ram Mohan Roy, the Hindu social reformer, who had published dictionaries in Bengali and Sanskrit, Shapurji published a *Grammar of the Gujarati Language*.

In 1866, at the age of twenty-five, Shapurji left the shores of his homeland and sailed for England to train as a missionary, paying for his passage from the sale of his dictionary of 'Guzerate and English'.[7] He arrived at St Augustine's College, Canterbury, marvelling at the sight of the famous cathedral, and began a three-year training course for 'accomplished Hindus, Muslims and Parsis'. His aim was to qualify as a priest and return to India to continue the work of the Church. He never returned to Bombay.

The next few years, Shapurji moved between different parish churches. Leaving Canterbury, he travelled to Oxford where he was ordained. He received his first curacy in the picturesque Cotswold town of Burford.

Oxford opened up a new world for Shapurji. He read avidly in the city's well-stocked libraries and sought to widen his knowledge.

He found himself in the presence of intellectuals with deep links to India, who appreciated the cultural wealth of the country. He met Sir Monier Monier-Williams, Boden Professor of Sanskrit, Persian and Hindustani at the university. Monier-Williams was born in Bombay and was a specialist in Indian languages. He stressed that Christian missionaries should learn Sanskrit so they could have discourses with Hindu priests. Shapurji also met the famed Orientalist Friedrich Max Müller. At his request, Shapurji published a translation into English of the *Pandnamah*, an ancient Zoroastrian work on morality. Müller wrote a personal preface. It was an important moment for Shapurji to relearn the teachings of Zoroastrianism, a religion he had rejected as a youth, and appreciate its moral guidelines of truthfulness and charity.

The young convert was soon noticed in Church circles and was seen as a shining example of the success of the missionaries in India. In 1868 he was asked to speak about his experience at a meeting called by the Bishop of Oxford in connection with the Society for the Propagation of the Gospel in Foreign Parts.[8] Watched by eminent parsons of the Church of England, Shapurji spoke about the work of the society 'amongst the heathen'.

He told the gathering that he had been a fire worshipper, but now he hoped he could say, 'By the Grace of God, I am what I am.' The freshly ordained priest gave an account of the work in the British dominions, saying there were neither grammars nor dictionaries, and the missionaries had to learn the language without any of this help. There were now, he said, 200,000 native Christians in India, double the number of Parsees. In a speech delivered in slightly broken English, Shapurji detailed the conversion of aborigines, who at one time 'were so uncivilised that they ate rats, monkeys and serpents' and praised England for conferring great blessings upon India. 'She has given her peace, education, civilisation, language, liberty and the art of self-government,' he said.[9] He called on the Church of England to now confer upon India the still higher blessing of the Gospel of Salvation and to 'save souls'. His speech was reported in the local press.

Shapurji had once said that he hoped to return to his native city of Bombay and carry on the work of the missions that he was so passionate about. However, he realised that he would never be given a senior position in India. Church services in India were largely attended by English men and women from the colonial administration, along with a handful of Indian converts, and there was no precedent of a brown priest leading the service. Besides, his health had suffered while working in the remote tribal areas of Maharashtra and he took the decision to stay on in England. From Oxford, he moved to New Bury in Farnworth in Lancashire, seeing for the first time the cotton mills of the industrial city. Over the next few years he moved between different parish churches up and down the country, passing through Toxteth in Liverpool and St Levan in Cornwall.

It was his curacy at St Thomas's Church in Liverpool under Reverend Reginald Yonge that would take him to the next stage of his life. It was there that he would meet his bride-to-be, Charlotte Stoneham. In 1872, Charlotte travelled to Liverpool with her elder sister, Mary Sancta, and their father, Reverend Thomas Stoneham, the Vicar of Ketley, in Shropshire. Thomas Stoneham was a friend of Yonge from his undergraduate days in Cambridge. The visit would be eventful. Charlotte and Shapurji were immediately drawn to each other. Both were in their early thirties at this time. Shapurji warmed to the vicar's daughter with the gentle and refined manner, who took an interest in his work. She in turn was attracted to the Indian man who had faced such hardships to follow the path of Christ. She also liked his kindly temperament. For Shapurji, it was the chance to finally find love and have his own family in England. Though she was not Indian, he felt Charlotte was the perfect match for him. She was the daughter of a vicar and would understand his work. In some ways, it might even be advantageous having a white woman by his side, as he negotiated his career in the church. Like most women of that era, Charlotte and her sister Mary had been educated at home and taught to paint, sew, knit and embroider. Charlotte had a quiet determination, as would be revealed years later when she would campaign for her son after his arrest.

Charlotte came from a family of priests. Her mother, Mary (née Compson), had two brothers, who were both vicars. One of her uncles was Reverend Edward Bate Compson, the Vicar of Hillesley and another, Reverend John Compson, the Vicar of Great Wyrley. Charlotte's ancestors had served for generations with the East India

Company as soldiers, merchants and sailors. Her great-grandfather Thompson Stoneham lived in Bombay in the mid eighteenth century. His father, Abraham Stoneham (1693–1752), was a captain in the East India Company. One of her great-uncles, Abraham Stoneham, had married an Indian woman.[10] Apparently she was a maharaja's daughter, but the register of the birth of their four children described her merely as a 'native woman' and did not even give her name.

Many Englishmen from the East India Company took Indian wives, the most famous being Charles 'Hindoo' Stuart (1758–1828), who was rumoured to have had sixteen wives in his harem. Charles regularly bathed in the Ganges, wore Indian clothes and smoked a hookah. Others included the Resident of Hyderabad, Sir James Achilles Kirkpatrick, who spoke fluent Urdu, and married Khair-un-nisa, the Muslim daughter of a nobleman. After his death, she was seduced and then abandoned by his assistant, Sir Henry Russell, who later had a liaison with another Indian woman from Hyderabad, and fathered a daughter with her in 1815, naming her Mary Wilson. Mary was brought secretly to Britain after he retired and was raised by Sir Henry's friend, Major Robert Pitman.

It was less usual for women from the British Isles to marry Indian men. In 1782, an adventurous young Indian, Sake Deen Mahomed, left his job as a subedar in the Indian Army and followed his captain, Godfrey Baker, to Ireland. He lived with the Bakers in Cork and met a young woman, Jane Daly, with whom he eloped in 1786, after her family objected to the match. Deen Mahomed soon became famous. He wrote his memoirs in 1794, the first Indian to be published in English. He eventually set up the Hindostanee Coffee House in Portman Square in London in 1810, the first curry house in Britain.[11] It catered to the returning nabobs of the East India Company, recreating the ambience of India for those who missed it. However, it closed down in 1812, as it was too expensive to maintain. The enterprising Mahomed relocated to Brighton, where he started a bath house and became the first to offer Indian head massage and aromatherapy. Mahomed's brand of exotica was popular among the elite in the early nineteenth century. Even the Prince of Wales was a client. He described himself as the 'Shampooing surgeon to the Majesties', wore his Indian clothes with pride and rode in his carriage down the streets of Brighton with a dagger in his girdle and his pretty Irish bride by his side. Today there is a green plaque outside the original premises of the Hindostanee Coffee House in London and an oil portrait of Deen Mahomed in the Brighton Museum.

Deen Mahomed seemed to have faced little criticism for marrying a white woman, perhaps because he was successful and popular and worked in a refined circle. After the Mutiny of 1857 and the imposition of direct rule from Westminster, interracial marriages with Indians were frowned upon.

Charlotte's family were familiar with India, where their ancestors had lived and worked. Even though it would be seen as highly unusual to allow their daughter to marry an Indian man, they felt no prejudice against the Indian convert who was courting their younger daughter. It is also likely that Charlotte's parents would have actually considered it a very suitable match, as their daughter was already in her thirties and had no other suitors. Charlotte's elder sister Mary Sancta had almost passed marriageable age. The prospect of leaving behind two unmarried daughters was not appealing. Shapurji was well-mannered and sincere, and could have prospects. Charlotte's father liked the earnest young man from India and he invited him to preach in Ketley in 1873. When the time came, he unhesitatingly gave him his daughter's hand in marriage.

Charlotte and Shapurji were married on 17 June 1874 in St Mary's Church in Ketley, where Charlotte had been baptised as a baby. The church was beautifully decorated for the occasion. The bride's uncle, Reverend Edward Bate Compson, Vicar of Hillesley, performed the ceremony. Shapurji, who had no family in Britain, was supported by Reverend Yonge from Liverpool. The bride wore a gown of white silk, and well-wishers and relatives packed the church, with many standing in the churchyard outside to watch the happy couple. The wedding was described in the local press as one of the 'most noticeable weddings in the district for years'.

After their wedding, Charlotte moved with Shapurji to Toxteth in Liverpool, where they lived for a year. Shapurji took up his next curacy in London, joining Bromley St Leonard's Church in east London. Life in the East End was a far cry from the scenic shires that Charlotte was used to. For Shapurji, it was his first direct contact with poverty and the Dickensian world of crime and destitution. It was not to last long, however. As Shapurji had probably calculated,

Charlotte's connections in the clergy would be helpful. Her uncle, Reverend John Compson, the Vicar of St Mark's Church in Great Wyrley in Staffordshire, wanted to resign on grounds of ill health. He recommended Shapurji's name to the Vicar of Cannock who had held the perpetual curacy of St Mark's Church since 1868 and had the power to gift the curacy.

With Charlotte's family backing him, the path was cleared for Shapurji. The Vicar of St Leonard's Church sent references to the Bishop of Lichfield in whose diocese the parish of Great Wyrley lay. He accepted the resignation of Compson. There were other hopefuls for the post, and it is possible that the transfer of the position to Shapurji on the recommendation of a family member may have led to early resentment amongst the clergy against Shapurji.

Leaving behind the smoke-filled factories and bleak terraced houses of east London, Shapurji and Charlotte arrived in the small mining village of Great Wyrley. Charlotte was pregnant and the young couple were looking to make their future home. Compson had already resigned and he died shortly afterwards. Shapurji immediately took over the baptisms and burials in the church and worked through the Christmas period without a break. On 22 January 1876, Shapurji Edalji, the Parsee from Bombay, was appointed the Vicar of St Mark's Church in the parish of Great Wyrley. He would make history as the first South Asian vicar of a church in England. Through the ups and downs of the years ahead, he would remain at the vicarage, keeping his job till his death in 1918.

A few days after her husband's appointment, Charlotte Edalji gave birth to a son, George.

The vicar and his family were soon to find that they were not entirely welcome.

## 2

# Great Wyrley

The village of Great Wyrley was set in a mining and agricultural area of Staffordshire in the Midlands. Miles around the vicarage stretched fields sunken with coal shafts and collieries, where miners and pit ponies would work through the night bringing the coal to the surface. Bells would ring out from these mines calling out the end of shifts. Dotting the landscape were a few large farms. The area was typical of most areas in the Midlands, with low literacy rates and a sizeable working-class population prone to industrial accidents and health problems. Horses, pit ponies, cows and sheep were an integral part of the landscape. Disgruntled workers would sometimes take revenge on their employers by attacking their livestock.

Into this world stepped an Indian vicar with an English wife, a brown man to preach the word of Christ to a white parish. The number of inhabitants at this time would have been around 2,500. Constructed in 1845, St Mark's Church in Great Wyrley served the parishioners from Landywood, Cheslyn Hay and Churchbridge. Shapurji plunged into his work as vicar, conducting forty-six baptisms, eleven marriages and sixty-three burials in his first year.[1] The number of deaths in the parish was high. The vicar often conducted services for workers killed in mining accidents or those fatally injured in factories, mills and brickworks. The most painful job was burying the babies who did not survive after a hazardous birth, some leaving the world in less than an hour. He buried children as young as one, victims of extreme poverty. Of the sixty-three burials in his first year, fourteen were infants under two months, a further twelve died before their first birthday and thirteen died before the age of five.[2] The pattern continued into the nineties. Many of Shapurji's parishioners were those who sought the comfort of the church mainly at times of birth, death and marriage, as the daily grind of their lives allowed them little time for much else. It was the rich landlords and mine owners of the area who had a say in matters of the parish.

Criss-crossed by the Wash Brook, the village was set between the parish towns of Cannock in the north and Walsall in the south. To the north-west lay the village of Cheslyn Hay, where the first pony would be found dismembered in 1903. A short walk from the vicarage was the branch station of Wyrley and Cheslyn Hay where eleven-year-old George would board the North Western Railway train to go to Rugeley Grammar School. The city of Birmingham was thirteen miles south. It was where George would work as an adult. In the census of 1811, there were eighty-two families living in the village, of which fifty-one were employed in agriculture and thirty-one in trade, manufacture or handicrafts.

The Victorian era had brought with it the demand for coal for the factories and railways. Already by 1817 several pits were in operation. By 1860, just over a decade before Shapurji took over as the Vicar of St Mark's Church, the Wyrley New Colliery Company had begun operations. The Wyrley Cannock Colliery Company started in 1872 and was working seven or eight shafts before it closed down ten years later. The Great Wyrley Colliery Company opened in 1872 and remained in operation till 1924. It was the maiming of a pony at the last colliery that led to the arrest of George Edalji. In 1896, William Harrison opened a large pit known as Wyrley No. 3 which remained in use till 1956. All the killings would occur in the collieries and fields in this region.

To the north of the vicarage lay Gilpin's Ironworks, a factory that employed many people in the area. The neighbouring district of Churchbridge also had a few factory buildings for the manufacture of tools. By the mid nineteenth century, several cottage industries had sprung up in the area. On the north end of Walsall Road was a steam mill owned by Thomas and Edward Hick. One of the farms closest to the vicarage was High House Farm, where the Green family lived and where a horse would be found dead in September 1903. Other farms like Landywood Farm and Fishers Farm dotted the area. The combination of factories, farms and coal mines created a soulless atmosphere. Discontent against the factory owners and landlords often simmered below the surface.

Years later, while investigating the case of George Edalji, Sir Arthur Conan Doyle would write: 'The appearance of a coloured clergyman with a half-caste son in a rude, unrefined parish was bound to cause some regrettable situation.'[3] The white English mining and agricultural community of Great Wyrley would not warm to the Indian vicar. The vestry committee of the parish was dominated at this time by two of the main players in the Great Wyrley Colliery Company, J. T. Hatton, the leading shareholder in the company and D. M. Munro, the manager. Shapurji would find it hard to find a balance between caring for his poor parishioners and catering to the demands of the rich landlords.

The problems started in 1872, when the vestry committee took possession of the rights to the iron-ore, coal and other mines in Cheslyn Hay after the death of its owner Joseph Brown. This was done on behalf of the ratepayers of Great Wyrley. However, instead of benefiting the parishioners as they were supposed to do, the committee invested the proceeds in securities, and cut the parish poor rates.

When Shapurji became the vicar four years later, he was not pleased to see the committee's actions. His poor parishioners were his priority and it led to a direct conflict with Hatton and Munro, who kept pushing for the sale of the mining rights held by the parish and sought to acquire it for the Great Wyrley Colliery Company. Hatton became a prosperous landowner as well as shareholder.

There were further grounds for conflict. Shapurji wanted to reopen the church school at Great Wyrley, another action that set him up directly against the vestry committee, who opposed it on financial grounds. Shapurji was one of the trustees of the Cheslyn Hay National School and he wanted only teachers of the Anglican faith to be employed to impart religious education. This brought him up against the newly set-up United District School Board who wanted to take control of the school. When the situation became impossible, Shapurji decided to join the board in September 1886. He then offered to sell the school and return the profits of the sale to Lord Hatherton, who had originally donated the land. The understanding was that Lord Hatherton would then release the funds for the benefit of the parishioners. It was a slightly muddled plan and did not please the aristocratic landowner, who wanted to reverse his grant and take back both his land and the buildings. Shapurji then dropped the idea of the sale, and Lord Hatherton did not get back his buildings, much to his displeasure. Once again the reverend had clashed with the influential men in his area. Local politics were soon going to entangle the family at the vicarage.

The Edaljis kept mainly to themselves. Charlotte said later that they had limited finances, as her husband had no independent means of income. Since her husband was keen to give their children the best education, there was not much left to lead a social life. It may also have been the case that the family at the vicarage were treated differently by the villagers and did not receive social invitations.

Victorian England was not kind to immigrants from the colonies. Though there was a smattering of Indian students, mostly studying law, medicine and preparing for the civil service examination, they were a privileged minority cushioned in university halls. In 1873, the number of Indian students in Britain was estimated to be around forty to fifty. By 1900, the number had increased to 336.[4] Most students were from wealthy families from Bombay and Calcutta, and faced little discrimination. However, the Indians visible in London were largely the sailors or lascars who had travelled as cooks and orderlies on the P&O ships from the 1830s onwards. They were paid one-sixth or one-seventh of the European rate of pay.[5] The lascars lived in crowded tenements around east London. They often had liaisons with white Englishwomen, who were subsequently dubbed 'Calcutta Louise' or 'Lascar Sally'.[6]

There were also many abandoned servants and ayahs, who had been brought to England by their owners, and then discharged when their work was done. Often homeless, they could be seen begging in Trafalgar Square, unable to raise the money to go home. In 1891, the Ayahs' Home was established in east London to look after abandoned ayahs at 6 Jewry Street in Aldgate. Owing to growing numbers, the home moved in 1900 to 26 King Edward Road, Mare Street, Hackney.

The rich pickings of Empire had created landowners, wealthy merchants and factory owners. Aristocracy rubbed hesitant shoulders with self-made businessmen. Exhibitions like the Colonial and India Exhibition of 1886, visited by 5.5 million people, cemented the views of the dominant race and Britain's position as a global industrial power.

It was the belief in the 'civilising' power of Empire that had led to the arrival of the first Indian on British shores. The nameless young Bengali boy arrived in the summer of 1614 with Patrick Copland, a chaplain in the East India Company. Copland's mission was to teach the young boy 'to speake, to reade and write the English tongue and hand'.[7] The British, he believed, were 'civilising the natives' and the boy would help him to convert his own people.

The young boy caused a stir in London. As he walked down the streets, he would be followed by children staring at him open-jawed; women would watch through tiny cracks in their doors. Even Shakespeare alluded to the disposition of Englishmen to stare at an Indian. In his play *The Tempest*, the ship-wrecked Trinculo, on seeing the dark-skinned native, Caliban, says: 'What have we here? A man or a fish? Dead or alive? A fish! ... Were I in England now ... There would this monster make a man ... When they will not give a doit to relieve a lame beggar, they will lay out ten to see a dead Indian.'

After two years in England, Copland suggested that his pupil, who had picked up both English and Christian texts, be publicly baptised 'as the first fruits of India'. The Archbishop of Canterbury, George Abbot, agreed to the proposal. On Sunday, 22 December 1616, a few days before Christmas, a boisterous crowd surged towards the Church of St Denis on Fenchurch Street in London to see the Indian being initiated into the Church of Christ. It was a star-studded affair attended by the members of the Privy Council, the Lord Mayor and aldermen, the shareholders of the East India Company and its sister company in Virginia. The boy from Bengal was christened Petrus Papa or Peter Pope, a name chosen for his baptism by King James I himself. The 'first fruit' was thus deemed 'civilised'.

Between 1800 and 1900, the largest immigrant communities were the Irish and the Germans, the former arriving in large numbers in the wake of the potato famine of 1849–52. In the late 1890s, Russian and Jewish Poles arrived in Britain. Anti-Semitism and anti-Irish sentiments were widespread in British society. 'No Irish, no blacks and no dogs' was a common sign outside ale houses in the country.

The English were fascinated and disgusted by Africans in equal measure, turning them into objects of curiosity as they displayed Bushmen in circuses and fairs. The term 'noble savage', coined by the eighteenth-century French philosopher Jean-Jacques Rousseau, who stated that indigenous people were inherently nobler since they were closer to nature and had not been corrupted, found mixed traction in Britain.

Charles Dickens himself emphatically threw out the romantic notion of the 'noble savage'. The writer, who so poignantly captured the conditions of the workhouses and debtors' prisons in Britain, had little sympathy for those from other climes. He wrote: '[The Noble Savage's] virtues are a fable; his happiness is a delusion; his nobility, nonsense ... and the world will be all the better when this place knows him no more.'[8] He recommended that all such people should be 'civilised off the face of the earth'. In 1878, Rev. J. G. Wood published the book *The Uncivilised Races of Men in All Countries of the World* covering the Bosjesman (Bushmen) of Africa, tribes of India like the Nagas, and the Gurkhas of Nepal, feeding into the perceived notion of Western superiority.

The Anglo-Zulu war of 1879 led to a keen interest in Zulus, who were depicted as spear-wielding savages attacking heroic British soldiers. Among those seeking to profit from exhibiting them was the famous American circus owner, P. T. Barnum, who wanted to include Zulus in his freak show. He even offered Queen Victoria $100,000 to exhibit their deposed monarch, Cetewayo, for five years. Wisely, Victoria refused.

Nevertheless, Zulus were exhibited at the Royal Aquarium in September 1880, drawing large crowds. In 1899, a play called *Savage South Africa* opened at the Empress Theatre in London with fifty Zulus in the cast re-enacting the Matabele Rebellion. But behind the spectacle of the show came the creeping unease in London circles that the exhibition had led to liaisons between black African men and white women. It led the *Daily Mail* newspaper to campaign to close the 'Kaffir kraals', the replica villages where the Africans lived. Eventually, the organisers banned all white women from entering the area. When it was revealed that one of the African men, Peter Lobengula, had married an Englishwoman, Kitty Jewell, the disapproval was thunderous. Even the American press expressed their horror, a Texan newspaper reporting that the incident had revealed that allowing the 'little band of savages' into their capital city, had revealed to the English for the first time 'the seriousness of mixed marriages'.[9] White women were supposed to bear the future children of the Empire. Racial intermingling was seen as threatening the purity of the race, and white mothers who bore them as unpatriotic.

If the Africans were portrayed as barbarians, Indians too were seen in many sections of society as the savages who killed British prisoners in the infamous 'Black Hole of Calcutta' in 1756 and massacred men, women and children in Cawnpore during the Mutiny of 1857. The high priests of Empire literature, like Rudyard Kipling, reinforced the notion of the superiority of the white race and the civilising force it represented in novels like *Kim*.

Charlotte had led a sheltered life in Shropshire. She would have known that her marriage to an Indian man would not be welcomed by large sections of society, but perhaps she was not fully aware of how strong these feelings could be. Having married Shapurji, she accepted her fate. The daughter of a vicar, she moved easily into her role as a clergyman's wife, immersing herself in looking after her parishioners and being a mother to her three children. All the Edalji children were schooled at home by their parents. George started formal school only at the age of eleven, when he joined Rugeley Grammar School, Horace joined him when he was eight and Maud went to school in Walsall from the age of fourteen.

The vicar was determined to work for his poor parishioners. His stubborn streak, which he had demonstrated as a teenager when he converted to Christianity in defiance of his family, continued into his working life. The reverend was known to be a Liberal Party supporter, even though he did not play a role in local politics and elections. During the general election campaign of 1892, Shapurji lent the church schoolroom to the Liberal Party for a meeting in support of Sir John Swinburne, MP for Lichfield. He himself presided over the meeting, possibly alienating the Tory-supporting landlords of the area. It was going to prove costly.

It has been suggested that when the horses belonging to Blewitt & Co. were killed on 29 June 1903, the first tip-off to the police giving the name of George Edalji was made by a local Justice of the Peace who was disgruntled with the vicar. It was none other than J. T. Hatton, landowner and main shareholder of the Great Wyrley Colliery, and the member of the vestry committee who had clashed earlier with Shapurji Edalji.[10] Race, class and parish politics would weave a tangled web for the Edaljis over the following years.

# 3

## *Letters*

### 1888

It all began with the letters. The first of them dropped through the vicar's letterbox in September 1888. It seemed fairly innocent, a mere advertisement for a newspaper: The letter said:

Express and Star ½d per evening and 3d per week.
Will be pleased with an order. Publisher, 50 and 5, Queen Street, Wolverhampton.[1]

The letter was signed 'TH'.

This was followed by further letters, also plugging the subscription to the *Express & Star*, and also signed 'TH'. It must be a very persistent salesman, thought the vicar. There was really nothing to it.

The residents of the vicarage at the time were the vicar, Shapurji Edalji, his wife Charlotte, his sons George, twelve, and Horace, nine, daughter Maud, five, and the maid, Elizabeth Foster. To the locals, they were an odd bunch, different from any family they had seen before. The dark-skinned vicar, who spoke with a marked Indian accent, worked tirelessly looking after his parishioners, arranging services, funerals and weddings. Charlotte was the perfect vicar's wife, the epitome of a well-educated Victorian lady, who threw herself into charitable work and supported her husband. They had lived in the village for over a decade, and the villagers had seen the three children being born and baptised in the church.

George, the eldest, was a dark stocky young boy with slightly bulging eyes. Horace, the second son, had inherited his mother's fairer skin and looked more like an English lad than his brother. Maud, the youngest, and the only daughter, was an earnest-looking girl, who combined the features of her English mother and Indian father. The children could be seen playing together in the grounds of the vicarage. The family kept to themselves and did not mix much with other locals.

One day the vicar and his family woke up to see the front of their house painted with the words: 'The Edaljis are wicked.' It was signed 'TH', just like the letters they had received. A feeling of misgiving swept over the vicar. He cleaned the graffiti off his walls, wondering who 'TH' could be.

In December, as he was preparing for the busy Christmas season, several more letters arrived at the vicarage. Even their maid, seventeen-year-old Elizabeth, received one. It said she was a fool and charged her with the writing on the wall. The letter was signed from 'Thomas Hitchings'. She showed it immediately to the vicar. Not surprisingly, he too had received a letter the same day, with the same signature. The mysterious 'TH' was now far more aggressive in tone: 'If you don't take The Star the *Express & Star* newspaper, I shall shoot you with a pistol I have in my house, or else I will break your windows. I shall watch you and shoot you dead. I have resolved to give you another chance. I will find out if there is an agent in Wyrley you can get it from.'

The letters – with their underlying tone of violence – worried Shapurji. The family were concerned that the maid was also receiving them. Gradually, the letters sent to her became more hostile in tone and took on a racist slant. She was called a 'traitor and tell-tale' and the writer threatened to kill her when 'her black man' was out.

Elizabeth was terrified and went to her employers in tears. Charlotte was sympathetic and immediately told her that she could sleep in her room, which she shared with her daughter Maud. The sleeping arrangements in the Edalji house had changed when George was nine years old. Horace had been ill for some time and Charlotte had moved into the children's room to be with him. George had moved into his father's bedroom to make way for his mother. Years later, the fact that the vicar and his son were sharing a room would lead to aspersions and comments intended to taint the family.

When the letter-writer started carrying out some of his violent threats, it could no longer be ignored as a prank. One day the windows of the vicarage were smashed, and the frightened vicar called in the police. Watched by the curious and nervous children, two policemen – silver buttons shining on their blue uniforms – sauntered up to the vicarage. It was the first of many visits that Sergeant William Upton and Police Constable Daley would make there. They assured the vicar that they would watch the house. The letters stopped briefly, but resumed immediately when the surveillance was lifted after a few days.

The missives turned up everywhere: in the yard, on the doorstep and inside the vicarage. Finding them became like a game for the children. They were usually small notes written in pencil. On New Year's Day 1889, when the village of Great Wyrley was in a state of slumber after generous amounts of ale had been consumed late into the night in most houses, the maid announced that she had received another letter. The vicar noticed that the gum on the envelope was still moist. This led the police to think that it was an inside job.

The children had grown jumpy. One day George shouted excitedly that he had seen a shadow through the door leading to the hall. Charlotte ran out and found Elizabeth walking in from that direction. On the doorstep lay a letter written on a flyleaf from one of the children's exercise books. More letters followed in quick succession. One of them was addressed to George. It was written on a page torn from an exercise book kept in the vicarage. Another addressed to the vicar was found by George and Elizabeth together. The common factor in all the letters seemed to be George or Elizabeth. Both had access to the study as well the children's school books.

The police were called in again. As the family watched nervously, they took samples of handwriting from everyone in the house by dictation, including young Horace and Maud. They asked Elizabeth to write on paper and with chalk on the school blackboard. They declared that her handwriting looked similar to that of the letter-writer. The police then proceeded to search her trunk, and to the surprise of the family found some papers there in the same handwriting as the 'TH' letters. They declared triumphantly that Elizabeth was the letter-writer after all.

Two weeks later, Elizabeth was charged at Cannock police station. She pleaded not guilty. At the hearing, her lawyer, A. Whitehouse, pleaded that if the case were committed for trial, it would ruin her reputation.[2] The vicar agreed to reduce the charge to one of using threats. Elizabeth pleaded guilty to the reduced charge and was let off with a warning. But the maid openly threatened to have her revenge on the Edaljis one day. Shapurji believed that Elizabeth had sent the letters to herself in the name of 'Thomas Hitchings' to throw the police off her trail. He dismissed her from his service and thanked Sergeant Upton and his team. He thought he could put the whole painful episode behind him and move on.

～

Wealth and success had not come easily to Arthur Conan Doyle. Born in 1859 in Edinburgh to parents Mary and Charles Doyle, he was one of nine children and had grown up in relative poverty. Two of his sisters had died in infancy. His father supplemented his meagre wages as a civil servant by selling his paintings, but he was often under the influence of alcohol and it was left to Arthur's mother, known as 'the Ma'am', to run the house and make sure there was food on the table. She remained a major influence on his life. His father would later be confined to a mental institution. As a young boy, Arthur, the elder of her two sons, was his mother's favourite. A voracious reader from an early age, it was on him that she pinned her hopes. His godfather was his great-uncle Michael Conan, a literary, theatre and music critic who lived in Paris. Michael regularly sent books from Paris to little Arthur, who eagerly devoured them. It was from Michael Conan that Arthur inherited the compound surname of Conan Doyle, the first in his family to do so. It would be used by his family for the next generation.

One day, Arthur sent his godfather his first short story, written at the age of six, about a Bengal tiger and a man. 'There was a man in it and there was a tiger, who amalgamated shortly after they met,' he wrote with characteristic dry wit in his memoirs. Conan Doyle recalled that once the poor victim had been consumed by the tiger, the six-year-old author did not quite know how to take the story forward. Young Arthur precociously told his mother that it was easy to get people into scrapes but not so easy to get them out again. This, Conan Doyle said later, was 'surely the experience of every writer of adventures'.[3]

In 1876, the year that George Edalji was born, Conan Doyle entered the University of Edinburgh to study medicine. It was here that he would meet Dr Joseph Bell, who would be a major influence on his life. He would model his most famous creation, Sherlock Holmes, on him. Bell, known to his students as 'Joe', was a doctor who used his sharp observational skills to work out every detail of the patient's background and history. He was known for his immaculate sense of logic, rational analysis and deduction and would use these tools to aid his medical diagnosis. Physically too, Sherlock Holmes resembled Bell, who at thirty-nine was 'thin, wiry, dark, with a high-nosed acute face, penetrating grey eyes, and angular shoulders'.[4]

Bell was a showman and often displayed his astute power of observation before his students. As Holmes would later do, Bell would deduce facts about his patient before he had asked a single question. 'He was a very skilful surgeon, but his strong point was diagnosis, not only of disease, but of occupation and character,' Conan Doyle said of Bell.[5]

Bell singled out Conan Doyle from among his students and made him his outpatient clerk. It meant he had to meet his outpatients, make simple notes of their cases, and then show them in, one by one, to the large room in which Bell sat surrounded by his team of dressers and students.

In one of his best examples, he said to a civilian patient: 'Well, my man, you've served in the army.'

'Aye, sir.'

'Not long discharged?'

'No, sir.'

'A Highland regiment?'

'Aye, sir.'

'A non-com. officer?'

'Aye, sir.'

'Stationed at Barbados?'

'Aye, sir.'

'You see, gentlemen,' Bell explained with a flourish. 'The man was a respectful man but did not remove his hat. They do not in the army, but he would have learnt civilian ways had he been long discharged. He has an air of authority and he is obviously Scottish.

As to Barbados, his complaint is elephantiasis, which is West Indian and not British.'[6]

It was from Bell that Conan Doyle would learn the power of observation. On one occasion the doctor pointed out the profession of his patient without asking a single question and later proudly told his students: 'Gentleman, a fisherman! You will notice that, though this is a very hot summer's day, the patient is wearing top-boots … No one but a sailor would wear top-boots at this season of the year … further, to prove the correctness of these deductions, I notice several fish scales adhering to his clothes and hands, while the odour of fish announced his arrival in a most marked and striking manner.'[7]

It was exactly the sort of deduction that Holmes would make in his mysteries. In *A Study in Scarlet*, Holmes tells Watson at their very first meeting that he must have arrived from Afghanistan, much to the man's astonishment. Holmes explains his train of reasoning to Watson in typical Bell-style: 'Here is a gentleman of a medical type, but with the air of a military man. Clearly an army doctor, then. He has just come from the tropics, for his face is dark, and that is not the natural tint of his skin, for his wrists are fair. He has undergone hardship and sickness, as his haggard face says clearly. His left arm has been injured. He holds it in a stiff and unnatural manner. Where in the tropics could an English army doctor have seen such hardship and got his arm wounded? Clearly in Afghanistan.'

Bell could identify accents, make out a person's trade by seeing his hands and had the knack of sniffing out every clue about his patient. Knowing their backstory helped him to take his diagnosis and treatment forward. It also gave the patient a sense of confidence in his doctor.

Working with Bell, the young Conan Doyle was able to watch his methods closely. Arthur would be Watson to Bell's Holmes. Later, when he wrote his books, the character of Watson would be loosely based on himself. The moustache, the parted hair and the slightly bulky persona of Watson – a doctor by profession – were all clearly modelled on his own physique.

To Holmes, the faculty of observation was key. 'By a man's finger-nails, by his coat sleeve, by his boot, by his trouser knees, by the callosities of his forefinger and thumb, by his expression, by his shirt-cuffs – by each of these things a man's calling is plainly revealed,' he says in *A Study in Scarlet*, emphasising the importance of the science of deduction.

*A Study in Scarlet* was published in 1888, the same year that the Edaljis woke up to see their house daubed with racist graffiti. Conan Doyle had been paid a mere £25 for the book, but Holmes and Watson had made their first appearance. He had written it in six weeks in Portsmouth where he had set up practice as a doctor from 1882. The three-storey house, 1 Bush Villas on Elm Grove in Southsea, which served as his residence and surgery had a lovingly polished brass plate on the door displaying his name – 'Dr A. Conan Doyle, Surgeon'. However, few patients walked through the door, and the bored young doctor spent his time plotting his books. His wife of three years, Louise Hawkins (or Touie as she was called), noted that he had written a 'little novel' of about 200 pages.[8]

His mind was already racing ahead, thinking of the next case that Holmes and Watson would embark on. He knew that he wanted his name on a volume.

In Great Wyrley, the dismissal of Elizabeth Foster saw peace restored to the vicarage for three years. The Edalji family got on with their lives. George had grown into a scholarly and shy sixteen-year-old. His voice had broken and the faint shadow of a moustache had appeared above his upper-lip. He had started taking the train to attend Rugeley Grammar School. He had few friends and mostly kept to himself. His brother Horace also attended the same school, while his sister Maud was taught at home. In the summer of 1892, the letters began again. Arriving by post or by hand, sometimes they had stamps or coins in them. One letter threatened to poison the water supply of the vicarage. It forced the worried vicar to have his pump protected by a wooden lock-up shed.[9]

The letter-writer now adopted a new method of harassment. Not only were the Edaljis receiving their supply of anonymous mail but Shapurji soon discovered that letters were falsely going out under his name to others.

The hoaxer cast his net even beyond the village of Great Wyrley. Postcards, supposedly signed by Shapurji or his wife were sent out to various clergy, medical practitioners and tradespeople in the neighbouring districts. This time the clear aim was to trouble the vicar's neighbours and colleagues. The police noted that all the hoax postcards were in the same handwriting as the anonymous letters. They were variously signed 'S. Edalji' or 'C. E. S. Edalji'.

Postcards were sent to clergy in neighbouring churches, saying that Shapurji was suffering from bronchitis and would be glad of their assistance at some funerals. No fewer than three clergymen from different parishes came to St Mark's Church, only to find that Shapurji was up and about and preparing to take his service as usual. Postcards were sent to doctors in the neighbourhood, asking them to call at the vicarage as Mrs Edalji was suffering from an attack of rheumatism. Two doctors answered the call, finding to their annoyance that there was nothing wrong with the vicar's wife or anyone else in the house. In fact there was not a single sickbed in sight, only a very embarrassed vicar trying to explain the situation.

One day Shapurji received a large supply of building material at the vicarage, sent by a tradesman at Cannock. Since he had not ordered anything, he returned it. A large supply of coal was also sent back. Suddenly the hapless vicar found that an endless stream of horses and carts were trotting up his drive bringing wagonloads of goods, none of which he needed. It was the latest trick devised by the mysterious letter-writer. Builders, plumbers and bricklayers arrived at the vicarage, apparently asked to mend leaking roofs, fix blocked toilets and lay new drives. Luckily, a number of tradesmen made enquiries before despatching their supplies of paint, varnish, tiles and other items. In frustration, the weary vicar called a reporter from the *Birmingham Post* and showed him the letters received from the tradesmen. Shapurji said he could not account for this persecution and said he was not aware that he had made any enemies in his parish. Even as the reporter was at the vicarage, a builder from Hednesford appeared at the door saying he had received a postcard requesting him to call to do some building repairs.[10]

The vicar finally wrote to *The Times* newspaper outlining the elaborate hoaxes that doctors, tradesmen, clergymen, solicitors and others were being subjected to under his name. 'The person who is engaged in this evil business seems to have no regard for the time, convenience or interest of any one,' wrote the vicar. He cautioned all persons against 'accepting, without inquiry, any letters or postcards which may come to them with my name and address'. Since the forged letters were being sent as far away as Ireland, he appealed to editors across the country to publish the letter as it would 'confer a favour not only upon myself but upon the public at large'.[11] The bewildered Shapurji could not understand why the prankster was targeting him. He was embarrassed that so many people had been inconvenienced on his account. The police, too, were puzzled by the letters. There seemed no logic to them, apart from the fact that the writer wanted to harass the vicar and his family.

The letter-writer was getting bolder. Around eleven o'clock one night, when Charlotte was having a last look around before going to bed, she saw a man near the back door. He had just pushed in a letter. She shouted out, but he ran away before anyone could follow. The letters resumed soon after. They kept on coming even in the depth of winter, when the ground outside the vicarage was covered in snow.

One morning, the children woke up to see a line of footprints clearly visible in the snow. A letter lay near the doorstep. They dashed out to see if they could trace the footprints, but the trail was lost outside the house as the prints got mixed up with those of others – colliers, tradesmen and ordinary people – going about their work. The police were informed again and they assured the family that they had a suspect and would arrest the culprit in a few days.[12] It is not known who the police suspected, or in fact if they suspected anyone at all. Perhaps it was just something they said to fob off the family. Upton, who was known to enjoy a drink in the local alehouse, was heard making dismissive remarks about the vicar. Elizabeth Foster's brothers had always claimed she was innocent. It was clear that Upton believed that Elizabeth had been set up and the dark-skinned Shapurji and his family were hiding the truth. Consequently, the police took only a half-hearted interest in the Edaljis' troubles.

The vicarage was surrounded by trees and shrubs and a considerable portion of the house and the church outside was covered in ivy. Sparrows roosted there at night and it was a favourite place for those wanting to shoot birds. Often their lanterns could be seen bobbing in the churchyard lighting up the dark nights. The police were known to hide among the gravestones watching the vicarage. One night they arrested two men who had been skulking with lanterns in the churchyard and brought them to Shapurji. But they had nets and implements for catching birds and were clearly not the letter-writers. They were dismissed. All the time the hoaxes, forgeries and anonymous letters continued.

# 4

## *A Key at the Doorstep*

The year was coming to a close and the December nights were getting longer. The story of the anonymous letters and hoaxes had been doing the rounds of the village. The vicar did not mention it in any of his Sunday services, but the villagers would look curiously at the family and wonder where the truth lay. Upton had always said that it was an inside job and pointed the finger at the Edaljis from the start. It was easy for the villagers to believe that one of the family members at the vicarage was playing the pranks, especially when the police seemed to think so.

One evening George walked back from the railway station after school as usual. Hiding in the hedges watching the vicarage was PC Joseph Poole. Shortly afterwards, a large key was found on the kitchen doorstep. It was handed over to the police by Shapurji. Sergeant Upton, stationed at Cannock police station, was not happy to receive it. He glared at the offending key. It had been discovered on Monday, 12 December, about five minutes after George Edalji returned from school. While Upton had no reason to think it, he had no doubt that it had been placed there by the boy himself and that the owner of the key would be traced to Mason College, Birmingham, where George was a pupil.[1]

On Tuesday, 13 December, on his return from school at 5 p.m. George said that he found twopence on the same doorstep along with a note. The following morning, the vicar informed the sergeant that he had found some excrement on the window of the bedroom occupied by him and George.

The window, which was in two parts, had been left open till about nine on the previous evening. The same night, excrement was also found on the inside of the door and just inside the window of the lavatory which was on the same landing as the bedrooms. Upton made a detailed report. He noted that the only person who used the lavatory between 8.30 and 10 p.m. was George. Around 10.20 that night a note was found inside the entrance hall. Notes were also found on Thursday and Friday nights. The note on the Friday contained a sixpence and said that Fred Brookes must pay back the fourpence and George Edalji must pay back the 10s 6d which they had stolen from the desks in the schools or all would be known on Monday. It was the first time that the name of Fred Brookes, a local boy, appeared on a letter. He too would soon be targeted by the same letter-writer in a series of anonymous letters over the next few years. It would further add to the mystery.

An exasperated Upton called at the vicarage on the evening of 17 December and interviewed Shapurji for two hours. He reported that there was no note that night. He went to the bedroom used by George and his father and examined the window from where the excreta had allegedly been thrown in. The window was eighteen feet high from the ground and the opening was only twenty inches. A yew tree partly covered the window and Upton was convinced that no one could have thrown it in from the ground. It could only be done if the person climbed the tree. He examined the tree and concluded that no one had climbed up or down it. Upton was convinced that George, the dark, awkward boy with bulging eyes, was the one behind the letters and the key. He had disliked him from the start, even during the charging of Elizabeth Foster. Upton was certain he could nail the blame on George. He started watching the vicarage closely.

On Sunday, 18 December, after the evening service at the church, Charlotte and Shapurji had just sat down for a quiet supper at 9.15 p.m., when there was a loud banging on the door. Outside were Sergeant Upton and Constable Jackson, who demanded to see the vicar. The policeman said they had been sitting on the steps outside the front door. At about 9 p.m. they heard someone with slippers going upstairs. Then they heard the sound of someone coming very quietly down the stairs in 'stockinged feet'. They lay quiet for some time waiting for the person to go back and then had looked under the door with a lamp. There was a letter on the floor, an inch from the door. Jackson had stayed near the front door and Upton had raced to the side door to alert the family. Shapurji rushed down the corridor and picked up what turned out to be a small pamphlet called 'Character Readings'. This was folded into the shape of a letter. Inside was a bit of dry excreta.

Upton told Shapurji that he believed the person who had placed the letter had gone upstairs. Shapurji said his son was in bed and had been for some time. Upton then asked if he could go up and see him. George was lying in his bed, and in reply to his father said he had not been downstairs or put down any paper. Upton then went to the lavatory, looked into the water closet and saw some brown paper. He concluded immediately that someone had used the lavatory recently and put the excreta in the envelope. An argument followed. The normally mild-mannered vicar, who had actually thanked Upton after the Elizabeth Foster case, now lost his temper. For months he had heard the rumours in the village that Foster had been innocent. The police had done nothing credible to investigate the letters and hoaxes and were now trying to blame his son. Shapurji told Upton that he had been trying to bring a charge against his son from the start. He said the letter must have been put under the door before the police came on their watch.

Shapurji vehemently denied that anyone inside the house had deposited the packet. He pointed out that the excreta was dry and could not have just been removed from the lavatory as suggested. The argument between the police officer and the vicar intensified. Shapurji said it was impossible to hear 'stockinged feet and breathing' through the thick oak door and see the stairs which were set a few feet back. He hinted that it was Upton himself who had pushed the packet under the door in an attempt to frame George. When Upton said it was not possible to push a letter under the gap in the front door, Shapurji took the letter and pushed it under the gap. The stand-off complete, the vicar did not allow him to search the house again, as the police had already questioned George on two previous occasions.

The incident terrified young George. Years later, his sister Maud would write that he would lie awake at night in fear thinking the police would come for him.[2]

Upton sent a detailed report to Anson, the chief constable of the Staffordshire police. He pointed out that the only people in the house that day were Mr and Mrs Edalji, the servant girl, George, and a younger son and daughter who were in bed. The younger boy had been in Lichfield the previous week, so could have had nothing to do with the incidents that occurred. The majority of the letters were posted in a pillar box close to the vicarage, reported Upton. He concluded: 'Should any proceedings be taken against the youth George Edalji, I have no doubt but that evidence as to his handwriting and probably an owner for the key may be got at Mason College Birmingham.'[3] Upton had immediately presumed that the key belonged to Mason College, where George was a pupil.

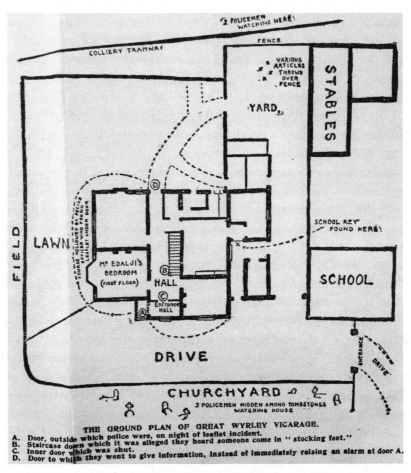

Map of the vicarage in *Pearson's Weekly* magazine

Meanwhile, Shapurji, too, had written to Anson. He had heard the villagers gossiping that the letters had been found on George. He informed the chief constable that this was completely untrue. The offending article – it was actually a pamphlet and not a letter at all – was found in the hall near the door. There was no clear view of the staircase from below the front door as there was an inner door in the entrance hall which was shut. It was clear that the police had been discussing the event with the locals and making false accusations. Shapurji asserted that the letter had been lying outside the door and that Upton had pushed the letter in himself. He invited the chief constable to visit the vicarage and see the layout of the house.

It was the first time that Shapurji had contacted Anson, the police chief who would play a key role in their lives in the years ahead. It did not start off on the right foot. Shapurji's letter accusing a member of Anson's force of a misdemeanour did not please him.

Anson replied curtly to Shapurji:

'I do not think we need seriously discuss the possibility of Sergeant Upton having himself placed anything under your door, with a view to fixing blame on some other person.'[4]

Anson – an arch-Conservative – was not prepared to listen to the arguments of the 'Hindoo vicar' of Great Wyrley.

Charlotte tried to take a more moderate approach. She even suggested that perhaps Upton had heard George walking in his room upstairs which was directly above the hall. George was a heavy boy and his footsteps may have been heard below. But Upton was unconvinced.

In fact, Upton was wrong about the key. It did not belong to Mason College, Birmingham, but to Walsall Grammar School. Though there was no reason to think that George Edalji, a pupil at Mason College, would go six miles away to the grammar school, steal the key and lay it on his own doorstep, Upton remained convinced that George was the culprit. He had decided – without a shred of evidence or logical reasoning – that the key was stolen by George Edalji and nothing would convince him otherwise. Nor was he bothered by the irksome possibility that since the key belonged to Walsall Grammar School, a prankster from that school could be responsible. He was not prepared to investigate further.

Upton advised Anson that the key was stolen by George Edalji. Though it was a relatively minor offence and the case went nowhere, the incident had been brought to the notice of the chief constable. It would bring George on to the radar of the Staffordshire police.

Anson wrote to Shapurji on 23 January 1893:

Will you please ask your son George from whom the key was obtained which was found on your doorstep on Dec 12? The key was stolen, but if it can be shown that the whole thing was due to some idle freak or practical joke, I should not be inclined to allow any police proceedings to be taken in regard to it. If however, the persons concerned in the removal of the key refuse to make any explanation of the subject, I must necessarily treat the matter in all seriousness as a theft. I may say at once that I shall not pretend to believe any protestations of ignorance which your son may make about this key. My information on the subject does not come from the police.

George would write later: 'Let it be noted that "it was not from the police" Captain Anson received his information. From whom then did he receive it? From whom more likely than the actual thief, who, despite Captain Anson's opinion to the contrary, was, I submit, undoubtedly connected with the offensive letter-writer.'[5]

Following the incident of the key, several other objects were left at the vicarage including a thermometer, a small leather purse and a pen. The family were convinced they were all stolen goods, but thought it was useless to hand them to the police as the thief would invent further stories and implicate other innocent people.

Arthur Conan Doyle was preparing for an important dinner meeting. He had been invited to the stylish Langham Hotel in London by Joseph Marshall Stoddart, the Philadelphia-based influential managing editor of *Lippincott's Monthly Magazine*. Stoddart was looking to start a British edition of his periodical and needed new writers. The meeting was to be eventful. Stoddart had also invited the Irish playwright Oscar Wilde, who at the time had published his stories in literary magazines. Wilde left a lasting impression on Conan Doyle. 'He towered above us all, and yet had the art of seeming to be interested in all we could say,' he wrote later.[6] The conversation stretched late into the night, aided by generous amounts of brandy and port. Stoddart went away with a literary coup. Wilde would deliver to him *The Picture of Dorian Gray* and Conan Doyle offered up Holmes and Watson's next adventure. The seed had already been planted in their first outing. 'I shall give Sherlock Holmes of *A Study in Scarlet* something else to unravel. I notice that everyone who has read the books wants to know more of that young man,' he wrote to Stoddart, who prepared the contract that very night.[7] Holmes, Watson and the Baker Street Irregulars were set for action.

Soon the stories were flowing. In 1892 *The Adventures of Sherlock Holmes* was published in book form. Conan Doyle would dedicate it to Dr Joseph Bell. He wrote to his former teacher: 'It is most certainly to you that I owe Sherlock Holmes and though in the stories I have the advantage of being able to place him in all sorts of dramatic positions, I do not think that his analytical work is in the least an exaggeration of some effects which I have seen you produce in the outpatient ward.'

Holmes and Watson had seized the popular imagination and Conan Doyle decided to give up medicine altogether. It was time for him to become a full-time writer.

The year 1892 would see two Parsees in Britain making the news. Dadabhai Naoroji would make history as the first Asian to be elected as a Member of Parliament. The bearded and elderly Naoroji, a well-known economist, bagged the seat of Finsbury Central for the Liberal Party by a mere five votes. Watched by his colleagues, he took his oath on his copy of the Khordeh Avesta, the holy scriptures of the Zoroastrians.

Naoroji had arrived in England in 1855 as a partner in the Parsee-owned trading firm Cama & Co, and set up their offices in London and Liverpool. The firm was dealing in alcohol and opium and Naoroji resigned on moral grounds. In 1859 he established his own cotton trading company, Dadabhai Naoroji & Co., but soon preferred to follow his academic interests. He became Professor of

Gujarati at University College London at a time when there were hardly any Indians in British academia. His passion for politics led him to set up the London Indian Society, to discuss all areas of Indian literature, society and politics. Urged by his followers, Naoroji made an unsuccessful attempt to win a parliamentary seat in 1886, when he contested the Conservative-held seat of Holborn in London. In 1888, Lord Salisbury, the prime minister at the time, made a speech at the Corn Exchange in Edinburgh mocking the defeat of Naoroji, saying that an English constituency was not yet ready to elect a 'Black Man'. Salisbury told the large gathering:

> I doubt if we have yet got to that point where a British constituency will elect a black man to represent them.(Laughter) Of course, you will understand that I am speaking roughly and using language in its ordinary colloquial sense, because I imagine the colour is not exactly black; but at all events he was a man of another race who was very unlikely to represent an English community.[8]

His words would come to haunt him, as it only made Naoroji more popular. The 'Black Man' incident was splashed across several newspapers. The *Pall Mall Gazette* recommended that Salisbury lather his tongue with Pears soap.[9] The humour magazine *Funny Folks* carried a poem titled 'To "Black Men" Generally: A Salisburian Address':

> You may be cultured, worthy, and the rest,
> You may no quality of virtue lack,
> But though, of course, you try to do your best,
> You're Black, my friend, You're Black![10]

Naoroji's electoral triumph four years later was celebrated in India and Britain. The satirical magazine *Punch* referred to it in a cartoon depicting Naoroji as Othello and Salisbury as the 'Doge of Westminster'.[11] Naoroji would eventually publish his seminal work *Poverty and un-British Rule in India* where he would put forward the 'drain of wealth' theory.

On a quieter note, Cornelia Sorabji became the first woman to graduate in law from Oxford in 1892, taking her exams at Somerville

College. She would have to wait for thirty years before being admitted to Lincoln's Inn, as women were not called to the Bar. A contemporary of Mohandas Karamchand Gandhi, she became the first woman lawyer to practise in India.

⌒⌐

The Parsee Vicar of Great Wyrley was, however, making the local news for entirely different reasons. As the winter frost covered the village, the letters to the Edalji family were becoming more frequent and aggressive. The writer was now increasing the number of his targets. Letters were sent to other residents of the village, even threatening to kill them. Some of the letters were received by Fred Brookes and Fred Wynne, pupils of Walsall Grammar School. The school, whose key was found at the vicarage, seemed to be an important link in the letters and hoaxes. Fred Brookes was the son of the local grocer W. H. Brookes, and lived on Walsall Road in Great Wyrley. Fred Wynne was the son of William Wynne, a painter and decorator. Inevitably, George and his family were mentioned in the letters. The letters written to Shapurji often cursed him for letting George mix with Fred Brookes, the grocer's son. The police were informed and kept a watch on the two boys.

Also of interest to the police was a third pupil from Walsall Grammar, a known troublemaker called Royden Sharp, who was not mentioned in the letters by name, but was associated with Fred Brookes and Fred Wynne. Sharp was already familiar to the police as he had a criminal record even as a juvenile. He was always bottom of the class and was reported to have been caned twenty times in one term alone in 1892.[12] He once broke the windows on the train carriage but managed to blame Fred Brookes and Fred Wynne for it, both of whom were wrongly charged for the damage.[13] Sharp had a propensity for violent action from a young age. He once took out a knife and slashed the seats of a railway carriage, for which he was charged. In 1892 he had been suspended from school for twelve months for setting fire to a hayrick belonging to influential local landowner J. T. Hatton. Sharp was dismissed from the school on grounds of forging letters, cheating, lying, swearing and falsifying marks.[14]

Though George did not attend Walsall Grammar School, and at the time of the second series of letters was a pupil at Mason College,

Birmingham, the police were convinced he had a link with the other boys. All three travelled on the branch line of the North Western Railway to their school in Walsall. George would be on the same train, travelling further to Birmingham. They were typical schoolboys, boisterous and loud. George was the opposite, sitting quietly by himself. Though he knew the other boys by sight, he did not mix with them.

The link between the letters and the schoolboys became clear when Fred Wynne received some letters which referred to Farmer Hatton's hayrick being set on fire and damage to rail compartments. The letter-writer claimed that he and his mates had damaged three compartments in the presence of George Edalji who had stared at him but failed to recognise him. Fred Wynne was accused in the letters of being part of the gang that set fire to the hayrick belonging to J. T. Hatton in 1892. However, it was Royden Sharp who had committed the crime. The locals were puzzled. Village gossip revolved around why George Edalji, who did not go to Walsall School, or mix with the boys, was being linked to them in the letters. The clear trail for the police would have been to trace if and why the boys named in the letters were disgruntled with Walsall Grammar School. Was there any rivalry between the boys themselves? Did they even know George Edalji apart from travelling with him on the same train. If not, what was their connection to him? Why was he being mentioned in the letters? Who gained from discrediting him? Did anyone have a grudge against the vicar? None of these questions seemed to interest the police.

The headmaster of Walsall Grammar School was not spared either. James Aldis received a letter, full of spelling mistakes, threatening to kill him and set fire to the school: 'Sir, you headmaster me and George Edaljia [sic] are going to leave and join the army because we wrote the letters and so we are going to set the blasted school on fire if you toutch [sic] us we will kick you black and blue ...'

A letter was sent to the *Lichfield Mercury* newspaper allegedly signed by George Edalji and Fred Brookes in which they apologised for writing the anonymous letters and requested that all accusations against Sergeant Upton and Elizabeth Foster be dropped.[15] Shapurji immediately complained that it was a fraud and the paper retracted the 'apology' in the next edition. It was clear that the letter-writer was local and that he had a grudge against George and the vicar. Yet

Upton remained convinced that the seventeen-year-old George was behind them.

It was also clear from the false advertisement that the letter-writer was an admirer of Sergeant Upton and Elizabeth Foster, and the charges against the maid and her subsequent dismissal four years before, had not been forgotten.

## PUBLIC APOLOGY.

WE, the undersigned, George E. T. Edalji and Frederick Brookes, both of Great Wyrley, near Walsall, and in the County of Stafford, do hereby declare, that we were the sole authors and writers of the certain offensive and anonymous letters received during the past twelve months by various persons, both in, and around, the united parishes of Cheslyn Hay and Great Wyrley. Moreover, that we do unreservedly withdraw all the heinous charges which we have made against the persons of William Upton, sergeant of police, of Cannock, and Miss Elizabeth Foster, residing in the parish of Norton Canes, as there was not the foundation for any one of them. Further, in consideration of their extreme clemency in forbearing to bring action against us for libel, we are willing to pay their legal expenses already incurred, and also the cost of inserting this, our most humble apology, in the columns of the public Press.

Signed { GEORGE E. T. EDALJI, FREDERICK BROOKES.

Witnesses to both { SHAPURJI EDALJI, Signatures. C. E. S. EDALJI, W. H. BROOKES

Great Wyrley, March, 1893.

The false advertisement published in the *Lichfield Mercury*

Foster continued to swear she was innocent, and Upton reportedly gossiped to the villagers that he thought she had been framed. Perhaps her friends and family believed this claim too, and acted on her calls for revenge on the Edaljis.

For, very soon, a note went up outside the kitchen door of the vicarage: It said: 'God Bless Lizzie Foster'. Elizabeth Foster had surfaced again.

# 5

## The Vicarage Under Siege

What could have been dismissed as pranks now took a much more sinister turn. The letters became more violent, openly calling for the death of George. From July 1892 to December 1895, the mild-mannered Parsee vicar, his English wife and his three 'half-caste children' were at the receiving end of a series of threatening letters, written in different hands, some in red ink, calling for murder and invoking the Almighty, the Prince of Darkness and God-Satan in a constantly escalating tempo of violent abuse. As the Edaljis recoiled in horror, the letter-writer became even more aggressive. There was also an element of insanity to the persecution of the Edaljis. One night the letter-writer deposited seventy-four small envelopes around the vicarage filled with expletives and foul comments along with random objects like pieces of coal, a pocket knife, spoons, collar studs and a bundle of leather bootlaces.

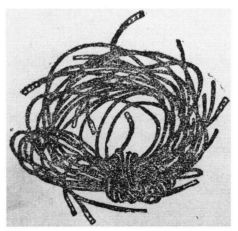

Bundle of bootlaces left outside the vicarage

A packet containing excreta was left on the vicarage doorstep. Sketches were left around the building. One of these of the 'The Black Man' referred to Shapurji. Magazine pieces were cut up into little pieces and scattered around the vicarage with offensive messages.

One of the offensive scraps of paper with 'Your Mother' scribbled next to the image of a beggarwoman

A crudely drawn sketch showed young George urinating. He, too, was sketched with a blackened face. All the letters and objects showed that the writer was obsessed with sex and bodily functions. George Edalji and Fred Brookes were accused of sexual relations with each other's sisters. Advertisements offering sexual services or matrimony were placed in newspapers with the vicar given as the contact person. Once again, letters requesting goods and services were sent out under his name.

Forged advertisements included one saying –

YOUNG LADY (25) handsome, agreeable and thoroughly domesticated, who has just been left £7,000 by an aunt and which is in possession of large freehold property wishes to correspond with kind-hearted gentleman, view early matrimony, address in the first instance in strictest confidence stating age, occupation, means etc., to S Edalji, Great Wyrley, near Wednesbury. N.B. No agents.[1]

Another, on a more risqué note, was sent out under the name of the ten-year-old Maud Edalji.

Accouchement, lying-in etc. Advertiser is in a position to receive women (married or single) for above purpose. Terms 9/6 per week (inclusive) every care and comfort. Write, wire or come immediately in any case of necessity. Miss Maud Edalji, Great Wyrley Vicarage, Walsall, Staffs. N.B. Unlimited accommodation.

The Brookes family also faced a tirade of abuse. Later, Anson would claim that the letter-writer was not motivated by race hate, as the Brookeses had also been targeted. Could this have been done to confuse the police, or was it someone with a grudge against both families? The Brookes family ran the grocery store in the village. For some reason, the letter-writer seemed to hate Fred and his parents. Though there was no connection between the Brookes and the Edaljis, apart from their living in the same village, they were often linked in the letters. Charlotte Edalji and Mrs Brookes were both wrongly accused of and damned for giving birth outside marriage. 'Unless you run away from the Black I'll murder you and Mrs Brookes,' was the threat in a letter received by the terrified Charlotte. Shapurji received a letter abusing him for letting George be friendly with Fred Brookes and letting his 'bleeding blasting kid talk to the grocer's kid'.

A chilling letter was also sent to him saying, 'Hurrah, we know now where your wife's relations live and their names!!! Hurrah for our "Tecs" ... We shall write to them now. They live at Wenlock. Miss Stonehams.'[2] Miss Stoneham was Mary Sancta, sister of Charlotte, who lived in Much Wenlock.

On Christmas Day in 1894, as the vicar prepared for the biggest celebrations of the year, his maid, Mary Ann, received a letter marked 'Urgent' that left her in tears. It informed her that her sister was dead. The letter was addressed to 'Miss Mary Ann Whitehouse, Rev. S Edalji, Wyrley Vicarage, nr Walsall'.

LILLESHALL
DEAR MARY ANN,

I have great sorrow in informing you that your dear sister died here (at the above address) about 9.pm last night.

Her body is at the 'Museum' Public House, Wolverhampton and you must go there at once when you will receive about £100 or so which I had given her as presents for good conduct. You had better go without saying anything to Mr Edalji, or he might stop you.

You are the most lovely girl I have ever seen and if you go to Wolverhampton immediately, I will give you £10.

Believe me, Dear Mary,

Yours most sincerely,

W. REES[3]

The letter was a forgery, but there was no consoling Mary Ann. She felt she had been targeted for a very mean joke. The letter had the effect of spoiling the Christmas at the vicarage. Nobody had an appetite for Christmas lunch that day.

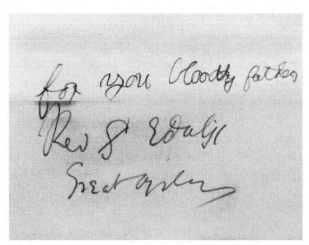

Offensive message on notepaper deposited outside the vicarage

When one dangerously hate-filled letter arrived at the vicarage, Shapurji sent it off to the local newspaper in despair.[4] The letter-writer now swore that he would take revenge and murder George Edalji. Inexplicably, he also wanted to murder Fred Brookes. The writer who signed himself as 'God' said he would bet £50 that George Edalji and Fred Brookes would be in their graves by the end of the year or disgraced for life. The letter celebrated Upton, the police officer who had investigated the first of the anonymous letters received by the vicar in 1888, which had resulted in the arrest and dismissal of Elizabeth Foster. Calling Shapurji a 'Pharisee' who would not be absolved because he was a priest, and referring to his wife and 'horrid daughter', the rambling half-crazed letter with its underlying threat of violence on his eldest son, would have been read by the vicar with horror. He wrote to the newspaper suggesting that the anonymous letter-writer was a dangerous lunatic and hoped that somebody would recognise his style and help to identify him.

Sir, the writer of the offensive letters still continues to send his letters to me and other persons in this parish. They are sent by post, and are much longer and more curious than those received last year. I beg to send you a copy of one received on Saturday last. It has been suggested to me that if I were to allow the public to see some of these letters in print I should be giving them an opportunity of rendering effective assistance in tracing the author. 'The style is the man' and there is no doubt that the writer talks much in the same manner as he writes. Many of these letters contain sufficient internal evidence to prove (1) that they are not written by an ordinary working man (2) that they are not the composition of a youth or a school boy (3) that they are written by a man who has received a good education and (4) that this man is a dangerous lunatic. I may, however, add that I shall not be surprised to find that the writer is a woman, and it ought to be noted as a most remarkable circumstance that in trying to torment me and others, the writer has become his own great tormentor, as is abundantly clear from what he says in the following letter.
Yours obediently,
S Edalji,
Vicar of Great Wyrley
20 March 1893.

The offending letter addressed to Shapurji was printed by the newspaper in full. Dated 17 March 1893, the letter-writer declared:

I swear by god that I will murder George Edalji and Fred Brookes damn soon, the only thing I care about in this world is revenge, revenge, revenge, sweet revenge. I long for, then I shall be happy, yes happy, yes happy in hell, in hell, in hell …

There were repeated threats that by the end of the year George and Fred would be 'either in the graveyard or disgrace (sic) for life.'

The letter-writer had praise for 'Good old Upton, good old Upton, blessed Upton,' and even wrote a poem to him:

Dear Upton thou wast watching
Outside the cursed door
And thou didst hear those stocking feet
Coming along the floor

The hatred for George and Fred is expressed with near frenzy:

Every day, every hour, my hatred is growing against George Edalji and Fred Brookes in particular. Revenge, revenge, revenge. I shall go mad, Christ, Christ, God have mercy on me … If I could get into an empty compartment (I mean with only your kid and FB in it) on a fast train I bet you £50 I would despatch them to hell in five minutes.

There was abuse for Shapurji too:

'Do you think, you Pharisee, that because you are a parson, God will absolve you from the iniquities; he will not absolve you.'

The letter ended on a hysterical note, bordering on insanity:

What makes Mr Brookes always look so sour? What makes you always look so silly? How old are you? Are you a Pharisee or Sadducee? Is your wife also a Pharisee? Were you born in the workhouse? Is your kid mad? Is Fred Brookes an escaped lunatic? Is your kid more ignorant than he looks? Is FB? Alas, alas, alas, I am a poor lost sinner. Christ have mercy on me …

Stand up, stand up for Upton,
Ye soldiers of the cross,

Lift high his royal banner,
It must not suffer loss.

Do not think that when we want we cannot copy your kid's and that grocer's kids writings. Our only reason for not forging their signatures and yours is that you will write such a vulgar hand that no managers of newspapers would suppose it was written by a person. I am God, God, I am God, I am God. I am Christ, I am Christ, I am Christ … Hurrah for Upton, hurrah for Upton, hurrah for Upton. I am dear Pharisee, yours faithfully,
God Almighty,
I am God, I am God

Though the letter-writer clearly stated that he could copy the handwriting of George Edalji and Fred Brookes, the police still continued to suspect George. The reference to the 'stockinged feet' was also crucial. It related to the specific incident when Upton visited the vicarage and claimed that a person with 'stockinged feet' had left the letter inside the vicarage door, and after which the sergeant had an argument with Shapurji. Clearly the village had been gossiping about the incident. To Shapurji, it meant that the family was totally isolated as the police seemed determined to accuse George.

Letter signed 'I am God'

The publication of the half-crazed letter in full in the newspaper did not stop the writer. The very next week Shapurji received another letter, viler than the earlier one. The vicar had to delete certain portions himself before sending it to the newspaper as it was 'wicked and blasphemous'.

The lengthy letter once again contained a threat to kill George Edalji.

> I swear by God that I will return from London next September and may the Lord strike me dead if I don't murder George Edalji and F__B_ [the name 'Fred Brookes' was cut out by George Edalji to protect their privacy]. … We are going to send a lot more advertisements to the papers. Now look here you Parsee, Pharisee, or whatever you are, if you are to escape having your house blown up by dynamite, you are to do this &c &c …

The letters arrived endlessly at the vicarage, threatening revenge and murder. The family felt besieged by the hate that seemed to be surrounding them. On 23 May 1895, the vicar received another letter:

> Revenge, revenge on you and your perjured kid damn son. How did you like me sending the postcards to those parsons. Are any of them going to prosecute you. Have you been returned not known, something decidedly unpleasant will happen at the vicarage in a day or two. 'S Edalji, the black'

With each letter and threat of violence, Shapurji and his young family grew more terrified. There was no telling when the letters would show up. George began to look out for anybody suspicious coming near the vicarage. He did not discuss the letters with Fred Brookes or the other children in the village and internalised his anxiety. Charlotte was in despair and young Maud could be seen quietly crying to herself. The only person not mentioned in the letters was Horace. The police did nothing to help the family.

The stakeholders of the British Empire knew that as they dominated the globe, one of the consequences would be the mixing of the

British races with the locals. In the mid- to late nineteenth century, the racial superiority of the white population was emphasised in every forum – whether it was theatre, grand exhibitions, or anthropological studies. John Beddoe, the President of the Anthropological Institute, wrote that all men of superior race were orthognathous (had less prominent jawbones). The obvious reference was to the Africans and Caribbeans, but Indians were not excluded. Nor were the Irish and the Welsh, whom he described as prognathous. In his book *Races of Britain* published in 1862, Beddoe also stated that the Celt was closely related to Cro-Magnon man, who was in turn 'Africanoid'.[5]

British children would be given the map of the Empire, proudly marked with the colonies their country ruled over. Mixing of races or hybridity was seen as something evil arising out of promiscuity. The Eurasian, or product of a mixed-race marriage, was an example of the evils arising out of racial promiscuity.[6] 'It is therefore clear that relative purity is something to be desired,' wrote G. R. Gair of the Scottish Anthropological Society. Gair was a fierce advocate of scientific racial purity. George, the product of an interracial marriage, was straitjacketed in this narrative.

The lamplit smoky streets of Victorian London had always been a source of inspiration for Conan Doyle. He had been living for some years at Montague Place near the British Museum, hoping to research historical subjects for his novels. London was where you could see the wealthy, dressed in their finest, riding in their carriages to the theatres, operas and clubs, crossing paths with grubby urchins, hawkers and peddlers. The counting houses of the City stood as proud edifices to wealth and power, while the workhouses in the East churned out poverty and disease. London was where the profits of Empire met those who had been left behind, and Conan Doyle kept a watch on both. His stories would feature the exclusive clubs, the Victorian mansions and the official buildings on Whitehall as well as the crime-filled alleys around the docks.

Life in London was an endless round of parties. Conan Doyle had applied to become a member of the Reform Club, a Liberal-leaning club. He had started contributing to the *Idler* magazine, a new style of literary magazine started by Jerome K. Jerome and Robert Barr.

At the *Idler* party in London he met J. M. Barrie, who would become a lifelong friend. However, he felt that in order to have the peace to write, he needed to be in the suburbs, a short train ride away from the throbbing capital. He soon moved to a large red-brick house at 12 Tennison Road, South Norwood, south of the Thames. It was here in his spacious study, surrounded by artefacts such as a bear's skull and a seal's paw from an expedition to the Arctic, and a war trophy from the siege of Alexandria in 1882 given to him by a former patient, that he contemplated his future as a writer. Though Holmes was popular and earning Conan Doyle his keep, he wanted to move away from crime stories.

On 6 April 1892, he wrote to his mother: 'All is very well down here. I am in the middle of the last Holmes story, after which the gentleman vanishes, never never to reappear. I am weary of his name.'[7]

～～

On 21 July 1895, the Rev. George Ward of Holy Trinity, Rathbury, Lincolnshire, received a letter from Shapurji.

> A woman who refused to give her name was found in my garden yesterday, weak and in a dying condition, she has only this morning recovered consciousness and she keeps on asking for you by name the whole time. From what I can gather she has wronged you in some ways and wants to make amends. She had on her £55 in bank notes and 11s 6½d in cash part of a PO Savings Bank Book name and number gone and a pocket handkerchief marked simply S. She is tall, aged about 62, has black hair, the front teeth projecting, doctor says the only thing is to get you over. I promised I would write and you would come on Tuesday. This seemed to pacify her and she is now gone to sleep. Could you manage to get here on Monday evening about 6. I should be most happy to accommodate you with a bed. Kindly address in reply to this to Walsall PO to be called for, so as I can get it on Monday. Letters do not get here till very late.

The letter was signed Shapurji Edalji and was a forgery. But it led to Rev. Ward coming over to the vicarage and being very annoyed with his time being wasted in this way.

The letter-writer also sent letters to the vicar's maid Nora, authoring them under the name of 'Thomas Hitchings'. The reappearance of 'Thomas Hitchings' was equally mysterious. Either the letter-writer was connected to Elizabeth Foster or there were others about. Or it was somebody trying to confuse the police and write copycat letters. The letters were far more violent in tone than the original Elizabeth Foster letters. Edalji was referred to as the 'infernal blackman', the most immoral man in creation who was responsible for starving, beating and torturing every girl employed at the vicarage and soon to be arrested for 'vile … gross immorality with persons using Vaseline in the same way as did Oscar Wilde and Taylor.' The accusations of sodomy against the vicar continued till the trial. Many innuendos were made about the fact that he and George slept in the same bedroom and that the vicar locked it from inside. Clearly, both the police and the village locals had been gossiping about the sleeping arrangements in the vicarage.

In further bizarre letters, the hapless Nora was invited to throw the cat down the toilet in her master's yard for which she would be rewarded with £50. Nora was also asked to report that she had found Mr Brookes sleeping with Mrs Edalji under Nora's bed at the vicarage and that they had held her down and outraged her. She had apparently managed to escape through the bedroom window where she met George Edalji and Fred and Edgar Brookes, who wanted to assault her and drink her urine. The offensive and deranged letter urged Nora to 'put shit with anything you may cook for the family and save all your piss and put it to boil potatoes.' Once again, Sergeant Upton took handwriting samples from George Edalji and Fred Brookes. He was determined to get to the bottom of this case.

Years later, Maud would write to the Home Office that it was impossible that her brother George could have written the letters and hoaxes. For one thing, the children did not get any pocket money. George would never have been able to afford the postage or to place hoax advertisements in newspapers.[8] It was one of those common-sense arguments that the police did not even consider.

Conan Doyle was standing in front of the thundering Reichenbach Falls. His face was covered with the icy spray. The tumbling waters,

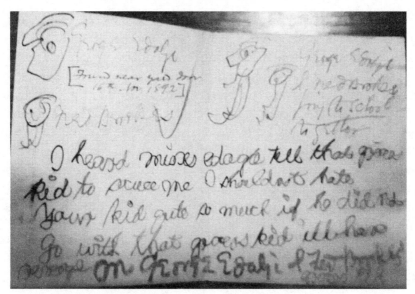

Letters with drawings of George Edalji and
Fred Brookes sent to the vicarage

and the mist that arose from the deep cauldron below, had a profound impact on him. He had a moment of revelation. This was the place he would kill off Sherlock Holmes.

Despite the pleas of his mother, who told him not to do so, he wanted to end the story of the man who, he said, had become a 'burden' to him and made his life 'unbearable'. He just needed a grand setting to do it. Reichenbach Falls was that setting. Holmes would die plunging off the falls as he grappled with his arch-rival Professor Moriarty in *The Final Problem*.

He was still in Davos when the story appeared in the *Strand Magazine*. Conan Doyle made a brief entry in his diary that December. It simply said: 'Killed Holmes.'[9]

# 6

## *A Period of Silence*

From his large country house a few miles from the village of Great Wyrley, Captain Hon. George Augustus Anson, chief constable of Staffordshire, was reading with disdain the report about the vicarage and the affair of the anonymous letters. The second son of the Earl of Lichfield and Lady Harriet Hamilton (daughter of the Duke of Abercorn), Anson was an aristocratic Victorian Conservative. Born in 1857, the year of the Indian Mutiny, he grew up in the grandeur of his family estate in Shugborough Manor, where Queen Victoria had stayed as a thirteen-year-old when she visited with her mother, the Duchess of Kent. His ancestor Lord Anson was First Lord of the Admiralty from 1757–62, and had played a key role in the Seven Years War and circumnavigated the world in the *Centurion*, bringing back a fortune from his travels in the East. The family house contained, among other antiques, the 208-piece porcelain dinner service which had been presented to Lord Anson in Canton for his help in fighting the huge fires that were destroying the Chinese port when he visited there in the *Centurion*. Another forebear, Lieutenant Colonel Augustus Anson, son of the first Earl of Lichfield, had been awarded the Victoria Cross for his gallantry during the Indian Mutiny at Bolandshahar (present-day Bulandshahr) and Lucknow in 1857, during which he had been seriously wounded. The family had a long connection with India.

Anson attended the exclusive Harrow School, joined the Royal Military Academy at Woolwich and served in the army till 1876. He became chief constable of Staffordshire in 1888, a few years before the Edaljis started receiving the anonymous letters and hate mail. He lived at Green Hall in Stafford, part of his ancestral estate, where he would later receive Arthur Conan Doyle. Anson was an imperialist to the core, brought up with the firm belief that the inherent superiority of Western civilisation was the foundation on which the British Empire had been built. The late nineteenth century had seen the flourishing of race science in England and on the continent. Theorists like Arthur de Gobineau had reinforced the belief that some races were naturally superior and that the mixing of races led to the dilution of intellect and the decline of civilisations. Published in 1853, *The Inequality of Human Races* was the sort of book that lined many a bookshelf in manors and stately homes in England. Also popular were writers like Francis Galton, who wrote *Hereditary Genius* in 1869, claiming that the great leaders, thinkers and scientists of England came from a small upper-class stratum and that arranged marriages between them would produce a superior race. Galton coined the term 'eugenics' or 'well born' in 1883, formalising the study of preserving 'pure' and superior races.

The chief constable was forged with the power of his privileged upbringing. He had no sympathy for the coloured family at the vicarage, and did not approve of the fact that a brown man had been given the role of preaching to a white parish. He had no hesitation in calling Shapurji – who had a blameless reputation – a liar. He was equally disdainful of Charlotte for marrying an Indian, and treated her with scant respect. He was particularly contemptuous of George and referred to him as 'niggerish in appearance' and his sister Maud as 'dumpy'.

Anson's deep-seated dislike for the Edalji family, and particularly George, would have serious consequences. At seventeen, George was already a marked person. In 1895, two years after the key incident, Shapurji was informed by a local parishioner, Mr Perry, that Anson had proclaimed that he knew the offender's name. He immediately wrote to ask him who it was. Anson replied to Shapurji, 'I did not tell Mr Perry that I knew the name of the offender, though I told him I had my suspicions. I prefer to keep my suspicions to myself until I am able to prove them, and I trust to obtain a dose of penal servitude for the offender … the person who writes the letters has overreached himself in two or three instances, in such a manner as to render him liable to the most serious punishment. I have no doubt that the offender will be detected.'[1]

Conan Doyle would later describe this letter as 'rather sinister' as it followed eighteen months after Anson had directly accused George Edalji by name. 'If the Staffordshire police took this attitude towards young Edalji in 1895, what chance of impartiality had he in 1903 when a culprit was wanted for an entirely new set of crimes?'[2]

Anson had no basis for his suspicions, apart from an unreliable report from Sergeant Upton. Yet, he was so convinced by it, that he had openly declared that he was watching George Edalji and would seek 'penal servitude' for him if he managed to catch him. It was institutional prejudice at the highest level, and George would eventually pay the price.

Charlotte Edalji was not ready to accept Anson's arrogance. She wrote him a sharp letter saying that 'your attitude and that of the police has been most trying throughout'. It angered Anson even more. The police chief replied sternly that he would disregard any future letters from her unless she gave an assurance to the police that she and her husband were doing their best to help. Given that the Edaljis were always ready to assist the police, it only confirmed that Anson had nothing but contempt for them. It made no difference to him that the family had been the target of hate mail and hoaxes for several years.

The turn of the century saw England in the grip of the Boer Wars in South Africa. The octogenarian Queen Victoria had celebrated her Diamond Jubilee in 1897, the first English monarch to do so, and the Empire was at its height. On 11 October 1899, the second Boer War began. The Boers were the descendants of Dutch settlers in South Africa, who refused to give political rights to non-Boer incomers, most of whom were British. Both sides wanted control of the gold and diamond mines of Transvaal and the Orange Free State. The British started building up their troops in the area, prompting the Boers to give them an ultimatum to stop. By 1900, British forces had captured a number of Boer cities and Boer soldiers were infamously put into concentrations camps, where many died. It was to be the first international war of the new century, fought by Britain for dominance in South Africa. Troops from Canada, Australia and India were drawn in by the British. Mohandas Karamchand Gandhi, who was based as a lawyer in South Africa, volunteered for the British and worked as a stretcher-bearer. The Boer Wars – in which even Queen Victoria lost her grandson – were seen as the victory of Empire and the unquestionable control of Britain over one-fourth of the globe. Critics of Empire saw it as an act of repression by Britain – crushing two small nations which were trying to govern as republics.

The writer-poets of Empire like Rudyard Kipling championed the British cause. In 1899 he wrote the fund-raising poem 'The Absent-Minded Beggar' appealing for donations for the 'gentlemen in khaki ordered South'. He travelled to South Africa in 1900 and wrote articles for *The Friend*, a newspaper started by Field Marshal Lord Roberts in Bloemfontein, aimed at trying to win the hearts and minds of the locals. Kipling had known Roberts – the British hero of the Mutiny – from his India days. He wrote several short stories during the Boer War including *A Sahibs' War*, and several poems.

Conan Doyle, too, had been cheerleading the British side. He volunteered for service but was rejected because of his age. He remained persistent and in February 1900 sailed for South Africa on the *Oriental*, as part of the medical team for a field hospital. He was listed in *The Times* newspaper as 'A. Conan Doyle M.D., M.C.H. physician with the Langman Hospital'. In Bloemfontein, which had just been liberated by the British, he found himself in the midst of a typhoid epidemic with between 10,000 and 12,000 people affected. Conan Doyle described it in his memoirs as 'death, in its vilest filthiest form'. He, too, was asked to contribute to *The Friend*. He submitted one piece, but then decided to focus on his medical duties. So absorbed was Conan Doyle in his work, that when one of his patients – a fan – asked him to name his favourite Sherlock Holmes story, he could not even remember the title. He replied that it was perhaps the one about the 'serpent' (*The Speckled Band*). Over the next few months he travelled on to Pretoria and Johannesburg, returning to England in August. His book *The Great Boer War* was published in October of that year.

As a war veteran as well as a popular novelist, Conan Doyle's standing in society increased even more. He became a member of the exclusive Athenaeum Club in London, hosting a dinner almost immediately, including on his guest list the newly elected Conservative MP,

Winston Churchill. In 1902 Conan Doyle published *The War in South Africa: Its Causes and Conduct.* The 60,000-word book was a strong defence of the Boer War and the English effort. The British, who had faced heavy casualties, had been criticised for their treatment of the natives and for the building of concentration camps. The camps had been widely criticised by Liberal MPs like David Lloyd George and John Ellis, and the campaigner Emily Hobhouse. Conan Doyle, contrary to his fellow Liberals, defended the concentration camps. He argued that they were really refugee camps used to house the displaced women and children during the war. He stated that the high number of deaths in the camp was caused by disease rather than bad treatment. The book – coming as it did from a doctor and a man of impeccable repute – went a large way to make the public see the Boer Wars in a more sympathetic light. His defence of Empire in the second Boer War would be useful to the establishment. He was offered a knighthood for his services to the country. Conan Doyle was tempted to refuse it as he did not care for government honours, but under pressure from his mother accepted it. In October 1902, he became Sir Arthur Conan Doyle.

One day, the letters, the hoaxes and the abuse stopped. For a few years, all was quiet in Great Wyrley. The talk in the public houses returned to harvests, mining disasters and other local issues. The threatening letters, the attacks on the Brookeses and the Edaljis soon became a distant memory. The local police went about their work rounding up burglars and other petty criminals. No longer did they have to chase an invisible person wielding a poison pen. Perhaps the letter-writer had left the area or was giving the Edaljis a false sense of security. After years of torment, the family could finally breathe freely. A sense of normality returned to the vicarage as the children continued their studies and their parents cared for the parishioners. Sunday services at the church were no longer a tense affair.

In all his adolescent years, George had never been a source of concern to his parents. A shy and retiring person who enjoyed reading, he had been a model pupil at Rugeley Grammar School. He went on to study as a day boarder at Mason College, Birmingham, finishing his schooling in midsummer 1893 with certificates in

Latin, French and English. George decided to study law and took the Incorporated Law Society Examination in 1898. He was one of ten students out of two hundred whose names were placed at the top having obtained a second-class honours degree (there being no one to score the highest marks needed for a first-class degree). His parents were proud when their shy boy was awarded the Senior Law Class Prize for 1897 by the Birmingham Law Society and the bronze medal in 1898. He was also awarded the second speaking prize of the Law Students' Society in 1898.

George continued to live at the vicarage with his parents, sharing the bedroom with his father. It is not clear why Charlotte never returned to her husband's bedroom and why the old sleeping arrangements continued. It may have been the reason for the gradual isolation of Horace Edalji from his brother, as he had to share a bedroom with his mother and sister and was separated from the men in the family.

While the shy and studious George had few friends and mainly kept to himself, his brother was more outgoing. Fair-skinned like his mother, Horace could pass as Caucasian. This may have been partly why, while George had the academic prizes, Horace had friends. One of his friends was Christopher Hatton, son of the local landowner J. T. Hatton, the very man who had clashed with Shapurji over the vestry committee. Christopher would play a role during George's trial. In contrast, George barely spoke to any of the neighbouring children. The relationship between the brothers was always slightly strained. Perhaps Horace felt his parents were more partial to his brother. His younger sister Maud was also closer to George. Horace was an impressionable nine-year-old when the first racist graffiti had been painted on the vicarage walls. He had watched in terror as their windows had been broken, excreta thrown through the letterbox, and abusive letters, calling his father a 'blackman' and threatening to kill him, arrived at their home. Though the children were not heckled in the streets or attacked in school, there was an underlying current of mistrust in the way the villagers interacted with them. At best they were objects of curiosity because of their colouring. At worst it led to violent feelings against them, as expressed by the letter-writer. Horace was never mentioned in the letters. They were mainly targeted at George, and consequently it was his older brother who was comforted by his parents. There was no counselling for the children, so they each lived with their fears. A feeling of resentment and self-loathing filled Horace from a young age and he grew up ashamed of his ethnicity. He was the first to leave the vicarage when he got a job, and in the future would distance himself from his family.

Meanwhile, George was slowly making his way in the world. With his law degree in the bag, he started practising as a solicitor with King and Ludlow in Birmingham, proudly displaying his bronze medal and certificates on his office wall. After work he would usually head back home and spend some time in the evening meeting local clients at the vicarage. He even wrote a book, *Railway Law for 'the Man in the Train'*. It was intended as a guide for the 'travelling public on all points likely to arise in connection with the railways'. The book was priced at two shillings and advertisements were placed in the local papers. The *Cannock Chase Courier* reviewed it saying it was 'somewhat gratifying to the public of this district that "one of us" has been the author'.[3] Things seemed to be running on track for the Edaljis.

~~~

Sportsman, journalist and author Fletcher Robinson was on holiday with Conan Doyle in Norfolk. Robinson had family in Dartmoor and told him about the legends of a phantom hound on the mysterious moors in Devon. Conan Doyle instantly saw potential. He accompanied Fletcher Robinson to Dartmoor. They were driven around by Henry (Harry) Baskerville, who would lend his name to the famous story. The vast expanse of Dartmoor, the ponies grazing among the tall grasses, the granite tors rising through the bleak landscape, the scattered public houses set among the hills, provided the perfect setting for a chilling murder plot. In the heart of the moors rose the high brick walls of Dartmoor Prison, its cold stone cells isolating some of the toughest criminals in the land. Conan Doyle visited the great bog, and watched in fascination as darkness fell in the area, enveloping it with a sense of gloom and the foreboding of evil. He listened to the sounds of the moors. Though Conan Doyle had vowed never to write about Holmes again, he was unable to resist the pull of the story. Mindful of the pressure from his publishers and fans, he decided to pen another adventure for Baker

Street's famous detective. He wrote to Greenhough Smith, editor of the *Strand Magazine* that he had a 'real creeper of a story to tell him'. He masterfully set it in 1889 before his hero plunged down the Reichenbach Falls. The book was everything his publishers wanted. By July 1901, the first instalment of *The Hound of the Baskervilles* was published in the *Strand Magazine*, leading immediately to the demand that Conan Doyle resurrect Holmes.

Over the last few years, George Edalji had built up a steady practice in Birmingham. He had a good list of clients, he'd published a book, which even though it was rather dull and academic had at least established him as a hard-working and reputed solicitor. Britain had changed in 1901. The eighty-one-year-old Queen Victoria had died quietly in Osborne House on the Isle of Wight, surrounded by her beloved Indian servants. The Munshi, Abdul Karim, her closest confidant, was the last person to see her in her coffin before the lid was closed.[4] However, within hours of her funeral, her son and heir, Edward VII, ordered a raid on his house. All the letters written to him by Queen Victoria were burnt outside his cottage and Karim was ordered to return to India like a common criminal. So incensed was Edward VII with his mother's Indian servants, that he dismissed all of them from service. There would be no more colourful turbans and curries in the royal palaces. The 'Black Brigade', as the Indians were called by the aristocratic members of the household, had finally been banished. Britain had become a colder place. The Edwardian era was going to leave its special stamp on Britain and its colonial subjects.

Far away from the royal palaces, things were not going well for George.

In December 1902, George made an error of judgement. A solicitor colleague, John William Phillips, misappropriated funds to the value of £900 entrusted to him by his clients. Phillips absconded and George naively and trustingly agreed to stand surety for him, borrowing foolishly from moneylenders at exorbitant rates to honour the bond. When Phillips defaulted on payment, George became liable. To recover the payment for the loan, George speculated on the stock market, but failed to recover the money. A firm of stockbrokers filed a summons against him.

The Edalji family, Easter 1892. Left to right: George, Maud, Charlotte, Shapurji and Horace

The Vicarage, Great Wyrley

St Mary's Church, Great Wyrley

George Edalji
as a teenager

George Edalji as a
young adult

Inspector Campbell (far right) and two other policemen, walking to the scene of the mutilation in Great Wyrley

Policemen scouring the field where the horse was attacked

Two workmen standing
near a cart used to carry
away the mutilated horses

Inspector Campbell
(second from left) and two
other policemen outside a
house in Great Wyrley

Crowds outside the court during the trial of George Edalji

A scene from the courtroom

Reporters being taken on a tour during George's trial

Shapurji Edalji

An anonymous letter addressed to Shapurji Edalji

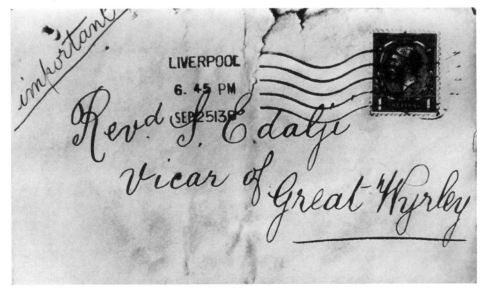

On 29 December he wrote a desperate letter to the MP for Birmingham East, Sir John Benjamin Stone, saying that he had been reduced 'from a fairly comfortable position to absolute poverty' and now owed a large sum of money (nearly £220). To pay off the loan, he had borrowed from three moneylenders 'in the hope of righting myself', but the extortionate interest only made matters worse. The moneylenders had now presented a bankruptcy petition against him, but were prepared to withdraw it if he raised £115 at once.

'I have no such friends to whom I can appeal,' wrote George Edalji, 'and a bankruptcy would ruin me and prevent me practising for a long time during which I should lose all my clients.'[5] He wrote that he was as a last resort appealing for aid to a few strangers. His friends, he said, could find him £20, and he could raise about £20 himself.

'I shall be most thankful for any aid, no matter how small as it will all help me to meet my liability,' he pleaded. He ended the letter apologising for troubling Sir John and hoped he would assist him as far as he could.

The bankruptcy charge would be one of the factors that Anson would point out to the Home Office to show that George had made poor judgements as a solicitor.

There is no record of whether George managed to raise the money. A new sinister mode of terror would now envelop the village of Wyrley, with direct implications for the family at the vicarage.

# 7

## *The Killing Fields*

Within a few months of George's desperate letter about his bankruptcy, the first of the animal killings took place in Great Wyrley. On 1 February 1903 a horse was killed in Cheslyn Hay, an area north of the vicarage. It was a two-year-old colt that belonged to Joseph Holmes, a local shopkeeper. The colt's stomach had been slashed and it had been left to die in the field. The incident would have passed as a one-off, or as a case of a grudge against the owner, which sometimes happened in agricultural communities, had not another offence occurred two months later. In a chilling repeat of the first mutilation, another horse was killed on 10 April.

Terror gripped the village of Great Wyrley as the killings continued in quick succession. Villagers watched in horror as the bodies of the mutilated horses were put on carts and removed from the fields. Photographers milled around the spot capturing the sights for local newspapers. There was something sinister about the mutilations and the torture. Who would do this to animals? asked the helpless villagers.

In the month of May a cow was attacked in Lower Landywood. This was followed by the killing of a sheep and a horse. It was as if a curtain of darkness was descending on the village, blackening the very heart and soul of the community. Farmers looked suspiciously at their labourers and miners searched for reasons for the madness. The small agricultural community had never seen anything like it. Suspicion bred suspicion and the very air seemed to be poisoned. Relentlessly, the killer went on. On 6 June, two cows belonging to Captain Harrison were killed. The Staffordshire police were now on high alert. On 8 June, on Anson's instructions, they brought in about twenty officers from different areas of the county to patrol the streets and fields.

On 29 June, police hid in the dark in the fields, keeping a look-out over Quinton Colliery. Two horses belonging to Blewitt and Company were usually kept in a shed in the fields nearby. At five in the morning, the foreman noticed one of the horses coming up to a pool of water to drink and was horrified to see its entrails hanging from its stomach. He looked for the second horse and found it lying dead. It had been brutally disembowelled. Once again the alarm was raised, locals rushed to the area and the injured horse had to be shot. The police seemed to be hopeless at catching the culprit. The terrified villagers started comparing the killer to 'Jack the Ripper', who had disembowelled prostitutes in east London only a few years previously and had never been caught.

Every killing followed a regular pattern. The killer would attack the animal with a sharp instrument and leave it to die. The same instrument seemed to have been used in every mutilation. It would have had a scimitar-like blade to cause the injuries it did. A drunk and disorderly miner named Thomas Farrington was spotted in the vicinity of the first two attacks, but the police did not follow through any investigation with him. The killer appeared and disappeared in the dead of night, and no one seemed to have any idea who was responsible.

There were angry mutterings about the police as well. At parish council meetings and elsewhere, the villagers complained that the police were wholly incompetent. The 'detectives' they had drafted in from the surrounding counties were basically constables out of uniform, who spent most of their time walking up and down, trying to look inconspicuous, but were given away 'by their very gait'.[1] Once a villager, hearing a disturbance in a bush, had looked to see what was up and found a group of plain-clothes policemen hiding there. On discovery, they tried to walk away nonchalantly, pretending to be locals.

The police seemed unable to stop any of the attacks. Nor were they prepared to consider any suggestions made to them. Local farmers even devised a plan: on the first night, all cattle owners would lock up their animals. Only one farmer would leave his herd free. His animals would be left to roam in certain fields which would be carefully guarded. Next night the 'trap' would be set on another farmer's field and so on. However, it was ignored by the police. Given the relatively small area of the crimes, the locals found it frustrating that the police could get no results. Panic and rumours continued to grow in the feral climate.

The day after the killings at Quinton Colliery, George was travelling to work as usual on the train to Birmingham. The train passed the field where the horses lay mutilated. 'They're the Blewitts', aren't they?' he asked. This simple, innocuous sentence would be held against him at the trial.

And then, as if on cue, to the horror of the vicar and his family, the anonymous letters started again. The vicar, who was trying to console the nervous and frightened people of the village, found that he too was under attack. This time the letters were also addressed to the Staffordshire police.

Sergeant Upton, who had carried out the earlier investigations during the Elizabeth Foster case and was behind the 'stockinged feet' episode, was no longer in service. He had been posted to West Bromwich, and by 1903 had resigned after being charged with drunkenness.

He had never taken the Edaljis seriously. When the second spate of letters started, the only family of colour in Great Wyrley could expect nothing from the police force.

George had few friends. A combination of his introverted personality and the racial prejudice against him meant that he lived a somewhat solitary life. As a young adult, his day consisted of going to his office in Birmingham and back and focusing on his work. He was a teetotaller and could not be seen drinking at a pub with friends or colleagues. He enjoyed going on walks. He had had a problem with his eyesight from a young age and as a child could not read the words on the blackboard if he was seated at the back. He always held his books close to his face when reading, which gave his eyes an unseemly bulge. His faulty vision meant he would sometimes fail to recognise somebody, and people mistakenly thought he was ignoring them. It increased his isolation. Occasionally he took a holiday with his younger sister Maud, who he was very fond of. He would also visit his aunt, Mary Sancta, who described him as her favourite nephew. However, he had a difficult relationship with his brother Horace. Years later, it was revealed that Horace had cast aspersions on his brother George and was cut off from the rest of the family. He did not go to university, and moved to Ludlow in Shropshire when he was offered a job with the Inland Revenue. By the time of the second spate of letters and the animal mutilations, he was not living at the vicarage.

The new officer on duty was Inspector Campbell. A well-built man with a thick moustache, Campbell would be at the centre of the investigation. However this would bring no relief to the Edaljis, as he had imbibed the prejudice of his predecessors and also viewed George with a jaundiced eye. With George's name appearing in the anonymous letters, Campbell would direct his suspicion at him. He would follow the same track of questioning as Upton.

The anonymous and pseudonymous letters now centred on George Edalji. They suggested that he was part of a gang that went out at night and mutilated the animals. The letter-writer constructed an image of George stealthily coming out in the dead of night and slashing the beasts. Police Constable Rowley at Bridgetown received one of these. It asked him to look out for a passenger who took the evening train from Walsall, a train in which George Edalji always travelled.

'A party whose initials you'll gess will be bringing a new hook home by the train from Walsall on Wednesday night ... he has got eagle eyes and his ears is as sharp as a razor an he is as fleet of foot as a fox and as noiseless an he crawls on all-fours up to the poor beasts, an' fondles them a bit, and then he pulls a hook smart across 'em, and out their entrails fly afore they gess they are hurt. You want 100 detectives to run him in red handed because he is so fly and knows every nook and corner ...' the letter said.

Some of the letters were written under the name of a schoolboy called Wilfred Greatorex. Letters were also sent to the real Wilfred Greatorex, who lived in Hednesford and who often travelled on the same train as George Edalji. These letters were slightly different in style from the 'God-Satan' letters of the 1890s as they had fewer religious maniacal references and were in different handwriting. But they also had many similarities. Once again, they were clearly written by a person with local knowledge. What was not clear was whether the killer and the letter-writer were the same person. They could have been different people and the letter-writer seized the opportunity to needle George again and link him to the killings. Or, it could be that a person with a despicably sick mind was committing both crimes.

In June, Police Constable Rowley received a letter which baited the police:

You made a mistake not keeping all the plain-clothes men at hand. You went away too soon. Why, just think, he did it close where two of them were hidin, only a few days gone by.

The police stepped up their patrol. They put a watch around the vicarage and looked out for George, as his name repeatedly appeared in the letters. They desperately needed to catch a killer and pacify the terrified villagers of Wyrley. Nearly six months had passed from the first mutilation and no arrests had been made. Given the local knowledge of the letter-writer, it was abundantly clear to the villagers as well as the police, that the killer and letter-writer (if they were the same person) were from the neighbourhood.

On one hand the sinister letter-writer was taunting the police. On the other hand, he was leading them on a trail. The police started watching a few people in the area. One of them was Royden Sharp, the former schoolboy from Walsall Grammar, a contemporary of George, who had shown potential for violent behaviour from his schooldays. After being expelled from school, Sharp had become an apprentice butcher and gone to sea as a mate on a cattle ship. He had been away from Wyrley between 1895 and 1903, the exact gap between the last anonymous letter and the latest spate of killings and letters. He also had a friend, John England Hart, a butcher from Cheslyn Hay, who was used to handling horses. Others in the broader pool of possible suspects included Harry Green, who was a member of the Staffordshire Yeomanry, a cavalry unit. Green was used to wielding a sabre and was the son of a farmer, T. J. Green. The Greens were neighbours of the Edalji family and Harry had been baptised by Shapurji. There was also the disgruntled and often inebriated miner Thomas Farrington, who had issues with his employers and was often seen lurking around the fields, but the police were focused on George. Much was made of the fact that he liked to go for long walks, a perfectly innocent pastime for a man who lived in the countryside. As the villagers discussed the situation in panic and fear, these 'long walks' were soon distorted and reported as 'prowling in the dark'.

Meanwhile, the letters continued:

'Now I'll tell you who are in the gang, but you can't prove it without me. There is one named Broell from Wyrley and a porter called Edgar of Wyrley station ... and there's Edalji the lawyer him as they say was locked up, there's Fred Wooton from Cheslyn Hay ...'

George's name was repeatedly mentioned in the letters. Some of them were addressed to him. Fatally for George, the police who had previously linked him with the anonymous letters from a few years ago, were now connecting him with the letters again, and this time the path was leading in an altogether more dangerous direction. George was not a seventeen-year-old schoolboy any more. He was a practising solicitor and any allegations against him would muddy his reputation. The terrified villagers were beginning to wonder whether the awkward and shy son of the vicar was behind the sinister crimes. In an atmosphere of fear, every rumour had legs. Everything seemed to be working against George: his lack of friends, his long walks and his appearance.

George heard the stories flying around in the village that his name had been suggested as being part of a gang and that he had been arrested. He put out an advertisement in the local paper offering a reward of £25 to anyone who had information on the person or persons who were defaming him. But nothing stopped the letter-writer and no one came forward to identify him.

The police called on George at the vicarage, pretending to be anxious to ascertain who had circulated the rumours about his arrest. They showed him a letter they had received. It was posted in a brown envelope without a stamp with the words OHMS (On His Majesty's Service) written on it in ink. A piece of paper had been pasted on the back of the envelope. On it were the words 'your affectionate friend, Fred Wooton'. Enclosed in the envelope was another envelope bearing the trademark of a well-known Birmingham stationer, Osborne & Son. It was addressed to 'G.E.T Edalji, Esq, 54 Newhall Street, Birmingham.'

The letter was addressed to 'The Sergeant, The Police Station, Hednesford', and stated that there would be 'merry times at Wyrley in November when they would start on little girls; they would do 20 wenches like the horses before next March.'

Inevitably, George was mentioned in the letter. 'Mr Edalji, him they said was locked up is going to Brum on Sunday night to see the Captain near Northfield about how its to be carried on with so many detectives about and I believe they are going to do some cows in the day time instead of at night.'

Watching George's reactions closely, the police asked him if he could throw any light on the letter. George said it had neither stamp nor postmark and he had not seen it before. The police said that it was probably written by the person who spread the rumour about his arrest. They asked George not to mention it to anybody and suggested that he might get another letter soon. After that the inspector engaged him in conversation about the killings. They asked if he had any idea about the killer. George said he had no idea, but he suggested to the police that they use bloodhounds to catch him. He asked the police if they were still watching the area and whether they had ever found a knife or instrument that it was done with. To the police, he seemed suspicious. They were convinced he knew something.

The letter caused panic in the village. Visions of young girls being attacked by a dangerous killer led to near hysteria. Mothers locked up their daughters and forbade them to go out after dark. The police were not silent about their suspicions either. While being shaved at a barber's shop in Cannock, a local man reported that he had heard a police constable say openly: 'If we could set fire to the bloody vicarage, there would be no more outrages.'[2]

The villagers had seen George every Sunday at church. They had seen him catch the train to Birmingham every morning, and seen him walking back home at the same time every evening. They knew he had written a book and had won medals. Some of them came to him for their legal matters. However, the seeds of doubt planted by the police started to grow as they desperately looked for a killer. Without logic or reason, they began wondering whether the son of the vicar was going out at night and slashing cattle.

Anonymous letter received by the police

Threatening letters to the police further added to local anxiety.

The letter to Sergeant Robinson said: 'I will shoot you with father's gun through your thick head if you come my way … I will murder you if I get a thick rope around my neck for it, but I don't think they would hang me but send me to sea …'[3]

On 23 July, George received a letter, slightly different in tone from the others. It was signed by 'A Lover of Justice' who said he did not 'like natives'. Written in a different, well-formed hand, it said:

George Edalji,
I do not know you, but I have sometimes seen you in the railway, and I do not expect I would like you very much, if I did not know you, as I do not like natives. But … I do not think you have anything to do with the horrid crimes … The people all about said it must be you because they do not think you are a right sort … If another horse is murdered the people will all say it was you …
A Lover of Justice

A few days later, another missive signed 'Greatorex' was delivered to George, the content of which was very similar to the 'Lover of Justice' letter. George informed the police. When Inspector Campbell called again at the vicarage, he handed over the 'Lover of Justice' letter to him, followed by the 'Greatorex' letter. He asked him if he thought that more than one person could have been involved in the mutilations and letter-writing. This was taken as evidence that he knew that there was a 'gang' in operation. While nearly all of Great Wyrley were discussing and trying to solve the crimes, every innocent utterance by George was seen as proof of his guilt.

George was beginning to dread the post. The letters were everywhere. They were at the vicarage and at his office. He was in despair when a postcard dated 4 August was dropped into his mailbox at his office. It was open for everyone to see. It contained crude sexual innuendos suggesting that George was having nightly liaisons with the sister of Arthur Quibbel, a local schoolboy, who was soon to marry the 'socialist' Frank Smith. It accused him of going back to his old practice of scribbling on walls, writing anonymous letters and killing cows. It was posted in Wolverhampton. Once again it was signed by 'Greatorex'. A postcard was also sent the same day to Inspector Campbell posted at Walsall. Despite George leaving early with his sister for Aberystwyth on the morning of 4 August, the police later accused him of writing both postcards.

George could feel the police waiting and watching. Years later, he would write: 'What was I to do? Was I to run away because some person had published a false report about me, and was sending letters which any reasonable being ought to know I should certainly not write?'[4]

From the overt racism of the anonymous letters found at the vicarage when he was a teenager to the current batch of mail naming him as the perpetrator of the violent crimes, George could only watch helplessly as the suspicions against him seemed to be building.

He continued to meet his clients and tried to carry on as usual. On the evening of 17 August he met a local client, David Hobson, at the vicarage between 7.30 and 8 p.m. He then went for a walk. It was to be his last walk as a free man in the village of Great Wyrley. On that wet and windy night another horse was mutilated and killed in the Great Wyrley Colliery, half a mile from the vicarage. It sealed George Edalji's fate.

Early next morning, the police called round. George had already left for work, Charlotte and Maud were having breakfast and the vicar was upstairs. Inspector Campbell asked Charlotte to bring him George's clothes and 'his dagger'. When no knives could be found, they left with a botany knife belonging to Maud which she used to collect flower samples. It was said to be so blunt that it could not even cut cheese. They found an old house-coat and a waistcoat that they said was damp and stained. They also found a pair of muddy boots. The police claimed that there were horse hairs on the coat, though no one in the Edalji family saw any when the coat was shown to them. The vicar took it to the window for a closer look and pointed out to Inspector Campbell that what he thought was a horse hair was actually a thread from the coat. Despite three family members and the domestic help saying that George had not left the house after 9.30 p.m. and that he had only left at 7.30 a.m. the next day on his way to work, Inspector Campbell remained unconvinced.

They called on George at his office in Birmingham, questioned him about his movements the night before, said they were not satisfied with his answers and arrested him on the charge of killing a horse.

Later that afternoon, the police returned to the vicarage and demanded to search all the rooms. They took away a box of four razors, which they said were wet. Shapurji said they were old and had not been used for a while. They also took away a pair of trousers they had seen earlier and which they had said were damp and muddy. They claimed that the trousers were not so wet now and were much cleaner than they were in the morning. Charlotte said she had not touched the trousers and they had probably dried on their own.

George was taken to the police lock-up in Steelhouse Lane in Birmingham, soon to be inhabited by the notorious members of the 'Peaky Blinders' gang. His pockets were turned out, yielding a pocket knife and a handkerchief. The police inspected the knife to see if there was any blood on it, but it was too small to inflict a wound. A police constable wanted to take away his handkerchief in case he strangled himself with it, but George assured them that he had no intention of committing suicide and was allowed to retain it. He was then placed in a cell for the first time in his life.

After about an hour and a half, he was taken in a cab to the railway station and then by train to Cannock. The policemen escorting him were not in uniform and fellow commuters were not aware that he was in custody. From Cannock station he was quickly transferred into a pony trap and driven to the police station. News of his arrest had not yet got around and there were few people in the street.

'I've copped one of them this time,' the inspector declared triumphantly as he led George into the police station. 'Ran away to Birmingham soon as he knew we were after him, but I followed him up and arrested him at his office.' George said nothing. He had not been running away. He had gone to work.

At the police station, he was measured for his height and photographed for police records. George asked to see the jacket and waistcoat they had removed as evidence from his house. At this, the Inspector sprang to his feet, declared he had already occupied too much time and told one of the police officers, to 'put him out of my sight for the devil's sake'. As George was being led away, the inspector shouted: 'I will show you that coat later on, Mr Edalji.'

Cannock police station had two small cells for the detention of prisoners. George was locked in one. He described it later as the worst cell he had ever seen or heard of. As they closed the door on him, it was almost pitch-dark. It had no gas or other artificial light. He was told he could not have a lamp or candle lest he set fire to himself. There was no bell, and the only way to attract attention was to thump or kick the door. This he did loudly at one stage in the night and was told that he had disturbed a policeman who was saying his prayers before he left on duty. The only furniture in the cell was a fixed bench, which worked as chair, table and bed.

A constable needled him: 'Well, Mr Edalji,' he said. 'I'm sorry to see you here, but how did you manage to slip by all our chaps? What time did you put the horse through it? Give the show away or someone else will.'[5]

Through the evening, the police tried to make him talk, so he could incriminate himself, but George would not oblige. His training as a lawyer had taught him that prisoners often had their words twisted out of context and ended up in trouble for what they said casually at the police station. Not getting anything out of him, the constable finally offered George a whisky, but he declined as he was a teetotaller.

In the evening he was allowed to go to the office-room in the station so he could write some letters and see a client. The police insisted on reading the letters and stood in the room while he met his client. Later he was allowed to see his father and a solicitor. Shapurji looked worried and tearful when he saw his son in the police lock-up. George reassured him that he would soon be out. All the while the police stood and listened to their conversation.

All night long the police kept a strict watch to see that he would not attempt suicide. The cell was pitch-dark and he could see nothing. Every hour, from 8 p.m. till 2 a.m., an officer would come with a lantern to check on him and try to make him talk. On the sixth appearance, George told him not to come again and he went away.

There was no water in the cell. When George asked for some, he was told he could not have any because prisoners tried to drown themselves by holding their heads underwater in the bucket. Finally, well past 2 a.m., tired, thirsty and worried, George fell into a troubled sleep.

It had been exactly ten years since the last anonymous letter declared that George Edalji would be sent to his grave.

# 8

# *A Public Spectacle*

George spent his first night in the dark claustrophobic cell at Cannock police station. Early next morning, the door was flung open and he was given a bucket of water, a mottled soap and a rag to clean up. Breakfast was sent from the vicarage, but he could only eat it after the beady-eyed police constable had gone through his milk and cereal and checked it thoroughly. It was time for him to be presented at the magistrates' court.

The news of the arrest of George Edalji had spread like wildfire in Great Wyrley. Crowds gathered outside Cannock Court and George had to walk through a dense crowd of people for about 150 yards before he could reach the door. An old lady followed him shouting a shower of abuse and had to be restrained by the police.

The first session was brief. The Edalji family would have been dismayed to see the magistrate – J. T. Hatton, one of those with a history of animosity against them. The two other magistrates present were Mr J. Williamson and Colonel R. S. Williamson. The charge against the prisoner was read out and he confirmed his name and address. The inspector recounted the interview he had with George at his office and with his parents at the vicarage. Shapurji swore that George was at home and in bed all night and that he slept in the same room as him. The magistrates set a date for further hearing of the evidence and bail was denied.

George returned to his cell and managed to have a brief conversation with his parents. He was then taken in a cab to Cannock to catch the train for Stafford. Once again crowds had gathered at the railway station. The police held them back from climbing on to the platform. As the train stopped at Hednesford, George bought a copy of the evening paper. It had a report of the case. A crowd of young boys immediately surrounded the compartment. 'That's 'im that killed the 'oss,' said one urchin pointing at George, 'and lor' help me if he ain't reading about 'imself.'[1]

At Stafford station a large crowd of railway officials were waiting for him. He was bundled into a cab and driven to the local prison. Small groups of people gathered to get a glimpse of him. 'The church clocks were just striking seven, as on the memorable evening of August 19th 1903 I reached the entrance to Stafford Prison,' George wrote later.[2]

It was the first time that he had seen the inside of a prison. The building was quiet as everyone was confined to their cells in the evening. He was taken to the reception room, where he was asked if he could read and write, whether he had been to prison before and what his religion was. He was then asked to strip naked to show that he had nothing to conceal. The humiliation was unbearable. The officers had the grace to apologise, saying it was the rule for every new arrival. George felt he was in the middle of a surreal nightmare.

He was sent to the prison hospital for the first night and stayed on one of the large wards. The governor and the doctor called on him and checked him out. In the neighbouring bed was a prisoner who told him that he had been in nearly every prison in the country including the famous Broadmoor prison and lunatic asylum. It wasn't the company George was used to.

The next morning he was transferred to a separate cell and only saw the other prisoners at exercise time. He was not allowed food from outside as he was in the hospital, but was allowed his choice of diet.

The arrest of George had put the village of Great Wyrley in the spotlight. The vicar found that attendance had increased at his church services. Horse carriages could be heard rumbling down the street as curious men, women and children chose to ride near the vicarage hoping to catch a glimpse of the family.

A few days after his arrest, George was taken to Cannock Court again, for the start of the pre-trial hearings. The excitement had been building in the surrounding area. Once again, a large crowd gathered round the station to catch a glimpse of the prisoner who would alight there. They strained out of curiosity to see the face of the man who had allegedly brought terror to the picturesque village of Great Wyrley. George arrived escorted by Inspector Campbell. A closed four-wheeled carriage was waiting to take him to the police court. The crowd roared as he alighted and boarded the cab. A group of small boys hung on to the back of the vehicle as it swung through the narrow streets.

The crowds outside the court were even larger. What had begun as a trickle in the morning, as groups of men and women stood around discussing the case, had turned into a mighty throng clamouring to enter the court. Even the rain did not deter them as they stood outside the door. The police constables tried to control the wild crowd. Soon the road became impassable. When the cab arrived, the crowds surged towards it, leaning up and battering against the door. 'It's him, it's him,' they cried out. Inside the carriage George sat with a detective on each side. He looked out at the screaming mob with a blank expression on his face. The crowd swept forward and wrenched the door of the cab. They made way as he was led inside.

The *Wolverhampton Express & Star* reported the crush: 'When the door was opened there was a rush that resembled nothing so much as the struggle for seats on "first night" at a popular theatre. Men were cursing, women were shrieking, and all were fighting, struggling and pushing making a veritable pandemonium. The police, as a result, lost their heads and tempers.' The reporter from the *Express & Star* could not even get in through the public entrance and entered through the magistrates' door, but was told that it was 'unheard of' do the same. He was promptly thrown out.

As the crowds struggled outside the courtroom, a policeman 'whose face was like a beetroot' shouted, 'You will have someone killed yet.'

'Murder!' shrieked a woman who was on the verge of being trampled underfoot. The representative of the *Express & Star* plunged into the 'swirling human sea', and was finally rescued by a policeman who managed to get him through.

Inside the hushed courtroom, George waited while the magistrates dealt with some trivial cases. Finally, it was decided to bring his case forward, given the attention it was receiving.

The courtroom was small, 'ill-arranged and inconvenient'. Reporters sat in a separate box where they could get a good view of the prisoner. George's parents, Shapurji and Charlotte, his sister Maud and brother Horace sat on the benches in the front. Horace had come down from his office in Ludlow to be present at the hearing. The family looked tense and worried. At 11 a.m. the proceedings began. They were very brief, formal and slightly confused. At the hearing, Hatton had been replaced by E. A. Foden. Foden was the agent of Lord Hatherton, another influential person whom Shapurji had clashed with. The other magistrates were once again John Williamson and Colonel R. S. Williamson. The prosecution was represented by Mr Burke and the defence by Litchfield Meek. The chief constable of Staffordshire police, G. A. Anson, the deputy chief constable, Longden, and Superintendent Barrett, were also present. It was the first time that Anson would see George. He was not impressed.

The police officer, Inspector Campbell, related the details of the arrest, stating that bloodstains were found on the prisoner's clothes and mud on his boots. A razor, the jacket and the boots were presented at court.

An application for bail was made by Meek. It was fixed at £500. Meek remarked that it was heavy bail, especially as the father was a clergyman and the prisoner a respectable solicitor.

'Well, it is the decision we have arrived at,' said John Williamson.

'Can they not abandon the surety [of £100]?' asked Meek.

'No, I don't think we can,' said Williamson.

'It is too high. My son will be ruined,' pleaded the vicar.

'No, we have already given our decision,' repeated Williamson.

George, however, decided not to pay the bail. He felt that since he was perfectly innocent, if another outrage occurred, it would help clear his name. Also, given the publicity and raw emotion around the case, he reckoned he would not be able to go about his work normally in Birmingham. He was remanded for a week. The next hearing would be at Penkridge.

Once again, he was led through the crowds and transferred in a cab to Hednesford railway station and from there to Stafford Prison. He managed to have a few words with his mother before he left the court. The vicar and his wife watched in silence as their son was escorted into the police van and the doors were shut. Tears streamed down Maud's face. Horace looked stonily ahead. The main street of

Cannock remained crowded for some time as people stood around discussing the events of the morning.

The next hearing took place a week later on Monday 31 August at Penkridge. George was taken from the prison to Stafford railway station in a 'Black Maria', the police van for prisoners. It seemed the whole district had turned out to watch his arrival at Penkridge. Watching the Edaljis had almost become a Sunday sport for the local miners. The case was attracting national coverage as well. Given that one of their own had been arrested, the legal profession, too, was keeping a keen eye. Every hearing was torture for the family and for George. Once again, Shapurji and Charlotte made their way to the court. Maud was not present. By now, three more magistrates had been added to the bench. They were E. C. R. Littleton and Lieutenant Littleton, sons of Lord Hatherton, and Mr A. Lane.

This time another charge was levelled against George Edalji. He was now charged with threatening to murder Sergeant Robinson via an anonymous letter: 'You bloated blackguard, I will shoot you with father's gun through your thick head if you come in my way ...'

George said he had never even heard of the policeman, let alone written to him. The police were determined to link the animal mutilations to the anonymous letters and close in on George Edalji. Anson, present at every hearing, and directing it from behind the scenes, was determined to get him sentenced to 'penal servitude'. Once again bail was fixed at the same rate. Once again, George refused it.

On the way back to Stafford, George and the escorting officers passed the excited crowds again. In the train, a constable provoked him: 'Well, if you aren't a clever 'un.' Turning to another constable, he added: 'This one here's the local De Wet; went and did the horse under with six men watching for him to come out. Tell us how you managed it, Mr Edalji.'[3]

George did not respond. He was getting used to the constant jibes from the police. On 2 September, George was presented for another hearing at a special court. Hundreds of people gathered outside. The story had inflamed the popular imagination and the locals were craving to get in on the action. Witnesses were produced in court. They said they had seen George Edalji near the area of the crime. The prosecution introduced further 'evidence': horse hairs on George's coat, and footprints that matched those at the scene of the crime. Sergeant Robinson recalled the alarm he had felt when he received the letter that threatened to kill him. A handwriting expert, Thomas Henry Gurrin, said that the anonymous letters were in George's handwriting. Though the police gave conflicting accounts of when the vicarage was watched on the night of 17/18 August, it was considered enough for the magistrates to commit George Edalji to trial. Once again he refused bail.

A police sergeant, who clearly felt sorry for George and was not convinced about his guilt, urged him to accept bail, saying that if he did not want to ask his friends, they could get three of the most honourable gentlemen in Cannock within an hour to stand for him. He simply had to pledge that he would stay at home before the trial. George refused and the sergeant remarked: 'It will be the worse for you. The inspectors will see to that.'

George had not anticipated that his decision to avoid bail would be twisted out of context and added to the thin line of evidence that would be presented against him in the months ahead. Back in Stafford Prison, he waited out the next few weeks. Still occupying a room in the hospital, he could wear his own clothes, exercise daily and have newspapers, magazines and books. He was allowed a visitor every week. All the letters were read by the constable and he was present at every meeting. George felt he had done the right thing by refusing bail.

In Great Wyrley, the killer was ready to strike again. On 22 September at around 1.30 a.m., a nightwatchman at Gilpin's Ironworks heard a horse neighing in pain. In the morning, John Jayes, a miner on his way to work going past High House Farm belonging to T. J. Green saw a horse lying dead with its stomach slashed. The horse had charged around the field in agony leaving portions of its entrails lying about. Once again, the veterinary surgeon was summoned. He said the horse had probably been killed around midnight. Once again, the news of the killing spread like wildfire. Crowds rushed to the scene of the crime, not far from the vicarage.

What chilled the villagers to the bone was the fact that George was in Stafford Prison awaiting trial. This was not his doing. It meant the killer was still out there.

The news of the killing gave some hope to Charlotte, who wrote to her son at Stafford Prison. George replied that he was 'overjoyed' that he had not accepted bail, but he remained sceptical about whether it would help his cause. He tried to remain calm as he prepared for his trial.

# 9

## A Trial in Staffordshire

To the gathered media and crowds, the man sitting in the front of the Staffordshire quarter sessions court on 20 October looked every bit the 'dark Oriental' with a 'deep secret'.[1] His eyes were slightly bulgy, his lips were thick and he had a prominent cleft on his chin. He had a thick moustache and his dark hair was neatly combed. It was two months since his arrest on that fateful August morning.

Present in the courtroom were his parents, Shapurji and Charlotte, and his sister Maud. His grey-haired mother took notes as the hearing progressed. His elderly father, who had conducted Sunday services for so many years in the local church, and who had married the residents of the village and consoled them at the funerals of their loved ones, now looked helpless and forlorn, the tension of the last few months clearly showing on his face. The family looked a model of righteousness and honour, unlikely relatives of a man accused of such heinous crimes. Also seated in the courtroom was Elizabeth Foster, the maid who had been fired from the Edalji house and sworn her revenge. It was not clear whether she had been brought in as a witness. The Staffordshire police were out in full force to give evidence, under the watchful eye of their chief, Captain Anson.

The tension in the courtroom could be cut with a knife. The killing of a horse on Green's Farm on 22 September, even as George was in Stafford Prison awaiting trial, had led to further panic among the villagers. Surely, George Edalji was innocent, they questioned. And the actual killer was still amongst them. The police had other ideas. They would claim at the trial that it had been done by somebody in George's 'gang'.

Before his trial, George had asked for permission to change his clothing as he had been wearing the summer suit he had been arrested in for the last three months. The request was refused. Prisoners were required to be tried in the clothes worn when apprehended. George was told that a prisoner on a murder charge in a nearby cell had to appear in his bloodied clothes, so the jurors could see the full horror of the crime. That, thought George, was an acceptable rule for a prisoner denied bail. However, as someone who had been granted bail and would have been allowed to stay at home if he had wanted, George questioned the rule. But the police were firm. He was not even allowed to change his shoes or the straw hat that he had worn in August and which was totally unsuitable for late October. George felt that his unsuitable clothes and appearance itself could prejudice a jury who were not aware of the rules.

The day before his trial, he asked to be shaved, but was told that such a thing was unheard of at Stafford. He could only be clipped with the 'nippers'. Since the court was sitting from early morning till late, there was no chance for him to get a 'clip'. Consequently, George appeared before the jury, the press and the public, sporting a light three-piece check suit, a worn-out boot and a rather overgrown moustache. The *Sunderland Daily Echo* reported: 'The prisoner was unshaven and his appearance was even more Oriental than before … His thick lips were pursed and his large black eyes fixed on the witnesses.'[2]

Most newspapers, however, did not remark too unfavourably on his sartorial choice as George took his place in the court. Sometimes he would lean back in his chair, his arms folded and his legs crossed, keenly watching the witnesses. Reporters noted that one of his boots was clearly worn down, a fact that would be brought up at the trial. There was a quiet demeanour about him, the air of a professional lawyer, they said, as he listened earnestly to the court proceedings. Occasionally he would say a few words to his counsel.

The hearing took place at the second court of the quarter sessions in Stafford. The October chill was setting in, but it had not put off the crowds. The press were present in full force ready to cover the trial of the man accused of bringing terror to Great Wyrley. Outside, the crowds milled in Market Square, discussing the case. A few days into the trial, two highly respected figures in the legal field, retired

Chief Justice Roger Dawson Yelverton and Sir George Lewis, a leading criminal lawyer, would criticise the fact that the most famous criminal trial in the area had been assigned to such a low court.

The quarter sessions sat every quarter through the year and were presided over by eminent local people in the area who acted as Justices of the Peace. Disputes between neighbours and small criminal cases were heard at the quarter sessions. Yelverton and Lewis claimed that the case should have gone to the assizes, where serious criminal cases were heard, or at least to Court One of the quarter sessions court, where the judge would have been far more experienced in legal matters and would have directed the jury in the proper manner, allowing only admissible evidence at the trial. However, Lord Hatherton, chairman of the quarter sessions court, withdrew from hearing the case on the grounds that he was a resident of the area and had known the Edalji family for some time, and handed the case over to the smaller Court Two, where Sir Reginald Hardy, vice chairman of the quarter sessions court, was in charge. Hatherton had clashed with Shapurji over the issue of local schools. Now he saw that the case was consigned to what the vicar described as the 'most inferior court with a jury in the county'.[3]

Justice Sir Reginald Hardy, a Staffordshire landowner and a man without any real legal experience, was thus put in charge. A sign of his own lack of confidence, Hardy appointed four judges to the bench for assistance. One of them was Vice Admiral Hon. A. C. Littleton, son of Lord Hatherton, who had been present at the pre-trials. He also enlisted the help of Bertram Brough, a junior barrister, who was invited as a legal adviser. However, Brough was busy acting for a client at another trial and spent most of his time running between the two courts. He was barely present at George's hearings. Yelverton would later question the suitability of Hardy to preside over such an important case. Hardy may not have been a legal expert, but he was well connected. His wife was the niece of former prime minister William E. Gladstone, and the cousin of the future Home Secretary, Herbert Gladstone.

There was also criticism later that the trial itself should have been held outside the area, given the strong local feelings about the case. It emerged later that it was Anson who had advised that the case be taken to quarter sessions rather than assizes. He had claimed that George had been anxious to get an early hearing and the dates available at assizes were two months later. The members of the aristocracy – Hatherton, Hatton, Hardy and Anson – had set the stage for a trial that would be disadvantageous to George Edalji from the very start.

The prosecution case was led by W. J. Disturnal, assisted by H. Harrison. They were instructed by A. W. Barnes of Lichfield. The defence was represented by F. S. Vachell and W. J. Gandy, instructed by Litchfield Meek of Messrs Walter and Meek. The twelve men of the jury were drawn from a wide area around Staffordshire, excluding people from Cannock as they would have too great an emotional connection with the case. It was, however, impossible to presume that the jury had not been following the media reports of the cattle killings of recent months. No profile of the jury exists. A plea by Yelverton for their names was denied by the Home Office.[4] Women were not allowed to be jury members in 1903.

Black men and women were often seen in the dock in trials in Britain in the eighteenth and nineteenth centuries, usually in cases of grand larceny or burglary. The colour of their skin was always brought up at trial and it often led to them being disadvantaged. When in 1737 George Scipio was accused of stealing Anne Godfrey's washing, the case rested entirely on whether or not Scipio was the only black man in Hackney at the time.[5] In 1909, when a twelve-year-old boy, William Worsley from Bolsover near Chesterfield was charged with stealing a chicken, the court was specifically told that he was 'half-caste'. Finally, his blind father, a resident of Bolsover for forty-two years, had to come to court and plead his son's innocence.[6]

At the turn of the century, there occurred a more serious case involving a black man, but the press coverage was quite sympathetic to him. In 1900, William Lacey murdered his white wife, Pauline, in Pontypridd in Wales. Lacey was found guilty and sentenced to death at Swansea Crown Court. The judge pronounced that it was a case 'not without its lesson and warning', implying that it could end badly if a white woman married a black man. But the press covered it as a crime of passion with considerable empathy for the accused.[7] The papers splashed the photograph of the couple in happier times with the caption 'Othello and his Desdemona'. Lacey was described as having a 'a kind, nay gentle face, even handsome as negroes go.' His last words to the court, which are said to have moved the packed courtroom, were headlined in the *Western Mail* as 'Bids Tragic Goodbye to the World'.

George's ethnicity would be very much part of the press coverage at his trial. The crowds gathered to stare at him not just because of the horrific nature of the crimes. They were there because of the dark man accused of committing them. Locals queued outside the court and rushed to get the best seats. Miners and farmers – dressed in their Sunday best – packed the courtroom. Women in large hats carried picnic baskets and reading matter, ready to spend the day watching the trial of the century. Public houses in the area did brisk business.

On Tuesday 20 October, George Edalji was driven the few hundred yards from Stafford Prison to the quarter sessions building in the Black Maria. This van was different from the other ones, as it was divided into individual compartments for the prisoners. The compartments were so narrow that there was barely room for a prisoner to sit in each. George commented later that a fat person would find it impossible to get out even if they managed to squeeze themselves in. Fortunately, it was a short drive. At the courtroom, he was led through a labyrinth of passages to the holding area, where he was asked to wait by himself for an hour. He was not nervous, having full confidence as a lawyer himself that his innocence would be declared.[8] He spent the hour reading some papers. Finally, he was taken upstairs. There was a hush of excitement as he emerged from the trapdoor escorted by two police officers and took his place in the courtroom.

The trial began with the naming of the prisoner and the charges against him. George was accused of having maliciously wounded a horse, the property of the Great Wyrley Colliery Company on or about 17 August, at Great Wyrley. He was also indicted for having on or about 11 July sent a threatening letter to Police Sergeant Robinson. He pleaded 'not guilty' to both charges.

Disturnal made his opening statements with the flourish of a prosecution lawyer, setting up the case for the jury. The charge against the prisoner was a serious one, he said, and when the jury saw that the accused was a solicitor and a distinguished member of the profession, they would see that the investigation was not an ordinary one. Disturnal gave a brief profile of the prisoner. He had been admitted into the profession in 1898 and had won a prize from the Birmingham Law Society. He was the son of Rev. S. Edalji who had been Vicar of Great Wyrley for nearly twenty-seven years. This gentleman was a Parsee; the mother of the accused was an English lady. The prisoner lived with them at the time of the commission of the crime for which he was charged. Disturnal then outlined the evidence he would present before the court.

He said he would prove that the prisoner was seen in the vicinity of the field after 9 p.m. on the night of 17 August. The police had recovered a suit of clothes from his house the next morning that were wet, bloodstained and smeared with horse hairs. They had found a pair of boots belonging to the accused which were very wet. A number of important letters would be exhibited, and Mr Gurrin, an eminent handwriting expert, would depose that these were written in a disguised hand by the prisoner.

Disturnal said that a number of killings had occurred in the district and the case had excited great interest. Urging the jury to look at the history of the case, Disturnal delved at length into the series of animal killings and mutilations that had occurred since February.

Though the prisoner was not charged with any of these crimes except that committed on August 17, Disturnal stated that it was important for the jury to know about these crimes so they could understand the meaning of many of the passages in the letters.

Speaking for an hour, Disturnal implied to the jury that the prisoner had been behind the writing of all the letters, as well as the cattle killings. Although George was charged with only two cases – the mutilation of a pony on the night of 17 August – and for writing the letter threatening to kill Sergeant Robinson (around 11 July) – Disturnal created the impression that all the cases were linked.

As the court watched him in silence, George shook his head, disagreeing with the claims of the prosecution. His defence lawyer sat quietly next to him, not raising any objection to Disturnal bringing up the previous cases. Taking advantage of Hardy's lack of legal expertise, and the silence of the defence, Disturnal carried on. From the outset he managed to instil in the jury's mind the link between the letters and the mutilations and pointed the responsibility for all in the direction of the prisoner. The prosecution claimed that the killing had happened between 9 p.m. and 10 p.m. when George was seen near the area.

Bringing up the prickly issue of the latest cattle-killing, which had happened on the night of 21 September while George was in custody, Disturnal managed a clever argument. It was very likely that there was a gang operating, he said, and one of its members would commit a similar killing in order to create evidence for the defence. The fact that Edalji had refused bail went to show that he was aware of the gang and knew that there would be another killing. In a swift stroke, the prosecution turned the latest killing to their advantage.

Having focused the minds of the jury on the letters and the killings, it was time for Disturnal to bring on the witnesses. Over the next few days witnesses were called from both sides and an array of exhibits shown to the jury: letters, shoes with one heel worn out, a jacket and a razor. The prosecution had commissioned an engineering firm to draw up a detailed map of the area, which was also produced in court.

The first to give evidence was Richard James Barnes, surveyor and architect, who produced plans and said that the distance from the vicarage to the field where the animal was mutilated was about half a mile.

William Wooton, a horse-keeper working for the company, said he saw a pony belonging to the company in the field near the colliery at nine o'clock on the night of 17 August. It was all right at the time. The next morning he found the pony in the field with a wound in its side. After the pony was examined by a veterinary surgeon, he shot it.

Henry Garrett, a youth employed at Gilpin's Ironworks said he was going to work at a quarter to six on the morning of 18 August and saw the pony in the field bleeding from a wound.

William Cooper, horse slaughterer of Cannock, said he examined the pony. The wound was about 14 inches long and extended across the belly. It must have been inflicted by a sharp, short-bladed knife. The bowels of the animal had not been penetrated.

William Brutch, another horse slaughterer, said he had cut a piece of skin from the horse.

The next set of witnesses gave evidence about when and where they last saw George.

William Danbury, groom and gardener, said he saw the prisoner in Coppice Lane going towards Cheslyn Hay about 9 p.m. on 17 August.

Frederick William Gripton, carpenter; Elizabeth Ann Biddle, dressmaker; William Charles Thacker, ironmonger; and Mabel Thacker said they had seen the prisoner near Cheslyn Hay between nine and half past nine on 17 August.

David Hobson, general dealer from Bridgetown said he had been with the prisoner at the vicarage from 7.30 to 8 p.m. on 17 August, at which time he was wearing the clothes that were shown in court.

Then it was time for the police witnesses to take the stand. First up was Inspector Campbell, the man who had led the investigation. Standing in the box for four hours, he recounted the case. He recalled that on the morning of 18 August he had gone with Sergeant Parsons and Police Constable Cooper to the field near the Great Wyrley Colliery and saw the chestnut-coloured pony.

'I examined the pony,' said Campbell. 'There was a large cut extending underneath the belly – extending up to the ribs on the near side 14 inches long. The bowels were partially protruding. I saw marks of blood in several places in the field. There was a large quantity of blood where the pony had evidently been standing at the time.' There were audible expressions of horror from the gathered crowds in the courtroom as Campbell gave details of the attack.

He described how he had gone to the vicarage the same morning, and the prisoner's mother had produced a jacket, vest and trousers belonging to the accused. On the cuffs of the jacket there was a dark reddish stain and on the sleeves were brown and white stains. He also found some brownish coloured hair like that of a horse on the jacket sleeves and front. The trousers were damp and dirty round the bottom. The boots were in the study. They were very wet and worn down at the heel, the left specially so. They removed the jacket, vest and the muddy boots.

Campbell produced the boots before the court, pointing out with an elaborate gesture that one of the boots had a heel that was worn down. The boot, he said triumphantly, was the exact fit for a mark on the field. There was a murmur from the visitors' galleries as he made the point.

Campbell said that around 2.30 p.m. he returned to the vicarage and retrieved the trousers from the accused's parents. The trousers, he said, were not in the same condition as in the morning, but had been thoroughly cleaned. In a box in the prisoner's bedroom they found four razors, all more or less stained. One was wet and appeared to have been recently used. The clothes and razors were taken to the police station and handed to Dr Butter.

Next Campbell brought up both the 'Lover of Justice' letter and the 'Greatorex' letters shown to him by George and suggested that George had written both. The prosecution implied that George had written the letter to himself to clear his own name.

It was time for the cross-examination. Vachell started with the shoe with the worn-down heel and the footprints on the field. Was there an image of the mark or proper measurement or cast of the footprint? he asked.

'No,' said Campbell.

How then had he measured it?

'With a straw and a stick,' said Campbell.

Vachell pointed out that Campbell had said that the ground near the footprint was hard. However, earlier he had claimed the ground was wet. He had also described the field as sandy. George's shoes were said to have clay on them. If the field was sandy, why would the shoes have clay on them? The spectators could be heard murmuring among themselves at this.

The proceedings then took a startling turn.

Vachell cross-questioned Campbell about the horse killed on 22 September when the prisoner was in jail.

'Has anybody admitted having done it?' asked Vachell.

'Yes,' said the policeman. There was an audible gasp in the courtroom.

'Is that person in court?'

'I believe he is here.' The crowds reacted again.

'Brought by the police?'

'Yes.'

'What is his name?'

'John Harry Green, the owner of the horse.' By now, the court had broken into an uproar, and needed to be calmed down.[9]

It seemed Harry Green, as he was known, the son of the owner of the farm, had confessed to the latest crime of maiming the horse. But the police did not produce him as a witness, adding further twists to the trial proceedings.

Vachell wanted to know why the prosecution had not produced Harry Green as a witness when he was present in the courtroom. There could not be two people in the county with such fiendish minds maiming horses, he said.

Disturnal tried to save the situation. He asked Campbell on his re-examination whether John Harry Green was the owner of the horse he had admitted having mutilated.

Campbell: Yes.

Disturnal: Did he make any admission as to any previous outrage?

Campbell: No.

And with that, Reginald Hardy brought down his gavel and adjourned the hearing at 7.30 p.m. It had been a dramatic opening day in court and there was a buzz outside, as people discussed the day's proceedings.

George thought it had gone rather well. He was still feeling fairly confident.

Court resumed at 9.30 a.m. the following day. The police continued giving evidence. First to enter the witness box on Wednesday was Sergeant Parsons, stationed at Great Haywood. He stated that on the morning of 18 August, he went with Inspector Campbell to the field near the Great Wyrley Colliery and saw the horse that had been injured. Parsons corroborated Campbell's account of the condition of the horse, the footprints and the visit to the vicarage.

One by one, the other policemen on the case entered the witness box. Constable Cooper, in his evidence, said that he pressed Edalji's boot down with a heavy hand into the soft ground to make an impression, at which a member of the jury rose and said there was a difference between the weight of a hand and that of a man wearing the boot. He was immediately stopped by Hardy and asked to direct questions through the bench, but was never given the chance to do so.

The defence would say later that the field had been trampled upon by many people once the news of the maiming spread around the village, and the evidence of the 'footprint' was thin. Much was made at the trial about the boot with the worn-out heel which matched the footprint at the site, with various versions emerging from the police themselves. Everyone craned to look at the prisoner and the shoes he was wearing in court. The worn-down heel was clearly visible. A large map of the area was produced. The prosecution had marked the trail of the footprints leading from the field towards the vicarage.

PC Rowley recounted that on 30 June, the day after Blewitt's horses were killed, he received a crude letter written in pencil, full of spelling mistakes, telling him to look out for a person carrying a 'hook' who would be on the train from Walsall. George Edalji was known to take the train from Birmingham via Walsall.

Disturnal reminded the court that on 5 July, a few days after Blewitt's horses were killed, George Edalji placed an advertisement in a Lichfield paper offering a reward of £25 for information as to the identity of the person or persons publishing defamatory statements about him.

The same month the police received a letter allegedly sent by a schoolboy called Wilfred Greatorex. The letter addressed to the police sergeant at Hednesford, Sergeant Charles Robinson, which was received on Saturday 11 July, was read out in court. This was the letter that George was actually charged with writing. It said there would be 'merry times at Wyrley in November when they would start on little girls; they would do 20 wenches like the horses before next March'. The letter also contained a threat to murder Robinson even though the writer would get a 'thick rope round his neck for it'.[10]

PC Cooper said that on 6 August he visited the prisoner at his home. The prisoner produced a letter purporting to have been written to him by 'Greatorex' which accused George Edalji of putting the police on his track. George Edalji had actually replied to the real Wilfred Greatorex and his letter was read out in court. He expressed regret that Wilfred had been annoyed by the police. In his opinion, wrote George, no boys were concerned in the case, and that when the truth became known, he would find it was somebody in a very different position. The prosecution asserted that the letter meant that George knew who the killer was.

More letters were read out in court, the prosecution producing an endless supply. One of these addressed by 'Greatorex' suggested the involvement of a gang in the maimings and named George as being part of the gang:

> I have got dare-devil face and can run well, and when they formed that gang at Wyrley they got me to join. I knew all about horses and beasts and how to catch them best. I had never done none before till those two horses near the line at Wyrley ... and then I caught each under the belly, but they didn't spurt much blood, and one ran away, but the other fell ... it is not true we always do it when the moon is young, and the one Edalji killed on August 11 was full moon.

There was much excitement in the court when the fifteen-year-old Wilfred Guy Greatorex was brought in as a witness. Wilfred, the son of a farmer, was a pupil at Queen Mary School, Walsall and travelled daily by train to Walsall. He denied writing the letters and said he was away in the Isle of Man when the letters were written. He was also away on 17 August, the date the horse was maimed in Wyrley.

Wilfred said that Edalji sometimes travelled in the same train as him, as did the schoolboys mentioned in the letters. Wilfred told the court that he generally took the 7.30 train in the morning, returning by the 5.10 train. 'I have known the accused by sight for three or four years,' said Wilfred. 'He has travelled in the same compartment with me and my schoolmates going to Walsall. This has not occurred many times during the last twelve months – about a dozen times in fact.'[11]

The last time he saw the prisoner was the morning that Blewitt's horses had been killed on 30 June. As the train passed the field where the horses lay, the accused, who was sitting on the opposite side said, 'They belong to Blewitt, don't they?'

William Greatorex, the boy's father, was next in the witness box. He said he had handed over the letters received by his son to the police.

Frederick George Wooton, a clerk in the Cheslyn Hay post office, whose name was given in the letters, was also called as witness. He denied writing the words 'Your affectionate friend, Fred Wooton' and pasting it on an envelope. He said he knew the prisoner very well by sight and had occasionally spoken to him. Asked whether he said 'good morning' to him, Wooton replied that he did say 'good morning' to people he met, at which there was much laughter in the court, including from George.

With considerable drama, Disturnal then brought in his key witness: a handwriting expert from London, Thomas Henry Gurrin. It was his principal evidence. Gurrin told the court that in his opinion all the letters were an attempted disguise and were written by the prisoner, George Edalji. A murmur went round the court and the villagers could be seen discussing this point with some agitation.

Next was the turn of the police surgeon, John Kerr Butter. The doctor declared that when he had examined George's coat at 9 p.m. at the police station, there were horse hairs on it. He said there were twenty-nine hairs on the coat and five on the waistcoat. He said he had compared the hairs taken from the piece of the pony's hide that the police had cut out, and found that they corresponded in length, colour and structure to those on the coat. The Edaljis had said there were no horse hairs on the coat when it was removed from the house.

About the stains on the coat, Butter could only say that the white marks on the coat were starch, other spots were food stains. Two stains on the cuff could have come from mammalian blood. They were not fresh, and could have come from a horse or from underdone meat. The mark on the razor was rust.

The prosecution continued their evidence. Police Sergeant Parsons said he had noticed a pony in the field at the Great Wyrley Colliery at 11 p.m. The pony was unharmed at the time.

Sergeant Parsons said the red stains on the cuff of the prisoner's jacket seemed to have been scratched or interfered with. The trousers which were wet and muddy had since been thoroughly cleaned. He said he had no doubt of the existence of mud and bloodstains when he first saw them.[12]

It showed the incompetence of the police, that having considered the trousers to be vital evidence, they had not removed them when they had called at the Edalji residence on 18 August. Instead, they sent for them later, by which time the muddy trousers had dried.

Further drama followed in the courtroom when the police sergeant who found the razor in the prisoner's bedroom said the prisoner's father, who was present when it was taken, tried to rub off some bloodstains with his thumb. At this, Shapurji Edalji, rose from his seat and emphatically said: 'This isn't true.'

He was ordered by the police to be quiet and resumed his seat.

Police Constable Meredith, who had met George in Stafford Prison, now gave evidence. He said that during a conversation with the prisoner in his cell after 4 September, Edalji had said he would not have bail, and that the next horse to be killed would not be by him. The prosecution contended that it proved that the prisoner had knowledge of the next attack which had been planned by his gang members. That concluded the case for the prosecution.

Meanwhile the press who were flocking to the courtroom were putting their own racial slant to the case of the 'black' vicar and his son. The coverage was predictable, detailing George's appearance and Asian heritage.

The *Daily Gazette* reported:

He is 28 years of age but looks younger. He was dressed in a shrunken black and white check suit, and there was little of the typical solicitor in his swarthy face, with its full, dark eyes, prominent mouth and small round chin. His appearance is essentially Oriental in its stolidity, no sign of emotion escaping him beyond a faint smile as the extra-ordinary story of the prosecution unfolded.

The reporter from the *Wolverhampton Express & Star* speculated about why George would have done the deed: 'Many and wonderful were the theories I heard propounded in the local ale houses as to why Edalji had gone forth in the night to slay cattle, and a widely accepted idea was that he made nocturnal sacrifices to strange gods.'

# IO

## The Case for the Defence

George had taken special care to groom himself on the third day of the trial. It was the day he would be stepping into the witness box. His hair was immaculately combed. He had still not been allowed to shave or trim his moustache. He was wearing the same three-piece check suit he had worn since the beginning of the trial.

At the start of the day, Hardy declared that the court would sit until 10 p.m. to conclude the case. It was clear that he wanted the case wrapped up as quickly as possible.

The court was packed as usual, the locals out in force to hear the accused give evidence. The strange-looking man who stood in the dock came from a religion that was alien to them. They had heard that Parsees worshipped the sun and the moon. Some of them believed they made nocturnal animal sacrifices to please their gods.

The *Wolverhampton Express & Star* had captured the mood when it reported: 'The average rustic can see no good in a foreigner – an Asiatic comes in the guise of an emissary of the devil.'

Vachell began the case for the defence, saying that never in all his long career had he been engaged in a case in which the responsibilities pressed as heavily as they did in this case. The first of the killings had taken place in February, but the police were at a loss to discover the perpetrator. The police, he said, were themselves on trial, unless they found a culprit.

On 18 August, they sent a policeman to intercept George at the station on his way to work, when they had no evidence to arrest him. What followed over the next few hours, said Vachell, was the police trying to match the evidence with the crime.

Finally, came the moment that everyone was waiting for: Vachell brought George into the witness box. The court fell into a hushed silence as he stood up and took his oath. For the next two hours and forty minutes, George spoke to the court. His voice was quiet but audible. The newspapers reported that he was very composed.

Vachell asked him why he had placed an advertisement in the local papers after rumours about him likely to be arrested for cattle-maiming started circulating.

'I had heard of the earlier mutilations, and in July a report got into circulation that I had been arrested,' he said.[1] He therefore issued an advertisement offering a reward.

He said that Inspector Campbell had called upon him on 14 July, showed him a letter and said he thought that he (Edalji) could assist him. They had a general conversation, but he could not say particularly what passed about the killings. He asked the inspector some questions and he suggested the employment of bloodhounds.

Vachell: The suggestion is that you endeavoured to obtain information from them for your own use?

George: Not at all. It was merely a general conversation.

Vachell: The mutilations were the subject of the keenest interest?

George: Naturally, everyone was talking about them.

George said that on 23 July he received the letter signed 'Lover of Justice', and in answer to a note from George to the police about it, Inspector Campbell and PC Cooper visited him.

He denied writing the 'Lover of Justice' letter or any of the others.

The questioning moved to the crucial evening of 17 August. George told the court that on that day he arrived home shortly after six o'clock in the evening. He changed his clothes and put on a pair of blue serge trousers. He took a pair of boots to the shoemaker's shop, arriving there about half past eight at night. He left Mr Hands's shop and walked along the road to Churchbridge, and turned to the right at Watling Street. He took a short walk to Walk Mill and then along the road. He saw some youths a little in front of him. On overtaking them he heard a whistle go, and one of the boys said that it was nine o'clock. He took out his watch and saw that it was. He went along the road and passed several people. He reached the railway station. At that time he looked at his watch and saw that it was 9.19 p.m. He went as far as Green's Farm, but did not go in. He returned home and saw a man named Whitehouse, near the gate leading to the vicarage. He got back home around 9.30 p.m. George Edalji told the court that he did not go out again that night.

The next morning he went to the railway station and while there he received a message from a policeman, who told him that Inspector Campbell wanted to see him. He asked the constable what the inspector wanted to see him about, and he said he did not know. He heard a man on the platform mention that a horse had been killed.

Vachell: Did you turn away and smile?

George: Not at that. I was asked if I could not take a holiday for a day, and I turned away smiling.[2]

He next detailed the interview with Inspector Campbell at his office in Birmingham. After Campbell had described the coat, he said he was not wearing it the previous night outside the grounds. The coat was an old one, and he only used it in the house and in the grounds. On the way to the police station at Birmingham the detective said: 'I know you very well, and you don't look like one who would do this sort of thing.' He replied: 'I did not, but I am not surprised at this as I had warning.'

Vachell: What did you refer to?

George: These reports which had been in circulation about me, the letters with the envelopes enclosed, also the letter: 'A Lover of Justice'.

Vachell: Why did you refuse bail?

George: I found I was all right where I was. I was in the hospital, and quite comfortable. There was such a commotion, and I did not see how I could do my business in Birmingham with this hanging over me, and I thought another outrage might occur.

George said that the policeman had a conversation with him while he was in the cells in Cannock and he said that plenty of people would put up the bail for him.

'It is possible another case may occur, which will be in my favour.'

He said he had nothing whatever to do with the mutilation of the pony and was not connected with it in any way, and did not know of anybody who was. He did not know how the stains got on to the coat, but it was one he used in and about the house. The bloodstains might have come from a cut. He certainly saw no stains on it the last time he wore it.

Assuming that there were hairs on the coat, he could only account for them by the supposition that he had been against a hedge in the garden where horses had been rubbing themselves. He was not in the field on the night in question.

It was time for the cross-examination. Disturnal walked over to the dock and began by reading the letter George had written to Greatorex: 'I am sure no boys are concerned in this wretched business. When the truth is known you will find it is somebody in a very different position.' Could the prisoner give an explanation?

George replied that he referred to the publication of the rumour about his being connected with the killings, and not to the commission of the killings.

Regarding the 'Lover of Justice' letter, he said it had probably been written by someone local to cast aspersions on him.

Disturnal: When PC Cooper told you that the farmers were carrying guns, did you say, 'You don't mean that?'

George: No, I did not.

Disturnal: Did you ask him if Harry Green was watching?

George: No, I did not.

Disturnal wanted to know about the curious sleeping arrangements at the vicarage.

His voice loaded with sarcasm, Disturnal said it was an 'extraordinary arrangement for a full grown-man without adequate reason to sleep in his father's room'.

George said he had occupied the same bedroom as his father for twenty years. He explained that it had started when his brother was ill as a child and his mother had to sleep in his room to nurse him. At that time he moved to his father's room.

Disturnal wanted to know why the arrangement had continued long after. George replied that it suited him all right. His brother had now left the home but was often at the vicarage. The bedroom was a large one and he and his father occupied different beds.

Disturnal: Have you heard it suggested by anyone in your family that your father has only begun to occupy that bedroom recently with you?

George: Certainly not.

The story of the sleeping arrangements were thus brought out in open court, leaving room for Anson and those opposed to the vicar to suggest an unhealthy relationship with his son. Rumours of sodomy began to circulate. Later, Arthur Conan Doyle would directly challenge Anson about what he had been implying when he mentioned the issue.

There was great interest in the court when Rev. Shapurji Edalji rose to give evidence. The vicar stated that his son went out on 17 August and returned around 9.30 p.m. He had supper and went to bed. The reverend said that he and his son slept in the same room, and when he retired to bed later on he saw George in bed. He sat up in bed about 4 a.m. as he was suffering from a painful lumbago and noticed that his son was sleeping. They always kept the bedroom door locked and if his son had left the room he would have heard him, as he was a very light sleeper.

Shapurji told the court that when Inspector Campbell pointed out some stains on the clothing, he told him they were cocoa or gravy stains. When his attention was called to some hairs on his son's coat, he examined the coat and said he could not see any hairs. The police pointed out some stains on a razor, and he told them they were old stains. He did not rub any of the stains off the razor as stated by the police. The razor was never out of Campbell's hands.

Next in the witness stand was Charlotte. Looking composed and dignified, she deposed that her son had come home on the night in question and gone out after tea. He returned home about 9.25 pm. He remained in the house after that until he went to bed. When Campbell, on the morning of 18 August, asked to see her son's clothes she brought down some of them, and the police examined them. Charlotte also added that one of the policemen asked: 'Where is your son's dagger?' to which she replied that he had no dagger.[3] This produced some amusement in the court.

Under cross-examination she said she told the police that her son never went out in the clothes they took away. The clothes were not wet or muddy. She let the police see whatever they wanted to see and hid nothing from them.

Maud was next in the witness box. Nervous and pale, slightly overwhelmed by the crowds watching her, she reconfirmed that her brother returned home shortly before half past nine on the night of 17 August. He had supper and then remained chatting with her till he went to bed.

Dora Earp, the domestic servant at the vicarage, said that when she arrived home about a quarter to ten on 17 August she saw the prisoner there. She had been a servant at the vicarage for two years, and the prisoner had always slept in the same room with his father. Dora Earp also testified that the boots of her master, George Edalji, were not as wet as stated by the police.

There were other witnesses too: John Hands, the shoemaker, who had seen George Edalji on the evening of 17 August. Locals, Harry Loach, Fred Cope, Joseph Barton and Walter Whitehouse all gave their versions of when they had last seen George on that fateful evening. John Hands confirmed that George was wearing a blue coat, not an old jacket when he visited his shop. Whitehouse, who had not been brought by the prosecution, confirmed that he had seen George enter the vicarage around 9.30 p.m. Whitehouse had looked at the railway-station clock at the time so he could be quite certain.

None of the witnesses had seen George either going towards or returning from the field where the outrage occurred. Vachell pointed out that the portion of the village where George was seen was an ordinary thoroughfare and it would be the regular route home of any man desiring to return from the upper part of the village to his home near the station.

The veterinary surgeon, Robert M. Lewis, who had also not been called as a prosecution witness, testified that the wound could not have been inflicted more than six hours before he examined the horse at 8.30 a.m. on 18 August. The wound, he said, could not have been caused by a razor, but by a curved and pointed instrument with a handle, so as to give the user a good grip. This would have placed the attack at 2.30 a.m. at the earliest.

Despite the fact that George was accused of threatening to murder Sergeant Robinson, the prosecution did not bring the police officer into the witness box. In his account recorded at the police station, Robinson had said that twenty policemen had been on special duty at Wyrley from 8 June until 18 August. Robinson said that the prisoner's house was under observation the whole time. He had asserted that it was not possible for anyone to leave the accused's house that night on the side that he was watching.

The police theory that the crime had been committed between 9 p.m. and 10 p.m. on 17 August when George was on his walkabout, was being blown away. If Hands had testified that George was not wearing an old coat, then it did not matter that there were horse hairs on it. If the crime was committed later, George had four witnesses testifying that he had not left the house. Moreover, one of the policemen on duty had said that the horse had appeared to be all right at 11 p.m.

On that note, the court was adjourned for the day. Despite Reginald Hardy's declaration that the hearing would go on till 10 p.m. if needed, the proceedings ended after the defence witnesses had all spoken. The court would convene again the next morning.

For the prosecution it was a godsend, as they could rethink their strategy.

By the fourth day of the hearing, the crowds had lessened. Perhaps they had surmised which way the verdict would go, and thought George would be cleared. The villagers were confused, but willing to believe that George had returned to his house by 9.25 p.m. at which time the horse was still alive. George, himself, was quietly satisfied at how things had gone. His fate would be decided that day. Surely the jury would see reason.

It was time for the final summing-up.

Over the last three days, witnesses had made their state-ments: Inspector Campbell, PC Cooper and PC Meredith of the Staffordshire police, Thomas Henry Gurrin, the handwriting expert, George's parents, Shapurji and Charlotte, and his sister Maud, as well as their domestic help. Twelve anonymous letters, in their full gory detail, had been read out before the shocked courtroom. George had given evidence.

As Disturnal started his summing-up, the tension visibly increased in the courtroom. A jury member was taken ill and had to leave the box for some minutes.

Finally, Vachell rose to sum up for the defence. On him depended George's fate.

'From the very commencement of these outrages in February, the Great Wyrley district has been in a state of alarm … and the police were at a loss to understand the outrages,' began Vachell. The theory that there was a connection to the prisoner had been exaggerated, he said. 'Only two spots of blood, the size of a threepenny piece, and some bread and milk stains, the result of careless feeding, had been discovered on the coat,' he told the jury.

He asked the jury whether they were not impressed by the prisoner's demeanour in the box, by his candour and whether they thought that the way in which he gave his evidence suggested to them that he was a man guilty of a hideous crime like this.

Vachell brought up the case of Harry Green. Was the prosecution going to suggest that Green was a member of a gang? They knew that Green had killed a horse while the accused was in prison. There was a man at large who was capable of doing this fiendish act. Why then should the jury say on such flimsy evidence and on the crumbling and shattered theories of the police that the prisoner was guilty of these outrages?

However, not once during the trial, did Vachell bring up the case of George's acute myopia.

Disturnal rose to speak for the last round. It was up to him to save the case which seemed to be falling apart after witness accounts. He realised that the theory that the pony was killed between 9 and 9.30 p.m. was not sustainable. At the tail end of the proceedings, he changed his argument.

Speaking for the final one hour and forty minutes of the case, Disturnal tried to sway the jury and impress upon them the link between the letters and the killings. The prosecution's 'trump card' was the evidence from the handwriting expert, Thomas Gurrin, who claimed that the letters were in George's handwriting. In contrast, the defence team had not brought any expert independent witnesses.

To the shock of the defence team, Disturnal now shifted the time of the alleged crime and placed it in the middle of the night. The jacket was wet, he said, because it had rained after midnight, the shoes were muddy because the ground had been wet. He implied that the vicar and his wife were lying to protect their son when they said he had not gone out at night. He also reminded the jury how the Edalji family had argued about the horse hairs being present on the jacket. All of it was designed to sow a doubt in the minds of the jury about the reliability of the family. It was Edalji who wrote the letters and he had a clear link to and knowledge about the killings, Disturnal told the jury.

As regards motive, Disturnal said the killings could not be attributed to spite or to some lust for blood. Rather, he would suggest that the perpetrator was activated by some desire for notoriety. With that dramatic statement Disturnal ended the session. Vachell had no opportunity to challenge him. Disturnal had had the last word.

Yelverton and Lewis would argue later that most of the evidence was inadmissible, but Hardy was not experienced enough to realise this. Nor did he direct the jury in a professional way. It was what Disturnal had gambled on.

The court waited breathlessly for Hardy to summarise for the jury. Justice Hardy began by saying that a reign of terror had prevailed, that it was a blot on the fair frame of the county. Coming to the motive for such a crime, he said, 'It really seemed as though the offence had been committed by some person possessed of a peculiar twist in the brain – some diabolical cunning – and it seemed impossible to arrive at any motive why the prisoner should have committed such a horrible act as that with which he had been charged. On the other hand, people often committed suicide without any apparent motive, the cause remaining a matter of conjecture.'

Hardy had failed to direct the jury towards the evidence, or lack of it. Instead he told the twelve white men sitting in judgement that the crimes could have been the product of a 'twisted brain'. The person they were directed to look at was a brown man of an ethnic origin that they did not understand. In not so many words, Hardy was telling them to consider that the 'Oriental' had committed this senseless and violent crime.

The jury left the courtroom at 2 p.m. and returned in fifty minutes.

Have you reached a verdict?' asked Justice Hardy.

'Yes, we have,' the foreman replied.

'Guilty!' he announced.

An audible gasp went around the courtroom. Rev. Shapurji Edalji and his wife looked stunned. They looked at their son. A slight pallor had come over his face. His composure seemed to have left him momentarily as he quivered, holding on to the dock.

'With a recommendation to mercy,' the foreman continued.

'On what grounds?' asked the chairman.

'His position,' said the foreman

'His personal position?'

'Yes, sir.'

Directed by Justice Hardy, the jury had no problem in concluding that George – whose Parsee ancestors worshipped the fire and the sun – had a 'peculiar twist of the brain' and 'diabolical cunning' and was capable of mutilating cattle. Such, they thought, were the mysterious ways of the Orient.

The bench then retired to consider the sentence. For a few moments George seemed to regain his composure and looked straight ahead. As they returned to pronounce their sentence, his face became an inscrutable mask.

Addressing George, the chairman said:

'You have been found guilty of this very serious charge and we think, very properly. The verdict of the jury is a right one. They also recommend you to mercy in consideration of the position you hold. We have to take into consideration your personal position and what any punishment means to you. On the other hand, we have to consider the state of the county of Stafford, and of the Great Wyrley district, and the disgrace inflicted on the neighbourhood by this condition of things.'

With that, Justice Hardy pronounced: 'Your sentence is one of penal servitude for seven years.'

As his words rang out in court, George seemed to pass into a hypnotic trance.

The *Mercury* newspaper reported:

He seemed to become darker, almost black, as he leaned over the edge of the dock, with the daylight streaming down upon him from the great window. His light check suit emphasised the black face and the staring wide-opened, gleaming eyes.

George lingered in the dock for about fifty seconds, as the full impact of the sentence began to dawn on him. At last one of the warders tapped him on the shoulder. He sighed and looked up.

Suddenly his body seemed to slump into resignation. He was led swiftly away. That was the last his parents saw of him that day.

'It was the Oriental's acceptance of fate,' reported the *Mercury*. 'He went down the trap-door with just the fringe of a placid smile upon his face, contented that all was over.'

~~~

The next day the *Daily Mail* reported:

> Those who closely studied this extraordinary criminal in the dock would have no doubt that he is a degenerate of the worst type. His jaw and mouth are those of a man of very debased life. Edalji has also gained for himself the reputation of being a lover of mystery – another Oriental trait, and one that goes far to explain the anonymous letters. Love of mystery rather than bloodlust was, according to the Crown, the predisposing motive.

The *Birmingham Daily Gazette*, reflecting on the extraordinary nature of the crime and the circumstances of the accused, ventured: 'The explanation of the choice is probably to be found in the circumstance that Edalji is of Eastern extraction. The subtle Eastern mind loves a mystery, and is vain … The Eastern mind is satisfied with its secret.'

The *Midland Express* concluded: 'We are glad to think that the district of Great Wyrley and the country is safe from such a monster for several years to come.'

Within a few weeks George, the nondescript, myopic lawyer from Great Wyrley, had been turned by the media into a 'monster' and a 'degenerate' whose very appearance betrayed the horror of his race and its dark mysterious ways.

~~~

George felt a sense of suffocation as he was handcuffed and led to the Black Maria to take him to Stafford Prison to begin his seven-year sentence. Soon, he had handed over his cotton check suit, turned out his pockets and personal possessions and was dressed in His Majesty's Prison clothes: a white jacket, trousers and a pillbox hat. The clothes were marked with broad arrows, the sign of Crown property. A warder in a blue uniform jangling a bunch of keys marched him through several doors, locking and unlocking them with a loud noise, all meant to instil a sense of fear in the prisoner. As he walked into the large central hall, George could see the cells arranged all round on the higher floors. The corridors outside the cells were screened off with wire to prevent prisoners throwing themselves down over the railings. Watched by other warders, he was led to the cell which was to be his home for the next few years. There was a plank bed, a heavily barred glass window high up, and a slop bucket. He was a star prisoner (first-time offender) and would have to spend his first nine months in isolation. With a calculated loud bang, the heavy iron door was shut and the key turned in the lock. There was a tiny peephole in the door. His eyes fell on the notice on the wall. It was a set of prison rules. There was one notice explaining how a prisoner could get marks for good conduct. He could get eight marks a day if he did nothing wrong. Trembling slightly, he sat down on the bed. Almost immediately he could see that an eye was placed against the tiny peephole. The warden was watching him. George's brain slowly started to whirr as he made a calculation. He would have to be here for 2,555 days.

# II

## *Prisons and Campaigns*

At the moment that Sir Reginald Hardy was sentencing George Edalji to seven years' penal servitude, Conan Doyle was assessing his chances of becoming a Member of Parliament. The night before, he had attended a political meeting at the town hall in Leamington in Warwickshire. Always eager to push himself a little further, Conan Doyle – the writer, war veteran, doctor and essayist – was considering joining politics. He had decided to stand as the Liberal-Unionist candidate from Hawick Burghs constituency in Scotland.

The Unionists had broken away from the Liberal Party after William Gladstone announced his support for Irish home rule. Though a long-term Liberal supporter, Conan Doyle now backed the Unionists and he took up their offer to stand for the elections.

*The Adventure of the Empty House*, announcing the miraculous return of Sherlock Holmes, had just been published a few days previously in the *Strand Magazine*. Like his fictional hero, Conan Doyle's life was taking a new turn.

～

Barely three days after George was taken to Stafford Prison, the offices of the Wolverhampton *Express & Star* received an anonymous letter:

I am very sorry that young Edalji who was convicted at the Stafford quarter sessions on Friday last is an innocent man the man who killed them cattle at wyrley is me and my name is G.h. darby the captain of the wyrley gang ... I will tell you how these cattle have been killed at wyrley there are 15 men in the gang and

9 men used to be on the watch every night while I killed them and we used to do the police down with their eyes wide open … we shall kill all the horses what we find out in the fields at night and do the police down.

It was signed 'G.h.darby, the captain of the wyrley gang'.[1]
It was clear that the letter-writer was still at large.

Time passed slowly at the vicarage after George was taken to prison. Within days he was moved from Stafford Prison to Lewes Prison in East Sussex, taking him further away from his family. He had to get used to the prison routine: first bell at 6 a.m., followed by a cup of tea and a small brown loaf handed to him in his cell. This was followed by inspection at 6.30 a.m. and exercise in the yard, which involved walking mechanically with other prisoners in a circle. No one was allowed to talk, but a few prisoners would manage to get a question in. 'What are you in for? How long are you here?' was the most common one. Inevitably they would stare at him as he was clearly a foreigner. Then it was back to the cell where they were given work to do. The prison authorities had noted his defective eyesight and George was given 'half-tasks' at cell labour. His job was picking coir for horse nosebags, a job he would not have enjoyed given the reason for his incarceration. Lunch was at 11.30 a.m. and evening meals were served at 5 p.m. Prisoners had to be in bed at 8 p.m. It was not easy to sleep. Through the night, the sound of the warders' canvas shoes could be heard padding down the corridors, as they looked through the peepholes. Sometimes, a scream from a distressed prisoner having a nightmare would shatter the silence of the night. The warders were on constant suicide watch.

Charlotte grieved for the quiet son who had to face seven years' penal servitude for no fault of his. The injustice was tearing apart the reverend as well. Was this the English legal system he had so admired, the Christian faith that he had devoted himself to? He resolved not to give up.

Barely a few weeks after his son – pale and trembling – had been led away to prison, the vicar started to mobilise signatures for a petition to the Home Office for his release. On a cold Sunday evening in November, while a strong west wind was blowing through the village, the vicar prepared to address his congregation at St Mark's Church in Great Wyrley. The church was packed to capacity; all the seats in the aisles were occupied, as well as all the standing room. Before the service, Shapurji told the gathered churchgoers that those who wanted to sign the petition on behalf of his son to the Home Office could do so in the schoolroom adjoining the church. As George served his term in Lewes Prison in Sussex, his parents were determined to fight on for justice.

The case against George had hung on four main points: the allegation that bloodstains and horse hairs had been found on his jacket, that there was a drop of blood on his razor, that his shoe (which had one of the heels worn down) fitted the footprints in the field, and that he was the author of the anonymous letters sent to the police. His parents disputed all these charges. The evidence was purely circumstantial and proved nothing, they said.

They pointed out that the catalogue of horror had not ended after their son was taken into custody. As had been revealed at the trial, a horse was disembowelled on 22 September while George was in jail awaiting trial. Harry Green had confessed to killing the horse. On 3 November, by which time George was locked away in Lewes Prison, another horse and mare were found mutilated at the 100-acre farm in Landywood owned by Herbert Stanley. The stable boy who found the two horses said the ten-year-old mare still had its eyes open in shock. The animal had an eighteen-inch open wound. Its intestines lay about 140 yards from the body, and the ground was covered in blood. The mare had limped along the field in pain before collapsing. Lying in the same field a little distance away was a newly born foal. It showed the sheer brutality of the killer. Three months later, on 8 February 1904, another horse was found to be injured and on 24 March two sheep and a lamb were discovered mutilated. This time, a coarse miner called Thomas Farrington was convicted and sentenced to three years in prison. What connection at all could there have been between Farrington and George Edalji and how could they have been part of an alleged gang? George had never even met Farrington. Their worlds were totally separate.

From his prison cell, George wrote to his mother saying that he had only discovered during the trial in which field the killing had happened, and it was impossible for him to have gone there at night given his poor eyesight.

'It would be well to arrange for a Home Office expert to properly examine my eyes as soon as possible as whoever committed that outrage must have had good sight. There is also the point that the footprints led towards Mr Green's and this may or may not be significant, but any way I do not like the idea of H. G. Harry Green going to South Africa in such a hurry. I certainly think my eyes should be examined. Of course, I had not seen the plan showing footprints till the trial,' wrote George.[2]

The Edaljis took comfort in the letters of support they received from members of the public. Shortly after George's conviction, his former teacher from Rugeley Grammar School wrote to Charlotte offering his sympathy to the family for the 'great trial and trouble' that had come upon them.

'During the five years your son George was at school here I never knew him to commit any act of cruelty or unkindness. I always found him a thoroughly upright and well principled youth, in whom I could have placed every confidence,' wrote A. D. Denning.[3]

Another solicitor from London, Henry Sutton Ludlow, wrote that George Edalji had served his Articles with him. 'I found him particularly studious and attentive to his duties and his conduct quite respectful and courteous to myself and left nothing to be desired.'[4]

A fellow student from Rugeley Grammar School, also vouched for George's character. S. Macgregor Grier said that from 1887 to 1889, he was a pupil at Rugeley Grammar School and knew George Edalji well as they travelled on the same train every day.

'He was several years older than myself, but always treated me with great kindness. I never knew him cruel to any animal, and from what I knew of him then, for I came to know him well, I should say that he was quite incapable of any act of cruelty to man or animal.

'My memory is that of a very quiet, good natured boy, always thoughtful and kind in his dealings with others. I find it impossible to believe that the character of the boy, whom I knew, can have become so utterly warped and altered.'[5]

The hapless Edaljis began a sustained campaign to free their son. Soon the petition started gathering support. The case of George Edalji had caught the eye of the retired former Chief Justice of the Bahamas, Roger Dawson Yelverton, who wrote a letter in the *Daily Telegraph* declaring that there had been a miscarriage of justice. Yelverton had served in the Caribbean and was not known to show prejudice against black people. He was a firm believer in justice being delivered. To him the Edalji case represented a classic case of a small-town magistrates' court being completely out of its league, a jury not looking carefully at the evidence and an inexperienced judge misguiding the jury.

Yelverton pointed out that no less than nine witnesses had established George Edalji's innocence, four of whom swore positively that he was in his father's house from 9.30 p.m. on 17 August until after breakfast on 18 August. The prosecution, said Yelverton, founded their case upon the extraordinary proposition that George Edalji wrote the anonymous letters to himself and to the police.

'I say "extraordinary" because such an allegation is a lie on the face of it, for what man would commit or contemplate the commission of a crime, and then write with oaths and imprecations upon himself (as Edalji is alleged to have done) to the police, unless, indeed the writer was a madman? That Mr Edalji is very sane is shown by numerous letters from his clients and friends in my possession. That he is an entirely innocent man I have after careful scrutiny, satisfied myself,' wrote Yelverton.[6]

An eminent lawyer, Sir George H. Lewis, backed Yelverton and wrote to him saying that a miscarriage of justice had occurred. It seemed that senior judicial figures in London were waking up to the Edalji case and ready to plead on his behalf.

I may tell you that Mr Edalji, being a solicitor accused of a heinous crime, his case attracted my attention at the time of the trial, and I carefully read the report of the case in *The Times*. And I was surprised to find that the jury had convicted him upon evidence before the court. I think and then thought, that Mr Edalji presented a very strong case in proof of his innocence ... I have carefully read the statement of facts which you have placed before me, and after a long experience of forty-seven years in the profession and a great experience of criminal cases, I wish to express my opinion that this conviction is wrong, and I hope the Home Secretary will see his way to put the matter right. I believe that a miscarriage of justice has undoubtedly occurred.

Grateful for the support, Charlotte Edalji wrote to Sir George Lewis at the start of the New Year, appealing to him to use his influence to release an innocent man.

Charlotte described her quiet son as someone who had never been in trouble or done anything disreputable in the past and felt that it was racial prejudice that had led to her son being falsely accused.

Our son always lived at home, going each day either to School, College or Office, only being absent at night when away for short visits or to London for his examinations. He was always very kind and dutiful to us, and from a child was always kind to any dumb creature; it would have been quite impossible for him to maim, or injure, any animal … Our son was thoroughly fond of his profession. My husband, daughter and I are deeply grateful to hear that you are kindly enquiring into the matter of what we feel to be a cruel and unjust sentence on one who is innocent.

I am an English woman, and I feel that there is among many people a prejudice against those who are not English, and I cannot help feeling that it is owing to that prejudice that my son has been falsely accused.[7]

Charlotte's sister, Mary Sancta Stoneham, also wrote to Lewis thanking him for his support and explaining why her nephew could never have committed the heinous crime he had been sentenced for. Testifying to the caring nature of her nephew and the good upbringing he had had from his parents, Mary Sancta also pointed out that her own family never felt any racial prejudice towards Shapurji for being a Parsee. In fact, he had been welcomed into their household.

'I always was very fond of my nephew and no woman on earth could have been more careful than my sister in the bringing up of her children, and Mr Edalji too, was such a fond father and so anxious that they should get on well with their studies, all three of them,' wrote Mary.

Whenever I have seen or heard of my nephew (until these abominable things were spoken of) I always found him nice and heard of his being nice, and clever also.

When we first became acquainted with Mr Edalji he was in orders in the English church, and had been for about 5 years, and my father himself a clergyman had such very good testimonials of him from the many people who had known him, several clergymen. There seemed then every hope of a happy and useful life for them both but they have had much to endure, from I suppose people who have, hardly any sense of religion in them – Our friends at that time too felt as we did that Parsees are of a very old and cultivated race, and have many good qualities.

She added: 'My father and mother gave their full consent to the marriage and they were deeply attached to my sister.'[8]

Moved by the plight of the family, the heartfelt letters from Charlotte and her sister, Yelverton was determined to do his best to seek justice for George. He took his campaign to the Home Office, pointing out the flaws in the police investigation and the case for the prosecution. Charlotte and her sister decided to travel to London to pursue the matter and took lodgings at 39 Woburn Place, Russell Square while they too appealed to the Home Office.

The opinion of the villagers had begun to turn after the verdict had been delivered. Many believed now that it was impossible for George to have killed the animals. Given that horses and cows were still being killed while he was in jail, it renewed their discomfort at the verdict. They also had the genuine fear that the killer was still at large, and that the police had not done their job. The support of eminent people from around the country for George also had its impact. It was clear that the case was moving out of the small mining village of Great Wyrley and having a wider reach. Powerful professionals in London and Birmingham were backing George, and many of the villagers began to agree with the view that the young solicitor had been wrongly imprisoned.

Meanwhile, the 'Petition for the Release of George Edalji' had gathered over 10,000 signatures. Yelverton pointed out that it was backed by the highest legal opinions such as those of Sir George Lewis, eminent civil servants including Sir George Birdwood, top medical authorities and the president of the Incorporated Law Society. Hundreds of solicitors, some knights commanders, MPs and Staffordshire residents had signed the petition demanding justice. The solicitors signing the memorials from Birmingham, Wolverhampton and Brindley alone numbered more than sixty.

A detailed appeal 'In the Matter of George Ernest Thompson Edalji' was submitted to the Home Secretary in December 1903. The 87-page document listed all the flaws in the police investigation and the trial, including the fact that key witnesses like the veterinary surgeon had not been called by the prosecution.[9] In the absence of an appeal court, the only way to contest a judgement was a direct plea to the Home Office. Though it was extremely rare for a case to be overturned, Yelverton and Lewis were determined on a course of action.

Yelverton asked for the names of the twelve members of the jury, but the Home Office refused to disclose these.[10] The absence of a jury profile is significant. All one knows is that they were twelve white men, who lived outside the immediate area and needed to take trains back to their homes every night. They would have been influenced by the newspaper reports, as they were not shut away from these.

A few months after the incarceration of George Edalji, a small parliamentary committee was formed to put pressure on the government for his release. While presenting the case for review to the Home Office, the committee pointed out that Edalji was convicted on circumstantial evidence and the testimony of his family was disbelieved in court. It was pointed out that there was a signed confession by a farmer's son called Harry Green, who had killed his horse. It was noteworthy that Green had not been called as a witness. Barely two weeks after his confession and appearance at the trial, Green sailed for South Africa. Before leaving, he said that he had been forced to confess by the police, adding another twist to the affair. The petition noted that if the confession had been extorted by the police, then such officers were not fit to remain in the force. If not, then proceedings for cruelty at least should have been taken against him. Instead, Green was allowed to depart the country.

A copy of Green's confession was attached to the petition:

> I Harry Green High House Farm Great Wyrley state that on the night of the 21 Sept 03 I had an aged horse in my Father's field which had been injured in the Yeomanry training. Thinking that it would never recover I killed it. No one else was with me. I passed Copestake when I was leaving the field. I am very sorry for what I did I have been to Mr Benton and told him. I would not have anything from the Yeomanry or any other source; the result of the accident. The horse was not valued at above £5. The horse was killed to keep the Game rolling.
>
> Cannock 5th October 1903 (Signed) H. Green

Meanwhile, distinguished retired civil servant Sir George Birdwood, an old India hand, also espoused Edalji's cause.[11] The support for George from Yelverton and Lewis was having a snowball effect. The posh members of the Athenaeum Club seemed to be sinking into their leather armchairs and conferring over their cigars and brandy as to how the very bastion of the Empire – British justice – had to be saved. Charlotte's plea to Lewis, that as an Englishwoman she felt that racial prejudice had been the reason for her son's arrest and conviction, had clearly struck a chord among the liberal elite.

The support for Edalji from the great and powerful of the land excited the media. The tide was turning in favour of the young solicitor. The press – who had rushed to condemn him and place his crime as being led by his ethnic background and sun-worshipping Parsee faith – now started backtracking, as powerful legal experts started questioning the verdict of the trial and the trial itself.

The *St James's Gazette* pointed out that Birdwood was a person who would throw himself into a difficult case if there seemed ever so small a chance that there was a wrong to be righted. He had half a century's connection with India and was said to be 'a master of more secrets of the people and their ways than possibly any other man ever associated with the Dependency.' It was clear that the impression that people from India had 'secret ways' still remained with the writer of the article, even though he was sympathetic to George.

Doctors, too, entered the debate over George Edalji. The *Medical Press Journal* reported: 'Under the circumstances, it becomes in our opinion incumbent on the medical profession as a whole to demand an enquiry into the mental condition of Edalji, who is now under a sentence of seven years' penal servitude, arising purely from circumstantial evidence. We shall be glad to carry out the suggestion that a memorial signed by medical men should be presented without loss of time to the Home Secretary. Any reader willing either to sign such a petition or to obtain signatures from brother practitioners will find the necessary form accompanying our present issue.'[12]

The local *Walsall Advertiser* now changed its tune on the 'dark Oriental' with secrets. The newspaper reported that it was considered farcical that a man should be so demented as to send the police an anonymous letter denouncing himself as the perpetrator of the outrages. Furthermore, one of the communications was known to have been posted in Wolverhampton, at a time when George Edalji was spending a brief holiday in Aberystwyth, and finally the cattle-maiming continued while the young solicitor was under arrest.[13] All these points had been raised at the trial, but were ignored by the news reporters in their rush to condemn George, but were now being produced as proof of his innocence.

The Birmingham Law Society entered the debate. They wrote in George's support pointing out that he had been awarded the Senior Law Class Prize for 1897 and the bronze medal for 1898, having taken second-class honours in the examination. He had also been awarded the second speaking prize of the Law Students Society in 1898.[14]

The momentum in favour of releasing George Edalji was growing, but the Home Office remained unmoved.

Locked away in his cell for a crime that he had not committed, George spent his free time reading. He had picked up a copy of *The Hound of the Baskervilles* by Arthur Conan Doyle from the prison library. The book had been published the year before. The mystery set on the moors reminded him of the evil that sometimes lurks in the countryside. Following a day of hard labour, George found himself lost in the pages. He was fascinated by the skills of deduction used by Sherlock Holmes. He searched for more books by the author. As a busy lawyer he had never had the chance to read crime fiction. Now, passing his time in the cells, the page-turning mysteries created by Conan Doyle had him hooked.

The solicitor in him would not sit silent, accepting his fate. He sent a petition to the Home Secretary, declaring his innocence. 'I have never had anything to do with horses and I have never even held one,' he wrote.[15] He said he had never been to the field where the crime was committed and no evidence had been given to show that anyone had seen him in or near the field. 'My eyes are so defective that I cannot see at all on a dark night, nor find my way on a main road after dark unless I know it by long usage ... I request that my eyes be examined by an expert as soon as possible, and that he then visit the field and state his opinion.'

George said he had bought the boots in the district and lots of people would be wearing the same make and size. He had wet the boots by splashing in some puddles as he walked between 8.15 and 9.30 p.m. It was also unfair to allege that his going to Birmingham on 18 August was proof of guilt. 'Had I been guilty I should have taken the opportunity offered of returning home and disposing of the coat etc,' wrote George. Despite the police searching his house they had not found a scrap of paper to connect him with the letters or crime. He had never used a razor in his life, and always went to the barber for a shave.

He said he considered the letters were written by some person in order to injure him and that this person had given false information to the police about him. He requested that Inspector Campbell give the name of the person who had given him this 'information', as he believed that the person was the writer of the letters, as he had studied his handwriting. From his prison cell in Lewes, George requested that his case be reconsidered with a view to his release.

The Home Office passed on the petitions and queries to Anson who scornfully dismissed George's pleas about his poor eyesight, claiming that it was thought locally that he could actually see better at night than in the daylight.

'I noticed, during his trial, that when it got dark in court his eyes came out with a strange sort of glow like a cat's eyes, and I should be very much surprised indeed to be told as in absolute fact that he cannot see at night at the very least as well as I can, and I have as good sight as most. The way which he is believed to have gone could be travelled almost blindfolded by anyone who had lived on the spot all his life, as he had, being all within a very few fields of the vicarage ...' said Anson.

The chief constable also said that a number of different persons had started writing wild, threatening letters after the Edalji incident, showing how far imitation would go. 'So I am not surprised that there were found people to imitate the cattle killing.'[16]

The police chief would not be moved from his conviction that George had committed the original crimes. What happened after his arrest was imitation, he said, and the wish of some unscrupulous farmers to make a quick profit by destroying their old horses and claiming a higher cost for it from the village funds for farmers whose cattle had been destroyed. Anson was convinced that the attacks on horses and cattle from February to August 1903 were of a different nature and could be blamed solely on George Edalji. The ones after his arrest were mere copycat killings, he said.

In March 1905, nearly two years into George's imprisonment, a public meeting was held in the Temperance Hall in Birmingham to discuss criminal administration in the country. Packing the hall were a number of men and women who were raising the issue of miscarriages of justice and demanding changes in the law. The crowds waited eagerly to hear from Adolf Beck, who had been recently released from Portland Prison in Dorset. Beck had been sentenced to seven years' penal servitude in 1896 for defrauding ladies and stealing their watches and bracelets. However, it had been a case of mistaken identity, and a wrong assessment by a handwriting expert. Beck shared similar physical features with the actual fraudster, but the real criminal had got away. But even as he was in prison, the fraudster struck again. This time he was caught red-handed and arrested. Beck was released from prison and later awarded compensation of £2,000. His case was similar to that of George Edalji. Both had been arrested without proper evidence and on wrong decisions by the same handwriting expert, Thomas Henry Gurrin. In both cases, the crime of which they had been accused happened again while they were still in custody.

Beck, however, could not attend the meeting as he had contracted bronchitis in prison. He sent a letter to be read out on his behalf. In it he stated that his experience had shown that no man was safe from a wrongful conviction. 'A court of criminal appeal was absolutely necessary,' his letter stated. The audience clapped loudly at this.[17]

A hushed silence fell as Rev. Shapurji Edalji rose to address the crowd. The soft-spoken vicar stated that shortly after his imprisonment, his son had written to him. In his letter he had said that when he was arrested, he did not have the slightest idea about which field the killing had taken place in. It was only when the trial took place in Stafford in October 1903 that he learnt the fact. The field was at a distance of half a mile from the road where he had been seen by two witnesses, and the way to it was across a railway line. The night of 17 August was a particularly dark one. Shapurji said that his son suffered from an affliction of the eyes, and it was a physical impossibility for him to have gone to that place.

He said it was only after many appeals that the Home Office had directed an oculist to examine George's eyesight. They had received a report. When he had asked to see a copy of the report, he had been told by the Home Office that there were no grounds for him to be shown this as it was of a 'confidential character'. The same answer was also sent to him when he enquired about other documents relating to the case, said Shapurji.

'Shame,' cried the excited crowd.

Resolutions were adopted in the meeting in favour of petitions being sent to the Home Office asking for new trials for Edalji as he was a victim of a miscarriage of justice.

The *Walsall Advertiser* took up the campaign. In a column called 'The Bystander', the Edalji family were profiled and a case made once again for George. Much was made of the physical appearance of the Edaljis:

The Rev Shapurji Edalji has the sallow complexion, the modest demeanour, and the patient expression which are the distinguishing features of his race. His son, George, too, in spite of the fact that his mother is English, and that he was born and bred here, resembles far more a young Parsee than a young Englishman ... We do think it right to ask whether a great cosmopolitan nation like ours is going to refuse justice to a poor prisoner because he happens to have Asiatic blood in his veins ...[18]

With members of the elite establishment backing George, the press was having a change of heart. Overnight, George seemed to be benefiting from the stardust sprinkled on him by his eminent supporters. The press had also found a change of mood among the residents of Great Wyrley, and they did not want to reflect a different perspective. No longer was George the picture-postcard villain, 'a degenerate of the worst type'. Nor were his jaw and mouth described as those 'of a man of very debased life'. Suddenly, the newspapers wanted to champion his cause and declared that he had been discriminated against because of these very same Asiatic features.

The next rallying call came from Henry Labouchère, the famous London-based politician, writer and theatre-owner, who wrote:

Even granting that George Edalji was guilty of the charge against him, the fact remains that a sentence of seven years penal servitude for a single offence of maliciously wounding a pony is a monstrous display of judicial ferocity.[19]

From January 1905, *Truth* magazine carried a series of articles about the case, outlining the details of the trial, the gathering of evidence and the incompetence of the police force. In the last instalment, Labouchère included the history of the anonymous letters received at the vicarage when George Edalji was a boy. The link between the letters of 1892–96 and the subsequent renewal of hate mail from 1903 could not be ignored, he said. Labouchère stated that it was clear that somebody, most probably the author of the anonymous letters, had been directing the police towards George Edalji and the police had followed suit. 'It is therefore of vital importance for the protection of the public that the whole conduct of the police should be inquired into, from the time when Captain Anson made his first charges against the boy in 1892, down to the time when he made his confidential report upon the case for the Home Office.'[20]

Two years after the imprisonment of his son, Shapurji published a booklet: *A Miscarriage of Justice: The Case of George Edalji*. In the preface to the publication, he wrote: 'I have never had a more painful task to perform than the task of writing the following pages ... I here express my belief that the prosecution wholly failed to prove their case against my son, and that he has been treated in a way to show that prejudice and unfairness had the upper hand ... I submit this case to the British public, – who hate injustice and oppression, – for their just and righteous consideration.'[21]

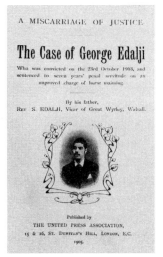

Frontispiece to Shapurji's published booklet, *A Miscarriage of Justice: The Case of George Edalji*

In December 1905, the Liberals were invited to form a government under Sir Henry Campbell-Bannerman, replacing the Conservative government led by Arthur Balfour. Aretas Akers-Douglas was replaced as Home Secretary by Herbert Gladstone, son of the Liberal prime minister William Gladstone.

Conan Doyle, however, lost the election as the Unionist candidate, securing only 2,444 votes against his opponent Thomas Shaw, who got 3,133 votes. He shrugged off the defeat, returning to his busy life of writing and lectures.

Shapurji had hoped that the new Liberal government would back his cause. He himself was a Liberal supporter. But he was disappointed. He found that the political elite had closed ranks against his family. Herbert Gladstone's cousin was married to Sir Reginald Hardy, the very judge who had sent George to prison.

On 6 October, Shapurji received a letter from the Home Office informing him that if George's conduct in prison remained good, he could be released on licence after he had served three years, i.e. in October 1906.

It would mean another year spent waiting for his son. The reverend replied immediately stating that he was 'wholly dissatisfied' with the decision: 'My son, George Edalji, has committed no crime ... I submit that my son is entitled to be released unconditionally and without delay.'[22]

Another year crept by at the vicarage. The petition by Yelverton and Lewis had not moved the Home Office, though the articles in *Truth* had made them consider early release on parole. Shapurji and Charlotte waited anxiously for the news of their son's release. Meanwhile, George had been moved from Lewes Prison and was now serving his sentence at Portland Prison, on the Isle of Portland, just off the coast of Dorset. It was a grim place. As the prisoners were driven the three miles uphill from the station, they could see the mass of grey stone rising darkly from the sea, flanked on all sides by high cliffs. It was as if nature had intended it to be a jail from which there was no escape. Soldiers with rifles stood on high posts ready to shoot down anyone trying to escape. Portland Prison was described by one inmate as a 'heart-breaking, soul-enslaving, brain-destroying, hell upon earth'.[23]

At Portland Prison, the authorities tested George's eyesight, and confirmed that he had a serious problem. They did not give him any close work in the jail. Further, on account of his myopia and astigmatism, he was not allowed to use the stairs and was placed in a medical ward, which was slightly less depressing than the regular cells.[24] Over the years, Charlotte and her sister made the journey from Great Wyrley in the Midlands to the Dorset coast in the south a number of times, spending twenty minutes with him at each visit. George assured them that he was fine. He did not want his family to be any more distressed than they already were.

Shapurji had been speaking to the newspapers about the letter from the Home Office offering the possibility of early parole for his son. In October 1906, three years after his conviction, the town of Wyrley was abuzz with the news that George Edalji was likely to be released. Once again the press gathered outside St Mary's Church. Shapurji told them that it was clear that the Home Office had doubts about the sentence, and if so, his son should have the benefit of it and not be released on ticket-of-leave.

'You know what a ticket-of-leave man is in England,' Shapurji told the *Mercury* newspaper bitterly.[25] 'He is a marked man, a man shunned by everybody. What can my son do when he comes out? He is a branded man; his character has gone, he can only earn his living by means of his own profession, and even that is closed to him, for he has been struck off the roll of the Law Society.'

His son was likely to come home soon, but Shapurji was uncertain of the future.

On 19 October 1906 the press started gathering outside Stafford Prison, expecting him to be released from his local jail. It was expected that George Edalji would be released that day. The excitement was mounting once again. But George was somewhere else. He had been quietly taken from Portland Prison and transported to Pentonville Prison in London three days before.

There was no one waiting for George when he walked out of Pentonville into the cold autumn air. It had been over three years since the fateful morning of his arrest. But he was not entirely a free man. He had been released on licence. The jail authorities had given him £2 9s 10d as a token grant. The terms for his release meant that he had to report to the police station every month until the end of his seven-year sentence in 1910.

George was relieved to avoid facing the press. He would prefer to meet them when he was ready. He headed for the London branch of the Church Army where his mother was waiting for him. It was an emotional reunion. Mother and son then headed for Mecklenburgh Street in Bloomsbury, where Charlotte had taken up temporary residence. George was in no hurry to return to Great Wyrley.

'It would not be safe to return,' Shapurji told local reporters who had gathered in Great Wyrley awaiting George's release. 'An outrage might be committed in a place like this at any time, and they would say in a minute that he had done it. It will mean trouble and expense for him to live elsewhere, but better that than to have any further worry.'[26]

Shapurji advised George to remain in London and paid for his lodgings there. George visited Great Wyrley for one day on 22 October to meet his father, stayed only for a few hours and made sure he was accompanied by a friend from the legal profession. Having come out of prison, George was determined not to simply accept his fate. He wanted to clear his name by publishing a pamphlet on his case. He also wanted to rally public support for his cause.

He wrote to the chief constable, Captain Anson, asking for a copy of Gurrin's report on the anonymous letters, which was given as evidence against him at the trial. George also wanted some clarifications from Anson, the man who had been instrumental in getting him a sentence of penal servitude. 'On looking over some old papers recently I came across a *Staffordshire Advertiser* of 5 December 1903 in which there is an article on "The outrages at Great Wyrley" where it is stated that: "The police are in 'possession of the strongest evidence' that I 'was implicit in the letter-writing of 10 years ago"',' he wrote.[27]

'This allegation is entirely false and I shall be glad to know if you caused it to be inserted in the press and if so whether you still adhere to it.'

George received a reply the very next day from Anson's office written by the deputy chief constable, E. W. Breton. It stated that it was not possible to supply George with a copy of Gurrin's report, as the police did not have it. Anson denied George's suggestion that he had inserted the information in the newspaper about the knowledge of the letter-writing of ten years previously. The letter showed clearly that Anson was not interested in any further dealings with George Edalji.

Disappointed at not being able to obtain a copy of Gurrin's report, George felt a sense of frustration. Unable to work, as his name had been struck off the roll and unable to return to his home and family in Great Wyrley, he was in the depths of despair. He had no earnings and was depending on his father to support him. All the petitions by the most reputed men in the legal profession had not moved the Home Office. He seemed to be in a dark tunnel from which there was no way out.

George's eyes fell on the book by his bedside. While in prison he had read almost all of Arthur Conan Doyle's works. He continued to follow the Sherlock Holmes stories in the *Strand Magazine*. In his despair, he grew convinced that if anyone could help untangle the mystery of the 'Wyrley Ripper', it was the author who had invented the master detective and who solved the most complicated of cases. He had read reports about Conan Doyle's lectures at the Society of Authors events and at venues around the country. He read the reviews of his plays being performed in the West End. Like many others before him, who regularly wrote to 'Sherlock Holmes' for help with a mystery, George picked up his pen and wrote to Sir Arthur Conan Doyle about the injustice he had suffered.[28] It was three months since his release. He asked for help in securing a pardon. Surely the man who had solved so many mysteries would be able to finally clear his name and overturn the verdict. He had nothing to lose.

# 12

# A Meeting with George

Winter seemed to have enveloped Undershaw in a blanket of gloom. Christmas was a few weeks away but Arthur Conan Doyle was not feeling the cheer. He looked out over his grounds. The leaves had fallen from the oak trees and they stood tall and bare in the garden, their branches stretching out like giant limbs. Most of the garden birds had left and only a few crows sat on the empty branches and called out to each other. A mist hung in the air, blocking his view over the rolling green of the South Downs.

His wife, Touie, had died in July after a long struggle with consumption. He had built the three-storey house for her in the Surrey countryside near the small village of Haslemere. The large windows provided plenty of light, the four acres of land a place to walk, play golf and reflect. London was forty miles away, a short train ride from Haslemere. Portsmouth could be reached in an hour. 'Her end was painless and serene. The long fight had ended at last in defeat, but at least we had held the vital fort for thirteen years after every expert had said that it was untenable,' he wrote later.[1] Even as his house and heart felt the emptiness left behind by Touie's death, he thought about Jean Leckie, the love of his life.

Despite all the comforts he had provided for Touie, Conan Doyle had struggled with his conscience for the past ten years. In 1897, at the age of thirty-seven, while married to Touie and father to their two children, he had met Jean Leckie at a party and fallen hopelessly in love. Jean was beautiful, witty and talented. A trained mezzo-soprano and an accomplished horsewoman, she was fourteen years younger than Conan Doyle, and enjoyed challenging him. She was everything that he looked for in a woman. The situation was complicated as Touie had been diagnosed with tuberculosis in 1893. With no cure for consumption available at the time, she was given only a few months to live. Conan Doyle would not give up. He took her to Davos in Switzerland for treatment, but they returned to England in 1897 as they missed their family and friends. He then built the large house for his wife in Haslemere, so she could enjoy the beauty of the Surrey countryside. In March that year he met Jean. She was the younger daughter of a family who lived in Blackheath in South London, who were known to the Conan Doyles for many years. He would later describe her as a 'dear friend of my mother and sister'.[2]

Though Conan Doyle was in love with Jean, he could not be unfaithful to his wife. For nearly ten years he kept the relationship platonic. To his friends and social circle, it was an open secret. Even his mother was aware of her son's love for Jean and was known to have comforted Jean as she struggled with the unusual relationship. She even acted as chaperone when her son met her in hotels in London, to give the liaison a stamp of respectability. He described his relationship with Jean as a 'fateful, heaven-sent thing and inspirational'.[3]

Jean had been patient, knowing his commitment to Touie. Yet it felt as though they were both waiting for her to die. And now she had gone, leaving them free to marry. Somehow, the guilt would not go away. They had decided to wait a year after Touie's death before tying the knot. The wedding would take place in September the following year. The creator of Sherlock Holmes was brooding just like his famous detective often did.

Conan Doyle's trusted secretary, Alfred Wood (Woodie), brought in the morning mail. He pointed out a particularly bulky envelope and suggested that it would interest him. It was a letter from George Edalji. The young lawyer had just been released from prison, where he had read Conan Doyle's books to pass the time. He now appealed to the author saying that he was innocent of the crime of mutilating a horse and writing anonymous letters, the crimes for which he had been incarcerated. George had enclosed a series of articles from a Birmingham newspaper.[4] Conan Doyle was used to receiving mail from his readers. Apart from the large amount of fan mail, there were also many letters addressed directly to 'Sherlock Holmes' appealing to him to solve a mystery. Some of these were personal problems, some were burglaries, others to do with missing items. Sometimes there were murders and other unsolved crimes. But the letter from George addressed directly to him was different. There was an urgency about the appeal, a need for justice to be done and seen to be done. The author felt a calling to come to the aid of the helpless young Parsee lawyer.

India had featured in some of the well-known novels and stories written by Conan Doyle and he had often done a considerable amount of research on the country. His fictional character, Dr Watson, friend and flatmate of Sherlock Holmes and narrator of his stories, had been posted in India as a surgeon with the British army. He served in the Second Anglo-Afghan War and was injured in the Battle of Maiwand. His hero, Sherlock Holmes, was so knowledgeable about Indian tobaccos that he could immediately tell when a man smoked an Indian hookah and if the ash left by a cigar was the black ash of Trichinopoly, all of which was crucial to solving his mysteries. Indians themselves, however, did not often feature in a positive light and their characters were depicted with all the trappings of a colonial mindset.

Conan Doyle's second novel, *The Sign of Four*, was set in a period after the Indian Mutiny and involved a plot revolving around three Indians and an Englishman who steal the valuable 'Agra treasure'. Agra during the Mutiny of 1857 is described as a place 'swarming with fanatics and fierce devil worshippers'. Conan Doyle's story references the infamous Cellular Jail – a colonial prison on the Andaman Islands in the Bay of Bengal – where Indian rebels, mutineers and criminals were incarcerated in the harshest of conditions. The islanders, who were usually around four feet tall, are described as 'naturally hideous, having large misshapen heads, small fierce eyes and distorted features'. The story moves from India to the grim docks of London and involves an islander called Tonga who is brought back by the Englishman. Tonga – who kills people with his poison darts – is painted to be worse than a ferocious animal. Dr Watson describes the native: 'That face was enough to give a man sleepless nights. Never have I seen a creature so deeply marked with all bestiality and cruelty. His small eyes glowed and burned with a sombre light and his thick lips were writhed back from his teeth which grinned and chattered at us with half animal fury.' He is killed in the story by Dr Watson.

In *The Adventure of the Speckled Band*, Holmes is called upon to investigate Dr Grimesby Roylott, a doctor who practised in India, who has returned with a menagerie of animals including a cheetah, a baboon and a deadly snake, which he is using to try to kill his stepdaughter. In Conan Doyle's works, India was a place of exotic creatures and treasures as much as it was a hot-bed of rebellion, thuggery, tribal wars and criminal acts. A strong defender of Empire, Conan Doyle would now be drawn into championing the cause of one who had been wronged by the racist attitudes of the establishment. For him, it was imperative to ensure that English justice prevailed.

Conan Doyle had asked George to meet him at the Grand Hotel in Trafalgar Square in London. George was nervous and excited. He had never met a celebrity in his life, and here he was now, waiting to meet the most famous writer of the time. The creator of Sherlock Holmes was late. As he entered the lobby of the hotel, he instantly recognised the young solicitor who had written to him. He was the only Indian man in the room. As soon as he set eyes on him, he also knew that George Edalji could not be the killer.

'I had been delayed, and he was passing the time by reading the paper,' wrote Conan Doyle. 'I recognised my man by his dark face, so I stood and observed him. He held the paper close to his eyes and rather sideways, proving not only a high degree of myopia, but marked astigmatism. The idea of such a man scouring fields at night and assaulting cattle while avoiding the police was ludicrous.'[5]

The condition was so bad that glasses did not help. It gave the sufferer 'a vacant, bulge-eyed, staring appearance, which when taken with his dark skin, must have made him seem a very queer man to the eyes of an English village, and therefore to be associated with any queer event.'

Like his fictional detective Sherlock Holmes, Conan Doyle made a quick appraisal of George, even before a single word had been exchanged between them. He knew that the man who was sitting in the hotel lobby had such defective eyesight that he could not have crept out in the dead of night, crossed village fields and disembowelled cattle. He also knew why he had been suspected. It was his appearance. 'There, in a single physical defect, lay the moral certainty of his innocence, and the reason why he should become the scapegoat,' wrote Conan Doyle.

He introduced himself to George and asked him immediately about his eyesight.

'Aren't you astigmatic?'

'Yes,' said George. He explained that he never wore glasses as even the strongest lenses could not alter the deformity of his eyeballs.

'Surely that was raised at your trial?'

George said he had wanted to call an oculist, but his counsel had felt it was not necessary as the case against him was so 'ridiculous' that it was not worth the trouble.

Over the next hour, George recounted the troubled history of the family at the vicarage, the anonymous letters with their racist abuse that had plagued them when he was a boy; and their recurrence from 1903 along with the cattle-maimings. He told Conan Doyle about the trial, how the evidence had been presented in court, and how he had been sentenced to seven years' penal servitude despite a horse being killed when he was still in custody, and the person who did it confessing to the police. He had now been struck off the roll, could not practise as a solicitor and could not remake his life as he was tainted. He had the support of several eminent people, but as long as he was released from jail on licence, he could do nothing. He pleaded with the author to help him to clear his name and get compensation for wrongful imprisonment.

Conan Doyle agreed readily. He had already read the newspaper articles and considerable coverage of the case before he met George. He immediately decided to read more, and investigate the case. He reassured the anxious young solicitor that he was on his side.

The tall and dependable figure of Conan Doyle, his kindly manner, the frank and direct way in which he spoke to George and the trust he clearly placed in him, filled George with a sense of hope. He had not experienced this sense of empathy and warmth from a stranger for a very long time. He walked back to his lodgings with a new lightness in his step.

The entry of Arthur Conan Doyle into the campaign for George Edalji attracted – as might be expected – immense publicity. The press reported with delight that 'Sherlock Holmes' had stepped into the investigation.

Conan Doyle wasted no time. First he wanted an independent assessment of George's eyesight. He sent George to the reputed ophthalmologist Mr Kenneth Scott of Manchester Square, London, to verify the extent of his myopia. To make sure that George could not lie about his sight or pretend semi-blindness, Conan Doyle asked Kenneth Scott to administer atropine in George's eyes and test them independently. His report convinced Conan Doyle of the severity of George's myopia:

Right eye – 8.75 Diop Spher.

–1.75 Diop cyclind axis 90 degree.

Left eye – 8.25 Diop Spher.

Kenneth Scott said he was prepared to testify to the accuracy of the result under oath.

The reading was even more acute than he had expected. The result confirmed to Conan Doyle that George was almost blind. Such a condition of the eyes would make the alleged crime practically impossible. A pair of glasses made to that prescription worn by somebody with normal healthy eyes would at once show the world through George's eyes. Conan Doyle was prepared to get such a pair of glasses made. It would prove the point that a person with such poor vision bordering on blindness could not make his way across dark country fields on a wet and windy night and slash animals in the way that it was done in Great Wyrley.

The next thing Conan Doyle wanted to do was visit the scene of the crime. If George Edalji had not committed the maimings, then somebody else had. He was sure the village of Great Wyrley contained the clues and the killer. Beneath the idyllic charm of the countryside, there lay a dark and sinister secret. Conan Doyle was well and truly on the case. It was a welcome distraction from the emotional upheavals of the last few months. Jean would understand. The wedding was not for a few months. He could spend the time investigating the strange case of the Wyrley Ripper. An innocent man's future depended on him.

# PART II

# 13

## *Elementary!*

On a cold winter morning at the start of the New Year, Arthur Conan Doyle travelled to Great Wyrley. On 3 January 1907, he caught the train from London to Birmingham and changed for the branch line to the village. He made his way to the vicarage and joined Shapurji, Charlotte and Maud for breakfast. The vicar told him about the anonymous letters, the hoaxes carried out in his name, the attitude of the police, the killing of the cattle and the arrest and trial of his son. He pointed out how the animal mutilations were still going on even while his son was in jail. It was heartbreaking for him to watch his son suffer even after his release: he could not practise as a lawyer, he could not even return to his home in the vicarage.

Conan Doyle was impressed by the sincerity of the Edalji family. He wrote afterwards: 'What aroused my indignation and gave me the driving force to carry this thing through, was the utter helplessness of this forlorn little group of people, the coloured clergyman in his strange position, the brave blue-eyed, grey-haired wife, the young daughter, baited by brutal boors and having the police, who should have been their natural protectors, adopting from the beginning a harsh tone towards them and accusing them, beyond all sense and reason, of being the cause of their own troubles and of persecuting and maligning themselves.'[1]

Conan Doyle was in full Sherlock Holmes mode. He needed to see the scene of the crime. After breakfast, he walked to Plant Pit Meadows to see the route that George Edalji would have allegedly taken that fateful night. The path involved crossing over the raised North Western Railway tracks behind the vicarage and clambering through clumps of prickly gorse bushes. It was clear to Conan Doyle that George with his partial blindness would never have managed to cross these barriers on a dark and wet night.

He knelt down in the field, picked up a lump of soil, crumbled it in his fingers and noted the colour: it was of a yellow-reddish hue, not the type that was found on Edalji's boots. He examined the field, and the shed where the police had found some blood. He could see no way that the young lawyer would have sidled up to the pony in the dark, grasped it and slashed its stomach. George had no experience with animals. He had never shown any cruelty to them. Conan Doyle noted that the journey was hard even for an able-bodied man like himself. For a severely myopic person to do it in the dead of night, in the middle of heavy showers, was impossible.

After the walk, Conan Doyle went to meet some of the residents of the village. He met William Henry Brookes, a local grocer, whose name had appeared in many of the letters. He also met William Greatorex, whose teenage son, Wilfred, had stood in court in 1903 and said he had not written the letters. He shared a pint with local miners at The Swan and picked up some of the village gossip. He called at the post office. Everyone was more than happy to talk to the writer.

It was soon time for him to make his last stop: Anson's house. Conan Doyle had written to Anson before his visit saying he wanted to write an article about the case for the *Daily Telegraph*. He told Anson that he had felt some 'uneasiness' about the verdict and he wanted to assure the public that George had had a fair trial. Anson was flattered by the request from the great writer and invited him to stay. He replied to Conan Doyle saying he would be happy to help him write an account of the end of the Edalji case and offered 'any amount of information for your own satisfaction if it would go no further than yourself'.[2] He even said he would be interested in 'what Sherlock Holmes might have to say about the real-life case'.[3]

Welcoming Conan Doyle to his stately home, Anson wasted no time in making the case against George Edalji and his family. He told him that George looked outwardly like a respectable lawyer but was in fact dishonest, had gambling debts and was practically bankrupt. He said that he falsely accused the police of stealing £200 from his office in Birmingham, but had actually cashed the money himself afterwards (this was not true as George was taken straight into police custody and never went to any bank). George, he said, had undoubtedly written the anonymous letters and his father had lied in the witness box to protect him. His eyes had been examined in prison and there was nothing wrong with them. At any rate he was so used to the fields that he could have got to Plant Pit Meadows blindfolded.

The police chief clearly had a low opinion of Shapurji. He dismissively told Conan Doyle that he did not know how a 'Hindoo' who spoke English with a marked accent had come to be the Vicar of Great Wyrley. He also cast aspersions on him, implying that he had inappropriate relations with his son, as they shared the same bedroom which he locked from inside every night. Anson told Conan Doyle that he 'presumed' that there was good reason for George to 'sleep with his father'. However, Anson had underestimated the astuteness of his famous guest. Conan Doyle listened to the chief of Staffordshire police without revealing any of the investigations he had already undertaken himself.

The meeting left Conan Doyle convinced that Anson was a racist and had single-mindedly targeted George Edalji. All the way back on the train, he thought about the elderly vicar and his wife, their shy and studious half-blind son and the arrogant police chief who had implicated him. Conan Doyle was ready to put pen to paper and do what he could to right this wrong.

Before sending the piece to the newspaper, he wrote to Anson telling him he was ready to publish his article, but warned him that the Staffordshire police would not come out well in it. Conan Doyle pointed out that he was 'honour bound' to do justice to his enquiries. He disclosed that he had had George's eyes tested and gave Anson the results of the tests. He reprimanded Anson for not having taken the trouble to visit the vicarage or the scene of the crime in the days before the trial. He told him that if he had done this, he would have then seen for himself that it was not easy to walk the distance that night. He rejected claims that the Edaljis were liars. As a final note, he cautioned Anson: 'If similar reports have gone to the Home Office and stand in the way of justice, then the Edaljis must find some public way of showing how baseless they are, in this they have my sympathy.' It would be the start of their acrimonious correspondence over the years.

On 7 January, exactly four days after his visit to Great Wyrley, Conan Doyle wrote a letter to the editor of the *Daily Telegraph*:

> I have been engaged for some time past in investigating the case of Mr George Edalji, a young solicitor of Parsee origin, who was condemned at the Stafford quarter sessions of October 1903, to seven years' penal servitude for the maiming of cattle. I should be much obliged to you if would aid the cause of justice by publishing the results of my inquiry in an early number of *The Daily Telegraph*. You would add to the favour if you would permit the statement to be headed 'No Copyright' for I hope that in that case other papers – and especially Midland papers – would copy it in extensor. Only an appeal to the public can put an end to a course of injustice and persecution which amount, as I hope that I shall show, to a national scandal.
> Yours faithfully,
> Arthur Conan Doyle
> Monkstown, Crowburgh, Jan. 7

True to his word, Conan Doyle sent his piece. 'The Case of Mr George Edalji' was published in two parts, starting on 11 January 1907. Dramatically displayed across the entire front page of the daily newspaper, the article had an immediate impact. Newspapers across the country reported that 'Sherlock Holmes' was investigating the Edalji case and that the vicar's son had a champion in none other than Arthur Conan Doyle. Copies of the article were reprinted in the *New York Times* and the *Washington Post* making George an international celebrity overnight.

Conan Doyle argued the case systematically and thoroughly, beginning with the account of his first meeting with George in the London hotel. In true Holmes style, he revealed that he had picked up a few things about the young man before having spoken a word to him. He had known immediately that he was innocent, when he saw George holding his newspaper close to his eyes and rather sideways, 'proving not only a high degree of myopia, but marked

The article by Arthur Conan Doyle in the *Daily Telegraph*

astigmatism'. Conan Doyle said that the idea of such a man scouring the fields at night and assaulting cattle while avoiding the police was ludicrous.

At all times while investigating the story, said the great crime writer, he had followed the truth rather than any preconceived theory. He was ready to examine any point made against the accused with as much care as the case made for his innocence. 'I have felt at last that it was an insult to my intelligence to hold out any longer against the certainty that there has been an inconceivable miscarriage of justice.'

Conan Doyle took his readers to the beginning of the story when Rev. Shapurji Edalji arrived as Vicar of Great Wyrley. 'Placed in the exceedingly difficult position of a coloured clergyman in an English parish, he seems to have conducted himself with dignity and discretion,' he wrote.

He recounted the story of the threatening letters in George's childhood. The history of the letters and the harassment of the Edalji family had not been discussed at the trial. Conan Doyle was now bringing this story not just to Britain, but to an international audience.[4] It was going to put the whole Edalji affair in a new light.

In his two-part article, Conan Doyle looked at every argument put forward by the prosecution and demolished it. He related how the maid Elizabeth Foster was accused of writing the letters, and she and her friends were filled with bitter feelings of revenge. 'There is good reason to believe that in this incident of 1888 is to be found the seed which led to the trouble of 1893–1895 and the subsequent trouble of 1903,' wrote Conan Doyle. He pointed out that the letters received in 1888 were in an adult's handwriting. As George at this time was a schoolboy of twelve, they could not have been his.

In 1892 the second singular outbreak of anonymous letters began. 'They were posted at Walsall, Cannock and various other towns, but bore internal evidence of a common origin, and were all tainted by the Elizabeth Foster incident.'

Conan Doyle made a detailed analysis of the letters and found the following characteristics.

1. That there was a 'diabolical hatred of the whole Edalji family, the 16-17-18-year-old George coming in for his fair share of the gross abuse.' He also noted that the hatred was insane in its intensity and coldly resolute as it lasted three years. Conan Doyle published a few extracts from the letters including: 'I swear by God that I will murder George Edalji soon. The only thing that I care about in this world is revenge, revenge, revenge, sweet revenge, I long for, then I shall be happy in hell.'

2. The second characteristic noted by Conan Doyle was that the letters had a frantic admiration, real or feigned, for the local police. Conan Doyle quoted the letters that went: 'Ha Ha, hurrah for Upton! Good Old Upton! Blessed Upton ...'

Also, 'I love Upton. I love him better than life, because for my sake he lost promotion.'

3. The third characteristic noted by Conan Doyle was that there was a real or simulated religious mania. In the same letter, the writer claimed to be God, while later in the letter he is eternally lost in Hell. 'So consistent is this that it is hard to doubt that there is a real streak of madness in the writer.'

4. The fourth characteristic was the intimacy of the writer with the names and affairs of the people in the district. Conan Doyle pointed out that as many as twenty names would sometimes be given with opprobrious epithets attached. No one could doubt that the writer lived in the immediate neighbourhood and was intimately acquainted with the people of whom he spoke.

Conan Doyle told his readers how even while the hate-filled letters were circulating, the vicar was subjected to a series of hoaxes. There was even a forged apology from George Edalji and Fred Brookes confessing to the hoax letters, which was immediately disowned by the Edaljis. Any reasonable man, said Conan Doyle, would be convinced that the 'Edaljis were not persecuting themselves in this maddening fashion'.

He also pointed out an important incident – the appearance of the key outside the vicarage – which may have seemed trivial at the time – but was important for one fact: for the first time it showed how suspicious Anson was of George Edalji. Conan Doyle was diplomatic in his reference to Anson.

Personally, I have met with nothing but frankness and courtesy from Captain the Honourable G. A. Anson, during the course of my investigation, and if in the search for the truth I have to criticise any word or action of his, I can assure him that it is with regret and only in pursuit of what seems to me to be a clear duty.

Conan Doyle described the incident of the key and how when it was brought before the chief constable of the county, he immediately concluded that young George Edalji was the culprit. However, George was not a pupil at Walsall School, having been educated at

Rugeley, and there was 'not the slightest reason' to suppose that he had procured a key from this 'six-mile distant' school and laid it on his doorstep.

'However, here is a queer-looking boy, and here are queer doings, and here is a zealous constable, the very Upton whose praises were later to be so enthusiastically voiced by the writer of the letters.

'If the Staffordshire police took this attitude towards young Edalji in 1895, what chance of impartiality had he in 1903, when a culprit was wanted for an entirely new set of crimes? It is evident that their minds were steeped in prejudice against him, and that they were in the mood to view his actions in the darkest light,' he wrote.

Conan Doyle then described the horrors of 1903 when the cattle-maiming was accompanied by further letter-writing. He also pointed out that the attacks continued after George was arrested. Finally, a rough miner called Farrington was convicted and imprisoned for three years. Farrington's arrest was followed by a complete cessation of the mutilation of cattle. 'How monstrous, then to contend, as the Home Office has done, that no new facts have arisen to justify a revision of Edalji's case,' wrote Conan Doyle.

Though there was no absolute proof that the letters of 1903 were by the same person who wrote those of 1895, there were points about their 'phrasing, about their audacity and violence of language, and finally, about the attentions which they bestow upon the Edalji family, which seem to point to a common origin,' said Conan Doyle. Though the second set of letters presented a variety of handwritings which were different from the 1895 letters, the original persecutor was fond of boasting that he could change his writing.

The 'Greatorex' letters pointing to a gang and the subsequent evidence given by the real Wilfred Greatorex should have been followed up by the police, said Conan Doyle. At the trial, Wilfred said he had seen George on his train about a dozen times in the last year. Given that they all took the same train every day, and they had been in the same compartment only twelve times in the year, it showed that it was purely incidental and that George was 'in their company but not of it'.

The two letters sent to the police threatening to kill Sergeant Robinson and the other received by PC Rowley, which gave a graphic description of the manner of killing the animals, were all certified by the expert at the trial to be in George's handwriting. Conan Doyle said it was absurd enough that 'these letters incriminating himself in such violent terms should be attributed to young Edalji'. The climax was the offensive postcard sent to George's office from Wolverhampton on 4 August. However, George was out of town on 4 August. The fact was attested to by the porter-signalman at Rugeley Town station, who spoke to George and his sister on their return from Aberystwyth on 5 August.

'It is certain then, that this postcard could not have been by him … yet it is included in that list of anonymous letters, which the police maintained and the expert declared, to be in Edalji's own handwriting. If this incident is not enough in itself to break down the whole case, so far as the authorship of the letters does, then I ask, what in this world would be sufficient to demonstrate this absurdity?'

Conan Doyle questioned the police assertion that George Edalji was 'an active member, if not the leading spirit, of a gang of village ruffians'. He pointed out that George was shy and studious and won the highest of legal prizes. 'Finally, he is as blind as a proverbial bat, but the bat has the advantage of finding its way in the dark, which would be very difficult for him.' In defence of George, Conan Doyle said: 'I have myself practised as an oculist, but I can never remember correcting so high a degree of astigmatic myopia as that which afflicts Mr Edalji.' Experts had said that in the dusk it would be practically impossible for him to find his way about in places with which he was not perfectly familiar.

'I appeal to the practising oculists of this country, and I ask whether there is one of them who would not admit that such a condition of the eyes would make such a performance practically impossible … And yet this all-important point was never made at the trial.'

Conan Doyle appealed directly to his readers: 'It is this studious youth, who touches neither alcohol nor tobacco, and is so blind that he gropes his way in the dark, who is the dangerous barbarian who scours the country at night, ripping up horses. Is it not perfectly clear, looking at his strange, swarthy face and bulging eyes, that it is not the village ruffian, but rather the unfortunate village scapegoat, who stands before you?'

The police had produced the evidence of the stained and damp coat that George had allegedly worn when he committed the crime. Like a skilled barrister, Conan Doyle tore into this argument, examining every point in detail:

'If the coat were damp and these were bloodstains contracted during the night, then those stains were damp also, and the inspector had only to touch them and then to raise his crimson finger in the air to silence all criticism. But since he could not do so it is clear that the stains were not fresh,' wrote Conan Doyle. As for the 'two stains' that were identified, he said: 'At any rate, it may be most safely said that the most adept operator who ever lived would not rip up a horse with a razor upon a dark night and have only two threepenny bit spots of blood to show for it. The idea is beyond argument.'

On the question of the presence of horse hairs, which had been vehemently denied by the vicar, his wife and his daughter, Conan Doyle presented the evidence of Miss Foxley, head of the high school attended by Maud, who vouched for her competence as a scientific observer: 'Wilful mis-statement on her part is as impossible in itself as it is inconsistent with her high principles and frank, straightforward character.'

The police, said Conan Doyle, should have immediately picked samples of the horse hair from the coat, sealed it in an envelope and produced it before the police doctor. 'But they did nothing of the kind,' he pointed out. Instead they carried off the coat, despite three reliable witnesses saying there were no horse hairs on it. The coat then disappeared for twelve hours. In the meantime, the pony was put to death, and a section of its hide with horse hairs was removed by the police. The coat was removed at eight in the morning. The police doctor, Dr Butter, saw it at nine in the evening. By then there were horse hairs on its surface.

'One need not fly to extreme conclusions. It is to be remembered that the mere carrying of the hide and coat together may have caused the transference of hairs, or that the officers may themselves have gathered hairs on their clothes while examining the pony, and so unconsciously transferred them to the coat.'

Conan Doyle also argued that the hairs on the coat corresponded to the type of hair cut from the horse's hide, whereas the horse had been slashed on the belly, and belly hairs were different from the longer, darker hair on the sides. Butter had said in his evidence: 'Numerous hairs on the jacket, which were similar in colour, length and structure to those on the piece of skin cut from the horse'. Conan Doyle could therefore say confidently that the hairs 'could not possibly be from the general body of the pony, but must have transferred, no doubt unconsciously, from the particular piece of skin.'

Then there was the issue of the trousers and boots. Once again, Conan Doyle pointed out that there were no blood marks on the boots, which there would have been if an animal had been slashed. Also, the colour of the mud on the boots was not the colour of the mud at the place of outrage which was yellow-red, a mixture of clay and sand. The boots were damp because George had said at the trial that he had stepped into a puddle. On the subject of the 'farce of the footprints', Conan Doyle said that hundreds of miners had swarmed in the area to see the pony and trampled on the soil from 6 a.m. Yet at 4 p.m., eight hours after the seizure of the boots Campbell was endeavouring to trace a similarity in the tracks. It was pointed out that the footprint was worn at the heel, as were George Edalji's boots.

'No cast was taken of the tracks. They were not photographed. They were not cut-out for expert comparison. So little were they valued by Inspector Campbell that he did not even mention them to the Magistrates on the 19th. But in retrospect they grew more valuable, and they bulked large at the trial,' wrote Conan Doyle. If the police had said the crime had been committed at 9.30 p.m. as was their original story, then the heavy rain on and off that night would have blurred the footprints. 'Every point in this case simply crumbles to pieces as you touch it,' declared Conan Doyle.

'How formidable it all sounds – wet razor, blood on razor, blood and saliva and hair on coat, wet boots, footmark corresponding to boot – and yet how absolutely futile it all is when examined. There is not one single item which will bear serious criticism.'

He then moved to the innocent comments made by George at various stages before and after his arrest, which were produced in court to prove his guilt.

These included George smiling at the railway station when the constable went to tell him that Inspector Campbell wanted to see him. It was referred to by the prosecuting counsel as 'the prisoner's extraordinary conduct at the station'. However, 'Edalji's account is that Markhew said: "Can't you give yourself a holiday for one day?" at which Edalji smiled. Which is the more probable version, I leave to the reader.'

Again, after his arrest as he was being driven to the police station, George remarked, 'I am not surprised at this. I have been expecting it for some time.' Conan Doyle contested that it was not a very natural remark for a guilty man to make, but in fact an 'extremely probable one' from a man who believed that the police distrusted him and who had been accused by name in malignant anonymous letters. After he was committed to Stafford Prison before his trial, George Edalji refused bail saying 'and when the next horse is killed it will not be by me'. This was brought up by the prosecution counsel, who said: 'In refusing bail the prisoner made use of a very significant observation, and it went to suggest that the prisoner knew perfectly well what he was about when he refused bail.' The inference was that it was prearranged that a friend of George Edalji would commit a fresh crime, in order to clear him.

'Was there ever a more unfair utterance! It was "Heads I win, tails you lose". If no crimes occur, then it is clear we have the villain under lock and key. If crimes do occur, then it is clear that he is deep in conspiracy with others,' said Conan Doyle. He concluded that both George's decision to remain in gaol and his remark were the 'most proper and natural things in the world'. George believed that there was a 'strong conspiracy' against him and felt he would be safest in his cell.

Conan Doyle then brought up the case of the killing of the horse on 22 September by Harry Green, who later, just before he left for South Africa, said he had been forced to make a confession. 'One or other statement of Green's must be a falsehood, and I have sufficient reason myself, in the shape of evidence which has been set before me, to form a very clear opinion what the actual facts of the case were.' He said he would bring these facts up when a renewed inquiry began.

'Meanwhile, the task which lies immediately before me is not to show who committed the crimes – though that, I think, is by no means an insuperable problem – but that Edalji did not and could not have committed them.'

Conan Doyle questioned why the police, who held the written confession, did not prosecute Green. Even though it was not a crime to kill one's horse for humane reasons, it was definitely a crime to disembowel a horse on a dark night, even if it was your own.

'The Home Office says that all inquiry has been made in this case, and that everything has been investigated and the matter closed. That is the official answer I received only a fortnight ago. Then can the Home Office give any good reason why Green was not prosecuted?' asked Conan Doyle.

Green had been subpoenaed by the police and was present at the trial. He was, however, not called as a witness. The reason, conjectured Conan Doyle, was that Green would probably have said he killed the horse because it had sustained injuries during Yeomanry training, but at no time would he suggest that he was acting in collusion with George Edalji.

Next Conan Doyle moved to the trial itself and questioned how such an important case could have been assigned to 'Court B' at the quarter sessions under Sir Reginald Hardy, who had no legal training. 'Here was a young man accused of one of a series of crimes for which the whole country was longing to find someone who might be made an example of. The jury would naturally have the same feelings as their fellow citizens. Hence it was peculiarly necessary to have a cold legal mind to cool their ardour and keep them on a firm ground of fact, far from prejudice and emotion. Yet it was in the court of the layman that the case was tried,' wrote Conan Doyle.

It was time for him to come down heavily on the prosecution's star witness – the handwriting expert, Thomas Gurrin – who had insisted that the letters were written by George Edalji, despite the evidence that one of the postcards could not have been sent by him. Gurrin had also been the expert witness at the trial of Adolf Beck, who had wrongly been accused of stealing. Beck was released from prison after the real culprit was caught and subsequently awarded compensation of £2,000.

'And who was the expert who expressed these views that weighed so heavily with the jury?' wrote Conan Doyle. 'It was Mr Thomas Gurrin. And what is the record of Mr Thomas Gurrin? His nemesis was soon to come. Within a year he had to present himself before the Beck Committee, and admit the terrible fact that through his evidence an innocent man had suffered prolonged incarceration. Does this fact alone not convince my readers that an entire reconsideration of the Edalji case is a most pressing public duty?'

Either Edalji did the crime before ten o'clock that night or after ten o'clock, said Conan Doyle. The latter scenario was laughable as the vicar spent the night a few feet from him, the vicarage was bolted and barred and no one heard him leave from inside the house. Nor did the police posted outside see anyone leave. The theory that it was done before ten was equally absurd, said Conan Doyle. 'You have to face the supposition that after returning from a long day's work in Birmingham, he sallied out in a coat which he was only known to wear in the house, performed a commonplace mission at the boot-shop in the village, then blind as he was, hurried off for three-quarters of a mile through difficult, tortuous ways, with fences to climb and railway lines to cross (I can answer for it, having myself trod every foot of it) to commit a ghastly and meaningless crime, entirely foreign to his studious and abstinent nature; that he then hurried back another three-quarters of a mile to the vicarage, arrived so composed and tidy as to attract no attention, and sat down quietly to the family supper, the whole expedition from the first to the last being under an hour.' He also pointed out that the pony had been seen to be alive at 11 p.m. and the veterinary surgeon had testified when he had seen the pony in the morning that the wound could not possibly be more than six hours old.

Conan Doyle also gently admonished George's defence counsel saying he had not been strong. 'The fact is that the consciousness of innocence was in this case a danger, as it caused some slackness in guarding every point. So far as I can find, the whole story of the early persecutions of 1888 and of 1893–5 was not gone into, nor was their probable connection with that of 1903 pointed out. The blindness of Edalji, a most vital fact ... was hardly mentioned at all ... But even granting that, one cannot but feel the amazement ... when the jury brought in "Guilty" and Sir Reginald Hardy sentenced the prisoner to seven years.'

After the conviction of George Edalji, the outrages continued, but the police were 'not too anxious to push the matter' as any conviction would disturb the one they already had.

Summing up what happened in the months after the conviction, Conan Doyle praised the work of R. D. Yelverton, former Chief

Justice of the Bahamas, for his petitions to the Home Office in favour of George Edalji and the public campaign he managed to organise. Though the petition in favour of Edalji was signed by many from the legal profession, it had no effect on the Home Office. The friends of Edalji, headed by Yelverton, demanded to see the dossier at the Home Office, but as in the Beck case they were denied access, said Conan Doyle.

He went further than the Beck case, instead comparing the Edalji case to the 'squalid Dreyfus case' which had caused a scandal in France and exposed deep anti-Semitism in French society. In 1894, a letter had been discovered in the German embassy offering French military secrets. The head of the French intelligence, a deeply anti-Semitic man, pointed the finger at Alfred Dreyfus, the only Jewish officer in the services. Dreyfus, an artillery captain, was convicted in a secret court martial in 1894 and sentenced to exile on Devil's Island, a penal colony in French Guiana. Baying crowds yelled 'Death to Dreyfus! Death to the Jews' outside the military court.

However, it was soon revealed that the real traitor was a French officer, Major Ferdinand Esterhazy. The case was reopened and Esterhazy was tried for treason. High-ranking French officials then engaged in a major cover-up and protected Esterhazy during his trial, through lies and forgeries. When Esterhazy was acquitted in 1898, the French writer Emile Zola wrote an open letter to the French president titled 'J'Accuse'. The 4,000-word essay was published in *L'Aurore* newspaper and delivered a scathing judgement on the French establishment and its inherent anti-Semitic attitude. It led to the eventual freedom of Dreyfus.

Conan Doyle correctly pointed out that George Edalji, like Alfred Dreyfus, had suffered on account of the same racial prejudice. While the British had taken the high moral ground in condemning the French police, they had failed to acknowledge that their own police and judicial system were guilty of the same crime. They, too, had formed a wall to support the establishment and covered up what was a blatant miscarriage of justice. (Over the years the Dreyfus case would be forged in people's memories, while the Edalji case would be forgotten, despite the cause being championed by a much-loved author and the widespread international coverage at the time.)

'The parallel is extraordinarily close,' Conan Doyle pointed out. 'You have a Parsee, instead of a Jew, with a promising career blighted, in each case the degradation from a profession and the campaign for redress and restoration, in each case questions of forgery and handwriting arise, with Esterhazy in the one, and the anonymous writer in the other. Finally, I regret to say, that in the one case you have a clique of French officials going from excess to excess in order to cover an initial mistake, and that in the other you have the Staffordshire police acting in the way I have described.'

Conan Doyle did not hesitate to highlight Anson's role in the Edalji affair either, though he said it was the 'most painful part of my statement'. He traced the negative attitude of Anson taking root against George Edalji during 1892–95 when Sergeant Upton sent him reports against the teenager. It made Anson determined to get for George 'a dose of penal servitude' as he was convinced that he was behind the pranks.

Giving the police chief the benefit of doubt – 'I have no doubt Captain Anson was quite honest in his dislike and unconscious of his own prejudice' – it led to the fact that Anson's dislike of George filtered through the rest of his force. 'When they had George Edalji they did not give him the most elementary justice, as is shown by the fact that they did not prosecute Green at a time when his prosecution would have endangered the case against Edalji,' said Conan Doyle.

He revealed that the police made every effort after the sentence to blacken George's character and that of his father so as to frighten off anyone who might be inclined to investigate his case. Conan Doyle stated: 'When Mr Yelverton first took it up, he had a letter [with] Captain Anson's own signature, saying, under date 8 Nov 1903: "It is right to tell you that you will find it a simple waste of time to attempt to prove that Edalji could not, owing to his position and alleged good character, have been guilty of writing offensive and abominable letters. His father is as well aware as I am of his proclivities in the direction of anonymous writing, and several other people have personal knowledge on the same subject."'

Both George and his father had declared on oath that George had never written an anonymous letter in his life. When Yelverton asked for the names of the 'several other people' he received no answer.

It seemed to be an attempt by Anson to 'nip in the bud' any move questioning the verdict.

Conan Doyle pointed out that in the fifteen years that the vicarage had been a centre of debate 'the chief constable has never once visited the spot or taken counsel personally with the inmates'.

After completing three of his seven years, George was suddenly released without pardon. 'Evidently the authorities were shaken, and compromised with their conscience in this fashion. But this cannot be final. The man is guilty, or he is not. If he is, he deserves every day of his seven years. If he is not, then we must have apology, pardon and restitution. There can be no middle ground between these extremes,' declared Conan Doyle.

He called for a small committee to reconsider the case, a complete reorganisation of the Staffordshire constabulary, an inquiry into the irregularity of procedures at Staffordshire quarter sessions and thirdly an inquiry into who was responsible at the Home Office for the debacle and the punishment that would be given for his delinquency. 'Until each and all of these questions is settled a dark stain will remain upon the administrative annals of this country,' said Conan Doyle.

'If the continuation of the outrages, the continuation of the anonymous letters, the discredit cast upon Gurrin as an expert, the confession of a culprit that he had done a similar outrage, and finally the exposition of Edalji's blindness, do not present new facts to modify a jury's conclusion, what possible new facts would do so? But the door is shut in our faces. Now we turn to the last tribunal of all, a tribunal which never errs when the facts are fairly laid before them, and we ask the public of Great Britain whether this thing is to go on,' he declared.

George read the articles with keen interest. He read the arguments over and over again, marvelling at the simple logic with which Conan Doyle made his points. Everything would now depend on how the public and Home Office officials reacted to it. Nervously, he waited for their verdict. Back at the vicarage, Shapurji, Charlotte and Maud also pored over the newspaper article. They knew that the whole village would soon be talking about it.

The Edalji case had sizzled on the back-burner of British society and politics for three years. A fiery campaign had been conducted by Yelverton, Lewis and Labouchère, there had been countless discussions in the newspapers and representations to the Home Office; the vicar had spent three years talking about the injustice suffered by his son. But it was the two-part serialisation of the case by Arthur Conan Doyle that led to an explosion. Overnight, the quiet, myopic George Edalji became a celebrity. No less than 'Sherlock Holmes' had come to his defence. A photograph of a smartly dressed clean-shaven George, taken on the day of his release, was published along with the article on 11 January.

THE DAILY TELEGRAPH, FRIDAY, JANUARY 11, 1907.

MR. GEORGE EDALJI.

TAKEN ON THE DAY OF HIS RELEASE.

Image from the *Daily Telegraph* newspaper

The article was reproduced in the *New York Times* and the *Washington Post*, and was replicated in its entirety in local newspapers across the Midlands. In public houses and in clubs, in town halls and churches, they discussed the case of George Edalji and the investigation by Arthur Conan Doyle. Letters of support came from famous writers of the day like J. M. Barrie, Bram Stoker and Jerome K. Jerome. John Churton Collins, professor of literature at Birmingham University and friend of Conan Doyle, wrote a passionate piece in the *English Review* demanding justice for George. Justice Yelverton offered his office space in Temple Chambers and soon it became the campaign centre for Edalji's supporters. A public fund to help the unemployed lawyer was formed by Conan Doyle with Sir Horace Voules (editor of *Truth* magazine) and Sir George Lewis, chair of the Law Society, one of George's earliest supporters. The Parsee community raised money for one of their own, who had been maligned and wronged. Hundreds of letters were sent to the Home Office, to the Staffordshire police and to Conan Doyle himself. It was as if a dam had burst, and people across continents were backing the Parsee lawyer and his troubled family.

The letters pages of the *Daily Telegraph* carried readers' opinions for days.

Responding to them was an Indian from Hull, who signed himself as Aroon Chunder Dutt, MA Cantab.

'From the letters appearing in your paper, it is evident that even in the present day the hardly-educated and un-travelled Englishman has an inherent prejudice against the peoples of India. He thinks they are uncouth and semi-savage, with tastes and habits far removed from Western ideals ... Edalji's personal appearance went against him at the trial.'[5]

Conan Doyle himself did not stop with the article in the *Daily Telegraph*. Within days he shot off a letter to the *British Medical Journal* giving the details of George's myopia and asking the experts to consider whether it was physically possible for such a person to have 'set forth without glasses on a pitch dark night with neither moon nor stars; to have crossed country for half a mile, climbing fences, finding gaps in hedges, and passing over a broad railway line; to have found and mutilated a pony which was loose in a large field, to have returned half a mile, and to have accomplished it all under thirty-five minutes ...'[6]

George was delighted with the initial response he was getting. He thanked Conan Doyle privately and publicly for taking interest in his case and for pointing out the important matter of his defective eyesight. In a letter published in the *Daily Telegraph* – which had become the platform for the Edalji case – George said that he could find his way on the main road after dusk without glasses, provided he knew it thoroughly.

'But the point in my case has nothing to do with semi-darkness or main roads, or even roads of any description.'[7]

The prosecution, he said, had changed its stand at the last minute and said he had committed the crime in the middle of the night, 'and that owing to the unusual darkness which the police had suggested equalled it if not exceeded, that which troubled Egypt, the three constables actually guarding the field (two of whom, Bradley and Weaver, the prosecution found it convenient not to call) could not have noticed me!' said George.

'There were also twenty other constables patrolling the immediate neighbourhood of the occurrence, and so we get the preposterous hypothesis that in complete darkness I sallied forth on the diabolical errand, found my way along a colliery tramway, with obstacles at almost every stop, across the London and North Western main line, over long rows of metals and sidings intersected with points wires and signalling contrivances of a varied description, than along the line over projecting "sleepers", to a flight of steps, and down the steps and under the archway into the field.

'All this way I should have to proceed so noiselessly as not to attract the attention of the army of watchers around me, and in the field make myself invisible to the three detectives there, find the animal, inflict the terrible injuries without the pony making any movement or sound likely to attract attention, and then return by an absolutely impossible route at night, over the fields, hedges and ditches where the alleged footprints were found.'

Ophthalmologists across the country responded to Conan Doyle's open query to them about George's myopia. H. Carer Mactier, a surgeon for nearly twelve years from the Midlands, wrote back saying it was 'not only improbable but impossible' that George could have seen his way around in the dark. George Ferdinand from Aberdeen wrote to Conan Doyle that in his opinion 'George Edalji could not with so high a degree of myopia have seen his way about under the conditions you mention'. Conan Doyle sent the letters to the Home Office who noted that of over thirteen opinions submitted, nine specialists said it was 'impossible', four said it was 'highly improbable' and only one said it was 'possible' that George could have walked to the fields in the middle of the night.[8]

# 14

## *Martin Molton*

Somewhere in the country, the letter-writer was stirring again. Did he know that Arthur Conan Doyle was going to burst upon the scene and take up the case of George Edalji? Or was it just a coincidence that he picked up his pen and wrote the first letter just before the articles were published in the *Daily Telegraph*? He also adopted a new name: 'Martin Molton'. The letters were posted in London and from the Midlands. Either the writer was travelling frequently or he asked people to post them for him. Once the articles were published, and the name of George Edalji and Arthur Conan Doyle were on everyone's lips, the letters increased in number. Letters were sent to Captain Anson, George Edalji and Arthur Conan Doyle.

The first of these letters was received on 7 January by Anson. It was signed by 'Martin Molton'. The letter-writer told the police chief that he had proof that it was Edalji who had killed the animals. He urged Anson to go to the vicarage where he would find the 'bloodied' coat. He left clues. The coat was lying upstairs, in a room where the police hadn't looked. The letter-writer also had inside information that he shared with Anson: that Edalji had gambling debts. He suggested that Edalji had taken a wager with some mates that he would slash some animals. That is how he would repay his debts. The mysterious letter was postmarked London NW and posted at 5.15 p.m. on 5 January.

The letter-writer gave Anson instructions on how to contact him in secret. He would do this anonymously through the advertisement sections of a daily newspaper. If he wanted to open channels of communication, Anson would have to place an advert in the *Daily Mail* where he would use the code words: 'Rats and Mice Jupiter'.

The letter-writer demanded a payment of £2 for information. 'I have seen Edalji several times and got incriminatory letters from him as I told him he must tell me the exact truth. He is in town and I am here till the 29th.' It was all very cloak-and-dagger.

Anson was in a dilemma. The letter, he thought, could be a trap for him; if he showed up at the vicarage looking for a coat, he might look like a fool, or if he sent money, it would look as though he was paying an informer. He gave the letter to Gurrin to analyse the handwriting. Gurrin immediately declared that it was written by George Edalji.

Meanwhile, four days after 'Martin Molton' had sent his letter to Anson, the *Daily Telegraph* announced the forthcoming articles by Arthur Conan Doyle on the Edalji case.

Anson consulted Sir Melville Macnaghten, assistant commissioner of police, New Scotland Yard, on how to progress on the 'Martin Molton' letters. Macnaghten thought they should call the writer's bluff. On 10 January, an advertisement was placed in the *Daily Mail* newspaper. It said: 'Rats and Mice Jupiter. Communicate further.'

On 11 January Anson received another letter postmarked London WC. The writer demanded that he send a £2 postal order to 'Martin Molton' care of the GPO London.

Further consultations in the police force took place. Again, it was agreed that Anson should post the £2 to 'Martin Molton'. It was decided that anyone coming to collect the letter should be arrested and the GPO was alerted. 'Whatever is done, I hope I shall not be accused of paying money to "crush G. E.",' Anson wrote to Macnaghten.[1]

Conan Doyle's articles appeared in the *Daily Telegraph* on 11 and 12 January, creating a stir.

On 15 January, an advertisement was inserted in the *Daily Mail* advising 'Rats and Mice Jupiter' to collect a letter from the GPO. The police thought they had laid a trap for the letter-writer.

However, 'Martin Molton' also had his own plans. Even as the police were in communication with him, he was writing to George. 'Martin Molton' informed George that he could prove who attacked the pony on 18 August 1903 and invited him to learn the names.

'On Wednesday, please come to the GPO and ask for a letter from me, which will be sent by a friend, and contain many proofs. When you have noted my name please destroy this letter for fear it should fall into wrong hands,' said the letter-writer. He was clearly setting up George to receive Anson's letter which would be sent to the GPO.

Ever since the publication of the articles, George had been in almost daily touch with Conan Doyle and Yelverton. The two men were working side by side running his campaign from Yelverton's office. For the first time in several years, George felt protected, knowing he could turn to these dependable people for advice. He immediately showed them the 'Martin Molton' letter. He was puzzled as to how the letter-writer knew his London address. As expected, both Conan Doyle and Yelverton strongly stated that he should not go to the post office by himself. It was decided that Yelverton would accompany George to the GPO.

Meanwhile, the letter-writer, who was clearly enjoying his game, wrote to Anson on 16 January saying that he had seen the advertisement and would call at the GPO on the 17th. He threw Anson a few more tantalising tips: 'the coat Edalji wore I told you of I now find was at the Rectory a year ago, but the witness don't want to come publicly. It was in the attic opening out of the servant's bedroom. I believe it is there now …'[2]

On the morning of 19 January, unaware that the police were waiting to arrest the person who asked for the 'Martin Molton' letter, George, accompanied by Yelverton, called at the GPO and enquired if there was a letter for Martin Molton. The post office clerk, who had been alerted, asked him if he was Martin Molton. George replied that he was not, but had been asked to collect a letter addressed to Martin Molton. He also introduced Yelverton. The clerk did not give him the letter, following which George said that he would apply to the postmaster general for the letter to be delivered to Conan Doyle and Yelverton, who were investigating his case. Sergeant McPherson was watching the event, ready to make an arrest if needed. When he realised that he did not need to, he spoke to Yelverton without disclosing his identity. The police officer then made a report to Macnaghten.

Yelverton made an intelligent guess that he had spoken to a plain-clothes policeman. The next day Yelverton wrote about the episode in the *Daily Telegraph*, describing how George had received a letter and how they had called at the GPO. The contents of the letter were printed in full. Yelverton even mentioned that two detectives had appeared at the end and said to him: 'That is sufficient sir.'

The following day, Yelverton and Conan Doyle called at Scotland Yard and handed over the letter to Macnaghten. The assistant commissioner explained the history of the 'Martin Molton' letters, and how Anson had obliged the letter-writer hoping to trap 'Martin Molton' (in fact, Anson had hoped to trap George Edalji). However, since Yelverton had made the whole episode public in the *Daily Telegraph*, the letter-writer would probably not call for the postal order any more. Yelverton apologised for his haste in publishing, and that ended the matter. However, the Home Office sent all the 'Martin Molton' letters to Gurrin for further analysis.

Following the meeting at Scotland Yard, Conan Doyle called at the Home Office and had a meeting with Ernley Blackwell, Assistant Secretary at the Home Office, and H. B. Simpson, the Home Office minister, and told them that he would soon bring them proof about the possible culprit.

Despite the failure of his plans, the letter-writer was not going away quietly.

On 22 January, George received another letter, this time addressed from 'One That Knows'.

> George Edalji,
> I write to tell you that it was I who wrote the letters in 1892 & 5 lest you should accuse the innocent man. I only wrote it because I hate all foreigners. The police are trying to catch me now so I am going to Melbourne and shall never write again … Take an old man's advice & write to those police who alone can help you if you tell them to arrest Greatorex. I have no personal grudge against the lad but I only want justice done and feel it would be such a pity to accuse an innocent man. One That Knows.

Once again George informed Conan Doyle and Yelverton. The letter was given to the Home Office who in turn handed it to Gurrin. The handwriting expert immediately declared that it was in George's handwriting.

Meanwhile, the public furore caused by Conan Doyle's articles had put enormous pressure on the Home Office. The newspapers were filled with letters to the editor from the public, supporting George's case. Several organisations were writing to the Home Office calling for a public inquiry. The press were covering the case with great interest. Local papers reported that the villagers of Great Wyrley were now convinced that George was innocent. By mid January Conan Doyle had received a letter from the Home Office saying his request to set up a committee was being given a 'sympathetic consideration'.

The Home Office still believed that the letters, including the latest spate in 1907, had been written by George. Home Office minister H. B. Simpson wrote to Anson warning him that a committee may be sitting soon to consider the case. He urged him to look at some samples of the anonymous letters which had recently arrived. These were being examined by the Home Office to see if they had the 'Edalji touch'.[3] One letter had been posted from Birmingham and the other probably from Walsall, so the Home Office thought that Edalji probably had an accomplice who posted these for him.

'Edalji by their means has taken in Conan Doyle and (probably) Yelverton,' wrote Simpson. 'What we are considering is whether we can get enough evidence to convince Conan Doyle that he is being fooled. I am afraid nothing will and then we have to look forward to something like a parliamentary inquiry in which at all events the Home Office and probably you will start with an enormous handicap of prejudice against us. I have little doubt as to the result but it won't do to omit any precaution.'

Petitions continued to arrive thick and fast at the Home Office. Professors at the University of Birmingham, led by Sir Oliver Lodge, petitioned the Home Secretary calling for a public inquiry into the Edalji case.[4] Letters were flying in from Ireland as well. A signed declaration from Dublin University professors and leading medical men in Ireland called for a public inquiry. The signatories demanded a thorough investigation of the conduct of the officials concerned, whether members of the Home Office or the Staffordshire constabulary.[5]

The world was watching. At last, the Home Secretary, Herbert Gladstone, relented and announced a three-man committee of inquiry to look into the case: Sir Arthur Wilson, a high court judge, the Rt Hon. John Lloyd Wharton, a Conservative MP, and Sir Robert Romer, a retired judge, who would be the chair. However Romer immediately declined to chair the committee when he heard that it would not be a public inquiry.

'I do not see any way to act as it were as judge and jury in trying the particular question of the guilt or innocence of Mr Edalji, and that without any proper legal power of summoning witnesses,' Romer wrote to Gladstone disapprovingly.[6]

Romer was replaced by Sir Albert de Rutzen, chief magistrate of the Metropolitan police courts. Ironically, the seventy-six-year-old de Rutzen was a cousin of Captain Anson, the very person who had ensured that George Edalji got a sentence of penal servitude. Familial, racial and class ties would bind the committee more than anything else. The working of the committee was described by the writer Compton Mackenzie, a friend of Conan Doyle's and a supporter of the Edalji campaign, in stark words: 'The white face of Captain the Hon. George Augustus Anson must be saved at the expense of George Edalji's brown face.'

# 15

## A Flawed Pardon

George had always been anxious to write his own story. A few weeks after Conan Doyle's defence of his case had made him an international celebrity, he published his account of the case in *Pearson's Weekly* titled 'My Own Story – The Narrative of 18 years' of Persecution'. The first article – written exclusively for the magazine – carried the bold headline in George's handwriting: 'I am innocent – G. E. T Edalji'. Beginning on 7 February 1907, the articles ran over several months recounting his traumatic story, from the anonymous letters of his childhood to his flawed trial and eventual sentencing. Sold for a penny, the popular weekly was read up and down the country. It even carried a small note: 'The correct way to pronounce Mr Edalji's name is *Ee-dl-gee* with the accent on the first syllable.' George was never one to hide away from his ethnic roots.

Even as the articles were being serialised, the anxious Edalji family were waiting for news from the Home Office. George had done everything he could to get the public on his side. He had the support of Arthur Conan Doyle as well as eminent jurists, academics, lawyers and medical men. On 23 April, the Home Office committee sent its report: they decided that George was innocent of the attack on the pony and recommended a free pardon. Arthur Conan Doyle had won the day.

The report incensed Anson, who reacted with undisguised rage. The Staffordshire police had been severely criticised and the report stated that they had carried out their investigation 'not for the purpose of finding out who was the guilty party, but for the purpose of finding out evidence against Edalji'.

The first article in *Pearson's Weekly* giving
George's own account of the case

'That is absolutely untrue,' Anson thundered at the reporters gathered outside his office. 'As a matter of fact Edalji was not suspected at all until some months after the outrages commenced,' he added.[1]

The committee declared that it was doubtful if the jury would have convicted at all, if they had not been, in some way, influenced by the anonymous letters. They said: 'The conviction was unsatisfactory, and after a full consideration of all the facts, we cannot agree with the verdict of the jury.'

But there was a sting in the tail.

The committee was not going to let George walk away with his pride intact. They ruled that George was guilty of writing the letters, and that he had brought his troubles on himself. The committee recommended that he receive no compensation for the three years he had been wrongly incarcerated. Gladstone released a dramatic statement: 'I have decided to advise His Majesty, as an act of royal clemency, to grant Mr Edalji a free pardon. But I have also come to the conclusion that the case is not one in which any grant of compensation can be made.'

With regard to the letters, the committee said they had carefully examined the letters themselves and concluded that while they were not the letters of a guilty man accusing himself in order to more easily accuse others, they thought it likely that they were 'the letters of an innocent man indulging in a piece of impish mischief, pretending to know what he may know nothing of, in order to puzzle the police and increase their difficulties in a very difficult investigation'.

In conclusion, they declared that they regarded the conviction as unsatisfactory, but could not disagree with the findings of the jury on the question of the letters. 'We cannot but see that assuming him to be an innocent man, he has to some extent brought his troubles upon himself,' the committee announced.[2]

The Home Office report was received with fury by George's campaigners. By not paying any compensation (in contrast Beck had received £2,000), the committee was all but declaring that he was indeed guilty. George described the report as the 'grossest insult'.

He told the clamouring press reporters that he was profoundly dissatisfied with the result of the inquiry: 'It is at least a step in the right direction,' he said. 'But the statement that I contributed to my conviction by writing some of the letters which played so prominent a part in the case is a slander – an insult. It is so far satisfactory to know that they are granting me a free pardon, but that statement about the letters is a baseless insinuation, and I shall not rest content until it is withdrawn and an apology tendered.

'Further I am disappointed to find that no compensation is offered. They have offered me a free pardon. They admit that I was wrongly convicted, and it is only just that I should be compensated for the three years' penal servitude that I suffered. I shall not let matters rest as they are. I want compensation for my wrongs.'[3]

The Home Office committee had deliberated for two months, calling in Gurrin to look at the letters again, including the latest 'Martin Molton' letters. The files have details of how the handwriting was analysed taking in every peculiarity of George's original handwriting and seeing if he carefully altered it. On the recommendation of the British ambassador to France, they hired the services of a French handwriting expert, Alfred Gobert, who worked for the Banque de France and the French Tribunal and Court of Appeal. Gobert was sent photographic copies of two anonymous letters (one sent on 13 July addressed to the police at Cannock station and the 'Martin Molton' letter dated January 1907 addressed to Captain Anson) and one of George Edalji's actual handwriting. He concluded that the writing on the anonymous letters corresponded with that of George Edalji who, he said, had a 'remarkable calligraphy, very clever, exceptionally rapid and very variable'.

On examining the reports of the handwriting experts, Simpson and Blackwell also gave their opinions about the case. Simpson recorded that if the letters were not written by George, they would have to be written by someone who was familiar with him in 1903, and inspired by such persistent hatred, that he pursued him again in 1907. This person would have been able to post or get letters posted in London and Birmingham, had the opportunity of studying George's writing closely and had spent a lot of time imitating his distinctive 'a' and 'o'. He would also know where George was living in London after his release from prison.

According to Simpson, these difficulties disappeared if they went with the police theory that George Edalji had written the letters. He could then be seen as a man with a love of mischief and especially a love of anonymous letter-writing which amounted to mania.

'We at the Home Office well know that similar manias – such as those of indecent exposure or for writing threatening letters – often exist in people who are in every other respect perfectly sane. If the letters are a result of mania, the mania may exist in a respectable young solicitor of blameless reputation as well as in anyone else.'[4]

Blackwell was more sceptical and his notes reveal that he was not entirely convinced that the letters were written by George. He felt that they could have been written by another person – a mysterious 'X' who wrote the letters in 1903 and repeated them in 1907, even though he saw no reason why this person would go through the laborious process of copying Edalji's writing instead of just sending 'Jack the Ripper' style letters revelling in the crime, or letters that simply accused Edalji.

The fiasco of the 'Martin Molton' letters in 1907 convinced him that the letters were not written by Edalji but rather 'X' who tried to implicate Edalji by sending him to collect the 'Martin Molton' letter from the GPO. 'X' would have known that the letter would contain nothing but the £2 sent by Anson. If his plan had succeeded, it would have led to George's arrest. That George did not introduce himself as Martin Molton, went with a friend, and was quite open about receiving the letter, proved his innocence.

At the end of the day, despite any personal doubts, Blackwell went with the report of the committee who refused to clear George of the charge of writing the anonymous letters, thus denying him compensation.

Back at the vicarage, Shapurji fiercely criticised the verdict. He vigorously denied that George had written the letters. He was furious that the Home Office had offered no compensation. Shapurji had spent £600 on George's legal defence. His wife, Charlotte, and sister-in-law, Mary Sancta, had all contributed despite their limited means of income.

Members of Parliament were not satisfied with the report either. For the next two months, Gladstone had to answer a volley of questions in Parliament. Conan Doyle had mobilised not just the public, but many of their representatives in the House of Commons.

On 28 May, Sir Gilbert Parker, the MP for Gravesend stood on the floor of the House and questioned Gladstone: 'I beg to ask the Secretary of State for the Home Department whether the Government will reconsider its decision not to compensate Mr Edalji, having regard to the fact that the verdict of the jury was unsatisfactory and that, by reason of this verdict, he has undergone imprisonment and suffered professional ruin.'[5]

Gladstone replied: 'No, Sir. I have most carefully considered all the facts of the case, but I have found it impossible to come to any other conclusion than that which has already been made public.'

Dissatisfied, Parker asked whether there was any precedent for compensation not being granted to a prisoner wrongfully imprisoned and who had received a so-called free pardon.

'I know of no analogous case,' replied Gladstone.

His reply was enough for Pike Pease, MP for Darlington, to ask a follow-up question. Did a free pardon mean that Mr Edalji did not commit the crime with which he was charged, and for which he had suffered imprisonment?

No answer was returned by Gladstone.

The tirade continued. MPs from different parties stood up in Parliament and badgered the government to reconsider the committee report. They demanded answers as to why George Edalji was not being given compensation. Papers were waved and 'hear hears' could be heard in the chamber as the lawmakers called for justice. The chamber of the Commons was resounding with calls for compensation for George. Gladstone's response was to stonewall them.

'I have advised the grant of a free pardon. No further interference with the sentence is within the power of the Government,' he replied to Wilfrid Ashley, MP for Blackpool, who wanted to know if the government would reconsider the sentence.

Not satisfied, Ashley came back: 'Does the Right Honourable Gentleman consider this man to be innocent?'

'I hardly think that is a proper question to ask me. It is on a matter of opinion,' replied the Home Secretary, clearly annoyed.

The Edalji case had riled many MPs. Over and over again they questioned Gladstone on the merits of the committee report.

George Younger, MP for Ayr Burghs, wanted the details of George's imprisonment.

'I beg to ask the Secretary of State for the Home Department how long Edalji was detained in prison, what character he bore during his incarceration, how long he was kept under surveillance after his release, and whether the surveillance was of such a character as to be prejudicial to his professional prospects'.

Gladstone replied: 'Mr Edalji was in prison for three years after his conviction. His prison character was good. From his release in October last until the grant of a free pardon a few days ago he was under police supervision, but he was allowed to report by letter instead of personally, and there was no interference of any sort on the part of police that could be prejudicial to him.'

Another MP wanted to know if the Lord Chancellor would take steps to reinstate George Edalji as a solicitor. Gladstone replied that he did not think that the Lord Chancellor had anything to do with it. The Home Secretary was being pushed into a corner. William

Mitchell-Thomson, MP for North-West Lanarkshire wanted to know whether he would think of appointing a committee to consider who wrote the anonymous letters in the Edalji case. 'I do not propose to appoint any such committee,' replied Gladstone.

Could the police witnesses be examined? asked John Joseph Mooney of the Irish Parliamentary Party.[6] Could the information and documents before the Edalji committee be made available to MPs? asked another. Some demanded that the newspaper reports of the Edalji case be printed as a parliamentary paper, presumably to examine how prejudiced the reporting was at the time. Gladstone remained firm: 'I do not propose to lay on the table any further papers connected with this case.'

Even the Prime Minister, Herbert Asquith, faced questions about the case.

Viscount Castlereagh from Maidstone cornered him. Reminding the Prime Minister that George Edalji had no means of income and was dependent on family and friends, he wanted to know if the government would order a public inquiry 'directed to the specific issue of whether or not he was the author of the anonymous letters'.

Gladstone replied on behalf of the Prime Minister: '… the Government are not prepared to take any further steps in the matter.'

Castlereagh was not to be put down.

'Will the Government do nothing to relieve Edalji of the suspicion of being the author of those letters?' he thundered.

To which Gladstone replied stonily: 'I am afraid I can add nothing to my answer.'

George would have been heartened to see how much support he had from MPs in the House of Commons. But they seemed to be firing cannons at an insurmountable wall. The Home Office had closed ranks and remained unmoved. Gladstone would stand and defend the committee report over and over again and refused to be drawn into any further discussion.

Conan Doyle was incensed. In his 18,000-word article in the *Daily Telegraph* he had virtually taken on the role of the defence lawyer, arguing point by point against every bit of tenuous evidence put forward by the Crown prosecution. He responded to the decision, writing once again in the pages of the *Daily Telegraph*:

'The position is absolutely illogical and untenable. Either the man is guilty or else there is not compensation which is adequate for the great wrong which this country, through its officials, has inflicted upon him … Could anything be imagined meaner or more un-English than that the mistake should be admitted but reparation refused.'[7]

He now wanted to take it further. With the Home Office committee giving their verdict on George, he was determined to carry on the fight. Clearly it was imperative not only to prove George's innocence, but to establish the identity of the real killer. It was time for Arthur Conan Doyle to solve this mystery once and for all. The game was afoot.

# 16

## Who Wrote the Letters?

Ever since his visit to Great Wyrley and his conversation with some of the residents, Conan Doyle had had his suspicions about the identity of the actual culprit. In January 1907, he wrote to his mother: 'All my energies have gone towards the capture of the real offenders. These are three youths (one already dead), brothers by the name of Sharp. The case I have against them is already very strong but I have five separate lines of enquiry on foot, which I hope to make it overwhelming.'[1]

But before he revealed the name of the killer, Conan Doyle wanted to convince the committee that George had not written the letters. He felt they had not been shown enough evidence to make them contradict the verdict of the jury.

'I do not know how the matter was laid before them, but I will undertake in half an hour, with the documents before him, to convince any reasonable and impartial man, that George Edalji did not write, and could not possibly have written, those letters,' declared Conan Doyle.[2]

He followed up his promise with a set of three articles in the *Daily Telegraph* on the subject of 'Who wrote the letters?'

The first article was published on 23 May 1907 along with several copies of the anonymous letters. Conan Doyle was putting the photographic copies of the letters before the public for the first time, trusting in their judgement as he argued the case. He published two examples of George's handwriting and two of the 'Greatorex' letters. He came down heavily on Gurrin, the handwriting expert, who had been mistaken in the Beck case, but who had testified that the anonymous letters were written by George Edalji. The letters by

Edalji, he said, were clearly the writing of an educated man, but the anonymous letters were certainly not so. 'The most superficial observer of character, as expressed in writing, would say that one and two were open and free, while three and four were cramped and mean. Yet Mr Gurrin and the Home Office committee contend that they are the same, and a man's career has been ruined on the resemblance.'

Analysing the content of the letters, Conan Doyle followed the trail of Wilfred Greatorex. Why was Greatorex, a local schoolboy, linked to George? Why were the letters written under his name? 'Young Greatorex and Edalji were practically strangers ... But it all becomes clear when we regard the letters as the work of a third person, who was the enemy both of Edalji and Greatorex, and who hoped by this device to bring down both his birds with one stone,' deduced Conan Doyle.[3]

The letters mentioned seven or eight people, all of whom lived in a group two stations down the line from Wyrley and were not in any way part of Edalji's circle. However, they were a group surrounding Greatorex. 'The entanglement of Greatorex was evidently the plotter's chief aim, and the ruin of Edalji was a mere by-product in the operation,' said Conan Doyle. Of the people mentioned in the letter, one was the village dressmaker, the second a doctor, the third a butcher: all in Greatorex's neighbourhood and with no links to Edalji.

The other observation made by Conan Doyle was that the letters had allusions to the sea ('I will murder you if I get a thick rope around my neck for it, but I don't think they would hang me but send me to sea.'). Edalji had no connection with the sea and there was no reason why he should write of it. How could this be accounted for? Conan Doyle explained the link saying that the first set of anonymous letters had ended abruptly in 1896 and peace had reigned for six years. Now the series of letters were commenced by someone whose mind was running on the sea. 'One would like to make inquiry as to the possibility of some sailor having returned to the neighbourhood. Should such a man exist ... it might be worth an investigator's while to trace the matter further ...'

In the second article, Conan Doyle took his readers back to the first spate of letters received at the vicarage between 1892 and 1895

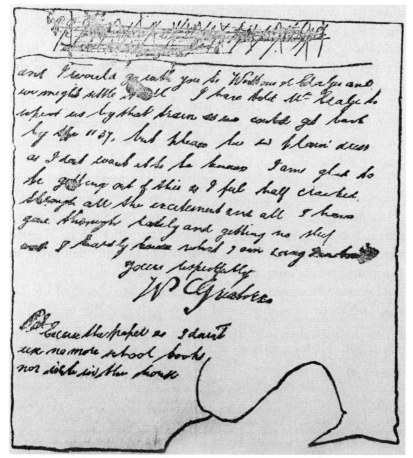

Part of a 'Greatorex' letter published by Conan Doyle in the *Telegraph*

to prove that they were written by the same person who later wrote to Edalji and his friends. Once again he printed copies of three letters for his public to see, including one of the 'God–Satan' letters and one of the hoaxes sent in the name of Shapurji. Conan Doyle reminded his readers that the cruel and violent letters continued for three years, while the Staffordshire police did nothing to shield the family from their tormentors.

On careful examination of the letters, he had come to the startling conclusion that they had been written by three people, two adults and a boy. He could trace three lines of thought and character, as well as three peculiarities of script. The boy could not have been less than twelve or more than sixteen. As for the adults, the fact that they devoted so much time to them and that the letters were of some length, showed that they had no settled occupation. It was obvious that they lived within a radius of a mile or two of the vicarage, since many of the missives were left by hand.

Conan Doyle briskly concluded that these three individuals undoubtedly lived under the same roof. Though he did not reveal the name of the alleged suspects to his readers, he was clearly thinking of the Sharp family: Royden Sharp and his two elder brothers, Wallie and Frank. He provided his reasoning to the readers: 'The epistles are continually on the same paper, and in the same envelopes. In some cases the rude scrawl of the boy comes in upon the very page which is taken up by the educated writing of the adult.' The rude drawings could only have been done by a lad. The adults appeared to pride themselves upon forgery. '"Do you think that we could not imitate your kid's writing?" they said exultantly on one of the 1892 letters. They most certainly could – and did.'

Conan Doyle went further, taking his readers along on his investigation. He said that it seemed that the three were relatives, probably brothers, and that the youngest developed at a later date some of the peculiarities of his elders. The first thing that was evident was that the younger one was connected with Walsall Grammar School. The Brookes and Wynne families were also troubled in the same fashion, and both of them had a son at Walsall School. The headmaster of Walsall was also a recipient of anonymous letters in the same rough boyish hand. George Edalji was a student at Rugeley Grammar and had no connection with Walsall.

The articles – read eagerly by the residents of Great Wyrley – had them immediately working out which family was being referred to. It was clear to the villagers that Conan Doyle was referring to the Sharp family.

It seemed highly likely that the young letter-writer was a boy who entertained a malignant hatred of the headmaster of Walsall School, suggested Conan Doyle. He deduced that the boy had probably often felt the headmaster's cane or possibly been expelled for his evil conduct. The boy's brother was clearly a scholar at Walsall School in the year 1892. The examination of the records of Walsall Grammar School would give a starting point for an investigation.

One of the other brothers could also have been at Walsall School but in a higher class. 'He joins his young brother in writing anonymously to the Brookeses and Wynnes, showing a certain community of interest where school matters are concerned.' Conan Doyle felt that the script and content of his letters showed a very alert and ingenious mind. In one of the letters there was a long quotation from Milton, which was part of the school exercise at the time. With the brothers being at the same school, it could narrow down the field of enquiry. The incident of the key which was laid at the door of the vicarage also proved that there was a direct link to Walsall Grammar School.

The specimens of writing of the two elders of the trio were examined next, with Conan Doyle maintaining that there was a possibility that the two older handwritings were actually by the same person. The 'God-Satan' letters showed mad effusions, grim humour, wild imagination and a maniacal turn of mind, said Conan Doyle. 'The writing in all these effusions is fluent and easy, with every mark of an educated hand. I can find no evidence that any particular care has been taken to disguise it, but it is naturally unformed, and does not set rigidly into definite characteristics.'

From 1896 onwards this individual disappeared entirely. However, said Conan Doyle, some interesting developments had happened recently: a newspaper containing some account of the Edalji affair had appeared in Long Beach, California, in the United States. A page of this paper had been sent back to George Edalji, with religious and blasphemous comments scribbled in pencil all around the margins. Conan Doyle was now convinced that the man was still alive and was a marked religious maniac.

'The general diameter of this script, the knowledge shown of the case, and the singular mental conditions, have all convinced me that, whatever be his name, God-Satan is now to be found on the Pacific Coast, and that he is an undoubted madman,' declared Conan Doyle dramatically.

With regard to the third individual, who sent the postcards out in the name of Shapurji Edalji, Conan Doyle could not be certain. He felt there was no fancy or madness in this person. He wrote a closer, smaller hand. He was not sure what had happened to this person, or indeed if he was the same person who wrote the 'God-Satan' letters, but in another hand.

On 27 May Conan Doyle wrote the last of his articles on the letters. Titled 'The Martin Molton Letters', this dealt with the letters that appeared after George's release. These were by the third 'foul-mouthed boy', who according to Conan Doyle continued the persecution. Once again he produced six examples of letters for his readers. 'The Martin Molton of 1907 and the bad boy of 1892 are the same individual is, as I will show, beyond all reasonable doubt,' he said.[4]

Conan Doyle declared that he too had received a threatening and violent letter, and he had no doubt that it was written by the same person who wrote the letters in 1892. The letter he mentioned was marked 'Private' and posted to the Grand Hotel in London dated 17 April addressed to Sir Arthur Conan Doyle. The writer said he was an admirer of Conan Doyle but threatened to cut his tongue and liver out if he continued to back George Edalji. It was signed 'A Nark London'.

'A line to tell you we are narks of the detectives and know Edalji killed the horse and wrote those letters. No use trying to lay it on others. It is Edalji and it will be proven for he is not a right sort nor is Greatorex who killed horses too,' said the letter.

The letter-writer told Conan Doyle that if he wrote to Gladstone and said Edalji was guilty, he would be made a lord. 'Is it not better to be a lord than to run the risk of losing kidneys and liver.' The writer said he was a Cockney from London and was always there to help police detect crimes and could also act as Conan Doyle's guardian angel. 'May you live for ever and those devils not cut your tongue or tonsels out.'[5]

Conan Doyle had by this time been investigating the Edalji case for nearly five months. Whether he was in his home in Sussex or travelling to London for meetings with Yelverton and others, it was George who was occupying his mind. He worked round the clock, writing articles and letters to newspapers, giving interviews and collecting more information from experts and local sources. The high-profile Edalji Committee, which consisted of Sir George Lewis, Horace Voules, Churton Collins, Jerome K. Jerome, J. Hall Richardson and himself, had already raised £350 from the general public to fight the case. Since no legal fees had yet been incurred, the committee decided to spend the money to compensate Shapurji

Edalji and Mary Sancta, George's aunt who had spent considerable amounts on fighting the case in 1903. George himself had refused to touch the money, even though he had no means of income at the moment, something Conan Doyle proudly pointed out to show what an honourable man he was.

Everything that he saw about George convinced Conan Doyle that fighting for him had been worth every minute of his time. The young, hesitant solicitor had come into his life like a fresh chapter in a book and lifted the author out of his melancholy after his wife's death. There was something proud and injured about George that called out to Conan Doyle. For George, there was a feeling of deep gratitude towards his protector. He felt lucky to be able to count on Conan Doyle's unwavering support and have him as a friend.

On 27 May, when Conan Doyle received another letter and a postcard written in pencil, addressed to him at the Grand Hotel, Trafalgar Square, he shot off a letter to the *Daily Telegraph* offering a reward of £20 to anyone who would enable him to say for certain where it came from. 'The letter was in a coarse yellow envelope, gummed up with stamp paper. A crease in both documents seems to show that though marked London NW they may have been sent up undercover, or possibly in somebody's pocket – a railway guard or other – and then posted.'[6] Conan Doyle urged the public and the papers in the Midlands to help him locate the sender.

Proving that George had not written the anonymous letters was the task foremost in Conan Doyle's mind. He stated that the letter-writer had committed a deliberate forgery in trying to imitate George's hand. By tracing the formation of the letters, Conan Doyle concluded that the letters had been written at the extremely slow rate of 13 words a minute (given a pulse rate of 70 this was extremely slow). Conan Doyle said he himself was writing the letter at 35 to a minute. This showed the 'deliberate nature of the forgery'.[7]

Determined to get his own handwriting expert on board, Conan Doyle sent the copies of the forged letters and those in George's handwriting to Dr Lindsay Johnson, who had been giving evidence at the Dreyfus trial at Rennes. Johnson replied within two days sending an elaborate report and asserting that all the anonymous letters were in the same hand, thus confirming Conan Doyle's own conclusions in this regard.[8] Conan Doyle then went a step further. He had already in his mind made an assertion as to who the ringleader was. He sent two signed letters in Royden Sharp's script to Dr Johnson. The handwriting expert at once confirmed that it was the same script as all the other documents. Conan Doyle submitted all the documents and the expert's certificate to the Home Office. Here was further proof, he said, this time from an independent expert witness.

Gladstone was not impressed by the pressure being applied by Conan Doyle. He referred to him as the 'commissioner of a newspaper' during the debates in the House of Commons, an insinuation that irked Conan Doyle. 'Might I be allowed to state that I have never been a paid agent at all in the matter,' the author declared.

His attack on Gladstone carried on in the newspaper columns, which had become a platform for his Edalji campaign. When Gladstone announced that the House of Commons was not a court of appeal in reference to the George Edalji case, Conan Doyle was immediately on the offensive again. 'To whom, then, are we to turn?' he questioned. 'Or are we to admit in despair that there is no tribunal of any sort in England, to which we can look to set a wrong right? The Home Office should itself be such a tribunal, but its own conduct is now just one of the questions which has to be judged,' he said.[9]

Conan Doyle was now ready to take this to the next level. The creator of Sherlock Holmes was certain he had discovered the real identity of the Wyrley Ripper. Anson was going to feel the force of the famous writer's argument.

# 17

## *Royden Sharp*

In May 1907, as the pages of the British newspapers were splashed with discussions of the Edalji case, Conan Doyle prepared to name his suspect. He had for some time had his eyes on Royden Sharp. Royden lived with his widowed mother in Cannock. His father was the late Peter Sharp, cashier of the East Cannock Colliery, who had died in 1893. Royden was three years younger than George, and had attended Walsall Grammar School. His school records showed a boy who was consistently bottom of the class. He was also given to violent behaviour and had reportedly caused considerable anxiety to his mother.

Ever since his visit to Great Wyrley, Conan Doyle had had his own team of 'Baker Street Irregulars' to help him on the Edalji case. From January he had been in touch with two locals in Great Wyrley: one was R. Beaumont of Wolverhampton Road, Cannock, the other was Frank Arrowsmith, owner of the Star Tea Company, also on Wolverhampton Road.

Among Conan Doyle's contacts was William Greatorex of Littleworth Farm, Hednesford, whose son's name was used in the 'Greatorex' letters of 1903. There was a direct link between Royden and the Greatorex family. After the death of Royden's father in 1893, William Greatorex, his uncle, was appointed as his trustee. The fourteen-year-old Royden had not been an easy boy to look after. Greatorex had sent him to be a butcher's apprentice. Royden had then taken a job on a cattle ship and left for the US. He returned to Great Wyrley in 1903.

Conan Doyle wrote to the headmaster of Walsall Grammar School, Mr Mitchell, and obtained Royden Sharp's report cards. It helped make a careful character construction of the schoolboy: Royden had a destructive trait in him and had shown marked criminal tendencies from a young age.

Born in 1879, he was only twelve years old when he set a hayrick on fire at Hatton's Farm in West Cannock and his father had been forced to pay a considerable sum in compensation.

In Christmas 1890, when he was in Lower 1 grade, Royden Sharp came twenty-third out of twenty-three students.

In Easter 1891, Lower 1, he came twentieth out of twenty. His report card described him as 'dull, homework neglected, begins to improve in Drawing'.

Midsummer 1891, Lower 1! He was eighteenth out of eighteen.

'Beginning to progress, caned for misbehaviour in class, tobacco chewing, prevarication and nicknaming.'

Christmas 1891. Lower 1. Order sixteenth out of sixteen.

His report card said: 'Unsatisfactory, often untruthful. Always complaining or being complained of. Detected cheating, and frequently absent without leave. Drawing improved.'

Easter 1892. Form 1. Order eighth out of eight. Report card: 'Idle and mischievous, caned daily, wrote to father, falsified schoolfellow's marks, and lied deliberately about it. Caned twenty times this term.'

Midsummer 1892. 'Played truant, forged letters and initials, removed by his father.'

It could be seen, said Conan Doyle, that forgery was familiar to Royden Sharp as a schoolboy. This played a part in the anonymous letters that he wrote later.

Royden was also known for his brutal violence and for the tendency to foist upon others the blame for the crimes he had committed. The anonymous letters to the school contained the sentences: 'I will cut your bowels out' and 'I will open your belly'. Both could be seen as forethoughts of crimes that would be committed later.

Conan Doyle also felt it was important to establish the weapon that was used in the mutilations. He felt that all the wounds were of a peculiar character and caused by a certain type of weapon. 'In every case there was a shallow incision which had cut through the skin and muscles, but had not penetrated the gut. Had any knife been plunged in and drawn along, it must almost certainly have cut the gut with its point.'

Conan Doyle made a sketch of the instrument and showed its sharp rounded cutting edge.

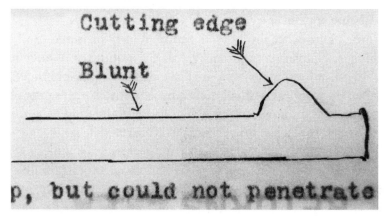

Arthur Conan Doyle's sketch of the instrument

He deduced that though the blade was very sharp, it could not penetrate further than superficially. He named two witnesses who could vouch for the nature of the cuts: one was Mr Sambrook, a butcher who lived in Wyrley, but had now moved to Sheffield, and Mr Forsyth, a veterinary surgeon of Cannock. Mr Sambrook, who saw the cuts during the outrage, was struck by the peculiarity of the cuts.

In a conversation with William Greatorex, Conan Doyle learnt the startling fact that in July 1903, Royden Sharp (then twenty-four years old) spoke to his aunt about the killings. Sharp then went to a cupboard and produced a horse lancet of unusual size. He showed this to Mrs Greatorex saying, 'This is what they kill the cattle with.'[1] Mrs Greatorex was horrified and told him to put it away saying, 'You don't want me to think you are the man, do you?'

Sharp had probably obtained the instrument when he served for ten months in 1902 on board a cattle ship between Liverpool and America. He had taken the lancet when he left. Conan Doyle suggested that the instrument was still in the house and should be secured in case of an arrest. In his view, Royden Sharp was in all respects 'peculiarly fitted to have done these crimes'.

Conan Doyle was convinced that the Sharps (brothers Frank, Wallie and Royden) were motivated by racism to write the letters against the Edaljis between 1892 and 1895, but he could not under-stand why another schoolboy, Fred Brookes, was also receiving letters. He sought the answers to this by seeking out a fellow schoolmate, Fred Wynne, a painter from Cheslyn Hay.

Wynne's name had also been mentioned in the anonymous letters of 1892–95. A former pupil at Walsall School, he was one of the group of schoolboys who occasionally travelled with George. Wynne described Royden as a small-built youth with sharp features who generally wore a sailor's suit, was very fond of chewing tobacco and was known to his schoolmates as 'Speck'.[2]

He then related an event confirming Royden's violent streak. 'One evening we were returning by the usual evening train. F. G. Brookes and myself got in the train when Speck came running into the same compartment . . . and put his head through the carriage window smashing it all to bits. We all made our way into another compartment. In a day or two after, Brookes and myself were charged by one of the railway officials of breaking the carriage window. We found that Sharp had told of us, that it was us, not himself. Then we sought the station master, and told him how it happened, and Sharp had to pay for it, and he was also caught cutting the straps of the window and had to pay, I think, more than once.'

Wynne said that if Sharp was let in a railway carriage, he would turn up the cushion and slit it on the lower side so as to let out the horse hair.

Conan Doyle calculated that it was after the railway-carriage incident that the first anonymous letters were sent to W. H. Brookes. Written in large school handwriting, the letter said: 'your kid and Wynn's kid have been spitting in an old woman's face on Walsall station' and requested money to be sent to Walsall post office. The second letter threatened to prosecute if the money was not sent.

The link between Brookes, Wynne and Sharp became immedia-tely clear. It explained to Conan Doyle why the letters were sent to those particular families.

Once Sharpe's father had been asked to remove him from school, Royden was sent as an apprentice to a butcher called Meldon, who lived in Cannock. Here he learnt to use a knife upon animals. His father died in November 1893 and William A. Greatorex of Littleworth Farm became Royden's guardian. He found the teenager difficult to handle and after two years sent him to sea as an apprentice. Royden sailed from Liverpool on 30 December 1895 in the ship *General Roberts*, belonging to Lewis Davies & Co, Fenwick Street, Liverpool.

Conan Doyle noted that from the time he left, the letters and hoaxes stopped completely and were not renewed until his return in 1903. All this time, George Edalji remained in Great Wyrley, but the police did not question the lack of letters written under his name, or draw any link between Royden and the letters. The last anonymous hoax played on the Edaljis was an advertisement placed in a Blackpool newspaper. It was significant, as Blackpool was the pleasure resort often frequented by the people of Liverpool.

Conan Doyle's enquiries revealed that Royden did not indulge in any violent activity on board the ship. He finished his apprenticeship in 1900 and gained a third mate's certificate. He returned home briefly in 1901 but left shortly after on board a cattle ship to America. He returned with a horse lancet.

The Wyrley outrages started when Royden came back. He was in a position to get in and out of his house at all hours of the night without being observed either by the police or by the other inmates of the house, if they were not conniving with him. His house was well suited for this. He lived alone with his mother and his sister. His brother Wallie was rarely there. There was no servant in the house to check on him. The back door opened into the garden which led into fields, so he could get away without having to go on the road and risk being seen. The man who mutilated cattle in the night would have been someone not just with reckless daring but also someone who was used to handling animals. As an ex-sailor and an ex-butcher, Royden Sharp united these qualities, said Conan Doyle.

Once the killings started, the letters resumed. Conan Doyle deduced that the second set of letters were sent by the Sharp family to implicate George Edalji as well as Wilfred Greatorex as the Sharps were resentful of their trustee who had regulated their money matters with a strict hand. One of the 'Greatorex' letters said 'I know Holton and Lyndop, Guy, Harvey, Phillips and many a score'.

Holton was a doctor from Littleworth, Lyndop was the local timekeeper at the colliery, Guy was the local butcher, Harvey an official at the colliery, and Phillips a shopkeeper who had fallen on hard days. None of these people would have been known to George as they lived miles away from him. They were known to Sharp, who put their names down. They were also known to Greatorex.

Conan Doyle said that he had proof that the police thought that Royden Sharp was behind some of the obscene letters which were circulating at the time. He had access to an official letter dated 3 August 1903 which revealed that a bank manager, coincidentally also named Greatorex, and Inspector Campbell had a meeting about the obscene letters. The letter said at the end: 'I believe that Royden Sharp will be arrested before evening.'

In the 'Greatorex' letter of 1903 there were two or three allusions to the sea. There was also a mention of a boy being sent to sea as an apprentice, which is exactly what happened to Royden Sharp. Conan Doyle pointed out that one of the letters also mentioned a 'hook' that would be carried on the train. The lancet that Sharp showed Mrs Greatorex had a hook that could be folded and carried shut. The writer also said that he felt the need to put his head on the rails where the train ran from Hednesford to Cannock. This was the actual stretch of rail that passed near Royden Sharp's house. Conan Doyle also concluded that the 'Lover of Justice' letter was written by Wallie Sharp, older brother of Royden, as it used phrases like 'you are not the right sort'. This phrase appears in another of the 'Greatorex' letters. Wallie Sharp died in South Africa in November 1906.

Some time after Edalji's arrest, a series of anonymous letters signed 'G.h.darby', claiming to be the captain of the Wyrley gang, were sent to newspaper offices. These letters, concluded Conan Doyle, contained the characteristics of Royden Sharp's writing, especially an 'r' made like 'x' which occurred from boyhood in his writing.

In November 1903, some anonymous letters posted in Rotherham were sent to the police, and the *Wolverhampton Express & Star* newspaper. Conan Doyle said that he had proof that Royden had travelled to Rotherham at the time. He had traced the porter, A. Beenham Drayman, who had carried Royden's luggage at Cannock station and observed that it was addressed to Rotherham. The Darby letters said that the 'captain' would return before Xmas, and Conan Doyle believed that Royden did too. It made him certain that the Darby letters were also authored by Royden Sharp. The creator of Sherlock Holmes had been meticulous in his investigation, tracking Royden's movements and linking them back to the letters and killings.

Conan Doyle had another clue. He looked carefully at the letter of 29 September 1903 in which there was a threat to 'slice up ten wenches' between 1 November and 20 November and a further ten after Christmas. Again, Royden Sharp was away from November to Christmas. The announcement – while George was already in police custody awaiting trial – had caused renewed terror in the district. There also happened at this time an incident in which a woman, Mrs Jarius Handley of Great Wyrley, and a little girl were walking from Wyrley station one evening when they met two men on the road. One of them caught the girl by the throat and held in his hand something that gleamed. They both screamed loudly and the man ran away, shouting out to his comrade, 'All right, Jack, I am coming.' Conan Doyle suggested that the man was Royden Sharp and his companion was Jack Hart, a dissolute butcher of the neighbourhood and a friend of his.

The girl told her mother that she had been stopped once before by the same man and described him in detail: he had a round face, no moustache, about five feet eight inches in height, and was wearing a dark suit and a shiny peaked cap. The clothes were identical to Royden Sharp's sailor-like costume. Conan Doyle was told by his informers that Sharp stopped wearing the sailor-like suit after this incident. He now urged that the girl be allowed to identify him.

Conan Doyle traced each letter and the circumstances around its posting. One was addressed from London and the writer said he had written it in Lockhart's Coffee House and that he had gone up to London from Birmingham for the day. Conan Doyle had reliable information that Sharp had actually left Cannock for Birmingham on the morning of the same day. The information had come from Beaumont of Wolverhampton Road, who had been informed of this by Mr Hunt, the stationmaster.

All his investigations over several months left Conan Doyle in no doubt that Royden Sharp was the man the police needed. He summed up his reasons:

He had shown his weapon to Mrs Greatorex, and the wounds could only be produced by the sort of instrument he held. Moreover, only this instrument fitted the description in the letters, and his training as a butcher and work on a cattle ship would have made it easy for him to handle animals. The anonymous letters contained internal evidence pointing to Royden Sharp, who had a proven record of writing anonymous letters, of forgery and diabolical mischief. He was in Rotherham at the time when the letters were sent from there, and he had been described by a girl who had been attacked as he pretended to carry out the threat in his letters.

Conan Doyle also said that Royden's normal handwriting was similar to that of the handwriting in the letters. He said that he had been informed that one of the letters carried the line: 'I am as Sharp as Sharp can be.'

The author was certain that more evidence could be gathered if Royden were arrested. He also suggested that two men who could supply further information that might lead to the conviction were Harry Green, now in South Africa, and Jack Hart, a butcher from Bridgtown near Cannock. They would know all about Sharp.

Others who could give evidence were Fred Brookes, formerly of Wyrley, now in Manchester, and Thomas and Grinsell, both of the local yeomanry. Conan Doyle suggested that Royden Sharp himself did not do any more killings after the arrest of George Edalji. The next killing in September was done by Harry Green. The mutilation of the ponies in November on Herbert Stanley's farm was done by Jack Hart in collusion with Royden Sharp, in his opinion.

Mrs Sharp told Mrs Greatorex that Royden was strangely affected by the new moon and that on such occasions she had to closely watch him. At such times he behaved like a maniac, and Greatorex had himself heard him laughing crazily. In this connection it could be noted that the first four killings occurred on 2 February, 2 April, 3 May and 6 June of 1903, which in each case immediately followed the date of the new moon. The connection between the outrages and the moon was referred to in one of the 'Greatorex' letters, so it was present in the mind of the writer.

Conan Doyle wrote the article 'The Case Against Royden Sharp' in his home in Undershaw, Hindhead. He was now ready to provide his evidence to the Home Office.

In May 1907, Conan Doyle received a letter from Bilton in South Staffordshire. The letter-writer, who said he was a 'well-wisher', had lived in the neighbourhood of Cannock and Hednesford for several years. The writer said that the 'mention of a "sailor"' in Conan Doyle's articles had set him thinking. He could only think of one sailor who could be mixed up in this affair: Royden Sharp.

'He appeared to me to have a "dare-devil face" & was coming and going frequently,' he wrote. 'Greatorex senior is his father's trustee & I believe did not agree very well with this youth.'

The letter-writer said that Sharp would know all about the district of Littleworth & 'West Cannock Farm' & 'Cross Keys' Farm', which are mentioned in the letters. He would have known all the schoolboys mentioned in the letters, as they would have travelled together by train. He would also know all about Wyrley.

The writer said the police were prejudiced against the Edaljis. 'Edalji was a suspect & the police would not listen to any other suggestion at all about the culprit being in any other direction,' said the writer.[3]

It reconfirmed Conan Doyle's theories about police prejudice and the involvement of Royden Sharp.

The summer days were stretching out before George. With still no progress on getting compensation, and unable to get a job, he decided to go on a short holiday to the coastal resort of Great Yarmouth. He was hoping that the sea air would help him to relax. George took the boat from London and arrived in Yarmouth at half past eight in the evening. However, there was no getting away from events of Great Wyrley. He had barely checked into the Town Hall Hotel when he was greeted with the news of another case of cattle-maiming, not far from the vicarage.

The editor of the *Birmingham Post* had sent a telegram to George via his hotel asking for his reactions. George replied immediately:

'I am not surprised at the repetition of the outrages after the ridiculous assumption of the Staffordshire Police that the last affair was accidental. Naturally, that assumption would encourage the maimers to commit further atrocities,' he said. 'Experienced officers are wanted to direct the constabulary. The best Scotland Yard detectives should immediately be sent.'

Great Wyrley had seen two more cattle-maimings in August. Both of these occurred before George arrived at Yarmouth. The first incident took place on 19 August at Cartwright's meadow. The veterinary surgeon, Mr Forsyth, had been called out to see a mare that had been gashed. However, Forsyth concluded that the injury was likely to have been caused by an accident rather than a malicious attack. The police believed that the mare may have been ripped by the horns of a cow in the same meadow. The second theory was that the wound was caused by contact with a sharp piece of glass or metal. The deputy chief constable of Staffordshire informed the press that such injuries were common enough in colliery districts where barbed wire fences largely took the place of hedgerows, and where the pastures were usually littered with broken bottles, earthenware and similar debris. He could not say whether any such fragments had been found in Cartwright's meadow. The wound, he said, was not of a serious nature.

The second incident happened on 26 August. At 11 p.m., residents near Harrison's Colliery heard horses galloping about the field and donkeys braying. In the morning they found that one horse had been killed and another wounded. A grey mare in foal was seen with a gash ten inches long across her stomach. The mares appeared to have been attacked and ran around the field in terror. A brown mare had dropped from sheer exhaustion and died. The grey mare was found in an exhausted condition. Police were informed immediately and once again Inspector Campbell reached the spot. The veterinary surgeon, Mr Forsyth, moved the grey mare to an adjoining stable and had no choice but to shoot her. Harrison Limited offered a reward of £50 for any information on the subject.

Not long after the second incident occurred, George Edalji was interviewed in London by the *Tribune* newspaper and told them he had not visited Staffordshire the whole year.

George Edalji, photographed after his arrest

# MR. GEORGE EDALJI.

The above photograph of the young Birmingham solicitor, sent to penal servitude in 1902 for cattle-maiming, was taken for 'The Daily Chronicle' yesterday after his release from prison.

Newspaper image of George Edalji on his release

Sir Arthur Conan Doyle

WEEK ENDING
Feb. 91. 1907.

512

# PEARSON'S WEEKLY.

To INTEREST.
To ELEVATE, To AMUSE.

No. 864.    TRANSMISSION AT DOOR RATES.    WEEK ENDING FEBRUARY 7, 1907.    ENTERED AT STATIONERS' HALL.    ONE PENNY.

"*I am innocent.*"

*G. E. T. Edalji.*

# MY OWN STORY.

*Written by*
*GEORGE EDALJI*
*Exclusively for*
*this Paper.*

The Narrative of
Eighteen Years'
Persecution.

EARLY in 1903 was perpetrated a long series of cattle-maiming outrages of the most revolting and hideous nature in the neighbourhood of Great Wyrley, Staffordshire. This crime was soon followed by others of a similar kind, and it was only too apparent from the nature of the wounds inflicted that all were the work of the same person. The police attempted to fathom the mystery, but failed.

One August 17th, 1903, came the outrage on a pony belonging to the Great Wyrley Colliery Company, and for this deed the police arrested George Edalji, the son of the Vicar of Great Wyrley. He was tried on evidence of the most unsatisfactory character, and finally sentenced to seven years' penal servitude. In spite of his arrest and imprisonment, however, the outrages continued for a time.

Many of George Edalji's friends used every effort to arrive at the truth, and chief amongst these was Mr. R. D. Yelverton (late Chief Justice of the Bahamas). The result is that after serving three years of his sentence he has now been released on ticket of leave. Sir A. Conan Doyle, who is firmly convinced of Edalji's innocence, is using his powerful pen on the young man's behalf.

Now for the first time Mr. George Edalji has put his pen to paper with the object of telling the whole history of his persecution. We publish this story in the sincere belief that the wide publicity it will naturally obtain throughout the British Empire will arouse further sympathy for the unfortunate victim of a cruel plot, and will result in the truth being discovered and proper compensation awarded to Mr. Edalji.

*Note.—The correct way to pronounce Mr. Edalji's name is Ee—dl—gee, with the accent on the first syllable.*

## THE FIRST SERIES OF OFFENSIVE LETTERS.

In order to enable the reader to understand the peculiar circumstances which led up to my arrest and conviction, I must make reference to events which happened over eighteen years ago. In the summer of 1888 my father received a letter which ran as follows:

"*Sir, EVENING STAR, every evening, 3d. a week. Will be very pleased with an order. Publisher, 50 and 51, Queen-street, Wolverhampton.*"

Letters of this sort were received for months, and it was ascertained that they did not emanate from the office of the paper in question. No notice being taken of these missives, the writer, who had so far appeared to have no name, suddenly became abusive, and ultimately, under the *nom-de-plume* of "Thomas Hitchings," threatened to watch my father and "shoot him dead."

About this time a window at the vicarage was mysteriously broken, and the letter-writer threatened to break more.

One day the words, "MOST OF THE EDALJIS ARE WICKED," was found written on an outhouse wall. The matter was placed in the hands of the police, who, after getting all the inmates of the house to write from dictation, arrested a girl named Elizabeth Foster (who died in 1905) employed as a general servant at my home.

On searching her box the police found some papers on which was writing similar to that in the letters. Before her arrest she burnt a number of documents, but what they contained is not known, and she gave no explanation.

When apprehended she threatened to have her revenge some day. Before the magistrates she at first pleaded not guilty, but subsequently agreed to be bound over to keep the peace for six months and to pay the costs, her solicitor stating that it was a mere foolish joke on her part.

This series of anonymous letters was, I believe, the first which had occurred in a district soon to obtain an unenviable notoriety for offensive communications of the most amazing kind.

### SECOND SERIES OF LETTERS.

In 1892 a fresh series of letters began to be received both at my home and by other people in the parish. There was a general election in the summer of that year, and the first of this lot of letters came to hand two days after my father had lent his schoolroom for, and presided at, a Liberal political meeting in support of Sir John Swinburne.

Most people connect this set of letters with that meeting, and I may add that the only occasions when any local feeling was aroused against my father were during election contests.

This series of letters (unlike the 1888 lot) were believed by those competent to judge to be the work of an educated person who apparently made no ...

In reference to ... ... ... ... and who was ... quotes Sir A. Conan Doyle's coming from some...

ceived the following extracts are taken at random from various communications:

In case the course we now purpose adopting acts upon your nerves and temper to too great an extent, pray rest assured that we have already communicated with the authorities at a certain lunatic asylum not a hundred miles distant from your thrice-accursed house, and thither you will be forcibly removed in case you give way to any strong expressions of opinion, or enter too warmly into any debate.

Revenge . . . . on you and —— and —— (here follow the names of certain persons in the parish, on whom to have vengeance I have sent a notice in his name to the COURIER that he will not be responsible for his wife's debts! I have sent Mr. B—— such a letter as will make her wish her husband in the lake that burneth with fire and brimstone. I have to-day posted in your name three packets of postcards of a most hellish nature, and also some in that grocer's name. I expect, therefore, there will be no need for the lunacy authorities to take you in charge, as some of those persons are sure to have you arrested, and more especially so because I have added in a postscript that if they write to you their letters will only be scribbled on and returned.

I am lost. God have mercy! Christ help! We are going to order 30lbs. of sausages to be sent to Mr. B——.

Every day, every hour, my hatred is growing against George Edalji and F—— B—— in particular. . . . I would despatch them to hell in five minutes.

Do you think that when we want we cannot copy your kid's and that grocer's kid's writing? Our only reason for not forging their signatures and yours is that you all write such a vulgar hand that no manager of newspapers would suppose it was written by a person.

May the Lord strike me dead if I don't murder George Edalji, your d—d wife, your horrid little girl. I will descend into the infernal regions showering curses on you all.

As in the 1888 letters, the writer at first appeared to be nameless, but afterwards he assumed various titles, sometimes declaring himself to be the Almighty and at other times the Prince of Darkness.

The above extract will give my readers some idea of the general nature of the letters, but I have only reproduced the least offensive samples, as most of the missives are unfit for publication.

In 1892, when these letters commenced, I was sixteen years of age, and attending Mason College (now the University), Birmingham. The editor of TRUTH (February 16th, 1905), after studying one of these documents, remarks:

The handwriting, although it presents certain strongly marked features, is in general character of a very ordinary type, such as one sees every day written by clergymen, lawyers, or other educated men who write freely and hurriedly. If it is a disguised hand, it could only have been written by someone who had cultivated the art of disguising his handwriting very carefully.

These letters were not (as in the case of the previous series) always posted in the district, but came from places all over the country. Several illiterate letters, in a totally different hand, were received at the same time.

As in 1888, police assistance was called in by my father, but they wholly failed to detect the writer.

Up to this time the letters had always come by post, but it is a curious fact that shortly after the police took matters in hand the nuisance, instead of diminishing, became more acute, and other forms of annoyance of all kinds were resorted to.

Some letters were now pushed under the doors after dark, and on one occasion the writer (or the deliverer it would be more correct to say, for it is doubtful if the actual writer ever came on the premises) got very nearly caught under the following circumstances: About eleven o'clock one night my mother was looking round according to her usual custom to see that everything was all right and the doors securely fastened. Just as she reached the back door she heard a sound outside, and astonished to see a letter thrust und...

*Mr. George Edalji was born in 1876, and had, except for occasional holidays, continually resided with his parents at the vicarage, Great Wyrley, Staffordshire. He was educated at Rugeley Grammar School and at Mason College (now the University), Birmingham, and in October, 1893, he was articled for five years to a solicitor in that city.*

*After obtaining a number of valuable prizes from the Birmingham Law Society and several other sources, he passed his final examination with second-class honours, became the local Law Society's Bronze Medallist for 1898, and started practice for himself in Newhall Street, Birmingham, in 1899, living at W...sley as before.*

*He is the author of a popular local handbook ...*

George Edalji's article in *Pearson's Weekly*

Advertisements for articles written by George Edalji in *The Umpire* (above) and *Pearson's Weekly* (left)

An older George Edalji

The Hon. Captain George A. Anson

Grave of Shapurji Edalji, St Mary's Church, Great Wyrley

The overgrown grave of George Edalji, Hatfield Hyde Cemetery, Welwyn Garden City

Here is fresh outrage, and after all the trouble and strife there has been about the matter, it surely affords the police a good opportunity to set right the injustice that has been done to me. Let them track the person responsible. The first question you will naturally ask is – Where was I? I am thankful to say that I have been here in London all the time. The outrage was discovered on Tuesday morning. It must have therefore occurred on Monday night or before. I have not been in Staffordshire this year. As for Great Wyrley, I have only spent one night there since my release from prison.

That was in October. I dare not go there, for fear that the opportunity should be seized by the person responsible for these outrages. I am not afraid for any other reason. Suppose by terrible chance I had gone home to spend last weekend with my family. Can you imagine such a position as mine would have been? The incident shows at least that my attitude in staying away from the locality was justified.[4]

Yelverton also spoke to the press saying that George had been in London when the killings occurred. Questioned about the motives of the outrage, Yelverton attributed them to love of fiendish brutality. He believed that if Sir Conan Doyle were to go down and act in the detective capacity of Sherlock Holmes and had some police officers and Scotland Yard at his back, the culprits would not long escape detection.[5]

Meanwhile things were developing quickly in Great Wyrley. The local newspapers had a startling revelation: Conan Doyle had uncovered the criminal.

'The Great Wyrley Cattle Maiming Mystery, Sir Arthur Conan Doyle Knows the Criminal' was the headline in the *Lincolnshire Chronicle*, much to the anger of the Staffordshire police.

The paper reported: 'Sir Arthur Conan Doyle who so ably championed the case of Mr Edalji, is fully convinced that he knows the perpetrator of the outrages.' It went on to quote his interview in the *Daily Mail* after the spate of killings:

I am not at all surprised at these new outrages occurring, for it is the best of my belief that the man who committed the original outrage is still living at GW.

I have the most conclusive evidence that he is a degenerate of a destructive and criminal type, a man who all his life destroyed things for the mere pleasure of destruction; and further, I am sure there have been other outrages that many have put down to quite different causes. For instance, some time after Edalji was sent to prison, a horse was found maimed in a field, but the police attributed the injuries to broken glass, and so gave an innocent turn to the affair. Last week there was another one, which was put down to a cow's horn. It is a curious coincidence that such a series of accidents should occur in the same parish. Besides a cow has usually two horns, and a trace of the other would have been found, if only a graze. The one course now by which the police can set themselves right is to admit frankly that in the first instance they made a very grave mistake, and then set to work, not to explain away every fresh outrage as they have endeavoured to do, but to try and find one single criminal on whom they can fix the guilt of the whole series. When they have done that they will find it is the work of the man who wrote the letters. Of that I am ready to convince any reasonable person in the course of a half-hour examination of the evidence.[6]

The paper reported that there was an almost painful anxiety among the local residents to learn whether any fresh atrocity had been perpetrated under cover of darkness. The chief constable of Staffordshire had assured the villagers that there was a large force of plain-clothes officers in the district. 'The police have proved so helpless through the history of these mysterious crimes,' the paper said.

A reporter from the *Mercury* travelled to Great Wyrley to see first-hand the effect of the latest cattle-maimings and found that there was 'an undercurrent of excitement in the district'. The porters at the station readily gave information and people stood around in huddles at street corners and garden gates trying to glean new information on the subject. The reporter noted that very few villagers now thought that George had something to do with or any knowledge of the recent attacks.

It is surprising to see that the great bulk of the inhabitants now side with Edalji and sympathise with his father and his family.

They consider the fact that Mr Edalji has been able to prove that he was at Yarmouth during the whole of Monday night is conclusive evidence that he had had nothing to do with this terrible deed, and they very clearly say that it is clear that he who did this deed was responsible also for those of four years ago, that Edalji has been wrongly convicted and punished. The theories they advance are that the perpetrator of the crime has a deep and unforgiving grudge against young Edalji, and when by his evil deeds he succeeded in obtaining Edalji's imprisonment, his desire for revenge was gratified and that now, when Edalji is once more a free man, he has commenced his fiendish tricks again. The 'gang' theory has very few supporters.[7]

The villagers of Great Wyrley had clearly changed their mind about George and the family at the vicarage. So had the press. Years of prejudice was gradually fading away. It had taken the championing of George by a famous writer to finally make the breakthrough.

The reporter from the *Mercury* visited Shapurji and asked him if he had any theories. He wrote later: 'Mr Edalji, his careworn face saddening, replied: "I have my theories, of course, but I have seen and known too much of the misery which is caused by the conviction of an innocent man to give utterance to anything which might directly or indirectly lead to the arrest of the wrong man who might not be the guilty person."'

The reporter asked Shapurji if there was any truth in the news reported by several newspapers that Sir Arthur Conan Doyle knew the guilty party and had communicated his name to the police. Shapurji replied that he could not answer that question. Conan Doyle had been kind and helped him in many ways, but he had no knowledge of what his theories, his actions or his plans might be.

He thought the police were now doing all in their power, but they did not have much evidence to work with. 'They had been too eager to accept evidence in the first place, and now were seeing to recover their lost prestige,' said Shapurji.

～⋗

The Home Office had put up a virtual blockade against the petitions of Conan Doyle. His carefully investigated report 'Statement of the Case Against Royden Sharp' had hit a complete dead end. In mid August, the Home Secretary, Herbert Gladstone, announced that there was no case 'even of a prima facie character' against the individual indicated by Sir Arthur and no action could be taken.

Conan Doyle was told by a high official of the government: 'I see no more evidence against these two brothers than against myself and my brother.'[8] The official added: 'I had one letter in sorrow and also in anger from the Staffordshire police complaining that I should be libelling this poor young man whose identity could easily be established.'

Reporting the Home Office decision, the *Mercury* newspaper was indignant: This on the face of it, seems as though the Home Office has played the last card.

> We do not think so. The general conclusion is so illogical that the public may depend that Sir Arthur Conan Doyle has, as yet, much to say, and that Mr Edalji's friends will break fresh ground in their determination to see the business to an end. From every point of view it is to be desired that the matter should be cleared. At present it is simply chaos. The freedom granted is a farce if Mr Edalji is not innocent, and if he be innocent he is entitled to the fullest reparation.[9]

George Edalji was suddenly being championed by the very newspapers that had maligned him.

# 18

## Conan Doyle v Anson

Fresh evidence was exactly what Conan Doyle had in mind. The public and the media had placed their faith in him. He was not going to be deterred by the Home Office's refusal to consider his argument against Royden Sharp. Bolstered by having obtained the free pardon for George, he carried on his investigations. He had worked tirelessly for the last eight months, looking at every angle of the Edalji case. He had spoken to local villagers, shopkeepers, butchers, post-office clerks, school headmasters, railway porters, and left no stone unturned. Single-handedly he had covered more ground than the police. He now decided to send his findings directly to Anson. Given that it was the Staffordshire police constabulary that had been criticised by Conan Doyle for not collecting information correctly and for accusing George without adequate evidence, Conan Doyle wanted to take his case straight to the man who had set out to get penal servitude for George Edalji. From August 1907, Conan Doyle began a series of exchanges with Anson.

The correspondence would start politely, but soon the insults began to fly as Anson made it almost personal. He did not want to be taught policing by an internationally famous writer of crime fiction. Conan Doyle flooded him with letters and telegrams written from his home in Undershaw and from his London hotel. The more Conan Doyle directed him, the more Anson would dig his heels in.

From the very start, Conan Doyle had been working methodically on the case looking first of all at the nature of the wound and the instrument that could have caused it. He was convinced that such a wound could only have been 'caused by a very large horse lancet'.[1]

If it had been a knife, it would have made a deep wound and penetrated the gut, stated Conan Doyle, but the rest of the wound would have been more superficial. However, a horse lancet would inflict a wound the same depth from end to end. There would also be signs of pressure or friction upon the skin on either side of the cut. Was anything of the sort visible? he asked Anson.

'My only desire is to help the police, if I can, to capture the man,' Conan Doyle wrote to Anson.[2]

Conan Doyle's suggestions flew thick and fast. Within days Anson received a lengthy letter giving him a list of possible suspects. He asked Anson to look out for two individuals: 'The one is Royden Sharp of Cannock, the other is John Hart, the butcher of Cheslyn Hay.'[3]

Conan Doyle informed him of his belief that it was Royden Sharp, who along with his brothers, Frank and Walter, had persecuted the Edaljis between 1892 and 1895, and that Royden was also the author of the letters in 1903. He gave Anson the same reasons he had given the Home Office: Royden's violent tendencies and his grudge against William Greatorex. The young man had been apprenticed to a butcher and knew how to handle animals, he had been on a cattle ship and there were references to the sea in several letters. He was quick-footed and keen-sighted as he had described himself in the letters. His mother said he often had uncontrollable fits. Their house backed on to fields and he could leave without being seen by anyone. She was stone deaf and could not hear him when he left the house by the back door. Conan Doyle also related the incident of the horse lancet and Mrs Greatorex.

There is no doubt that the letters annoyed Anson, who wrote his comments on the side. He meticulously numbered the various points made in the letter, taking up each allegation made by Conan Doyle. In all he listed nineteen points with which he wanted to confront Conan Doyle.

The chief of the Staffordshire police replied to Conan Doyle thanking him for his suggestions, but dismissing them as 'surmise'. His respsonse angered Conan Doyle, who replied:

Sir, I cannot admit that my conclusions are largely surmise. It is not surmise when an unpaid expert of the first rank without any prompting and after most elaborate examination declared in a report that the 'Greatorex' letters, the 'Martin Molton' letters and a letter signed by Sharp are in the same hand. That is positive evidence and not surmise.[4]

He said he had proof that Royden travelled to Rotherham and could produce the porter who carried his trunks at the railway station. The letters from the Wyrley killer were posted from Rotherham. He admitted that while he did not have enough proof to make an arrest, the police could at least investigate and see if there was a horse lancet or similar weapon in Royden's possession.

Despite his annoyance with Anson, Conan Doyle continued to give him leads in the hope that he would follow them. He suggested the police could watch or question a man called Emery, a betting man, who came and went from the Sharp household and was in Sharp's confidence.

Anson simply replied that he had 'no reason whatever' to believe Royden was guilty of any offence. Conan Doyle responded asking if it was not true that in August 1903 Inspector Campbell had had a conversation with a banker named Greatorex (no relation to William Greatorex) when they discussed whether Royden Sharp should have been arrested for writing obscene postcards. Anson did not respond to this query.

Conan Doyle had been getting information from various sources in Great Wyrley and the neighbouring villages. He met John Hart, the butcher, who called on him in London. Hart told him that he did not know Sharp, a fact that made Conan Doyle suspicious. He told Anson: 'He actually, as I understand, supplies the Sharp family with meat. Why should he lie in such a way, if he has no guilty conscience?'[5]

There were many people in the village of Great Wyrley who had information on the Sharps and were ready to speak. Their relations with the county police had been strained as Inspector Campbell had not listened to them. Conan Doyle suggested their names to Anson, saying they would be prepared to speak directly to him if he approached them. The list included two men, Grinsell and Thomas, who had information about Royden Sharp. Then there was Frank Arrowsmith, owner of the Star Trading Company, a shop in Cannock. Arrowsmith always had his ears to the ground and picked up information from customers who came and went from his shop. There was the dairy farmer, R. Beaumont of Wolverhampton Road, whose horse and cart regularly went through the village streets in the early morning. Beaumont often picked up local gossip on his delivery rounds. Mr Whitehouse, the insurance agent, also had information, as did Mr Plant who was known to Mr Whitehouse. A key informer was William Greatorex of Littleworth Farm, uncle and guardian of Royden Sharp. Arrowsmith, Beaumont and Greatorex were Conan Doyle's main informers.

Conan Doyle's marriage to Jean Leckie was fast approaching and yet the Edalji case was taking all his time. He found himself travelling regularly to London to meet his publishers and to make wedding arrangements. Yet he continued to write to a number of people who he hoped could still shed light on the case. No matter how dismissive Anson was, Conan Doyle would simply swallow his irritation and continue sending him tips.

There was one line of enquiry on the Sharp brothers that Conan Doyle was actively following. He did not want to share it yet with Anson, until he had made a positive discovery.

Early in the year, George had mysteriously been sent a packet from the United States. Inside was a page of a British newspaper carrying an advertisement of George's article in the *Pearson's Weekly*. On the margin of the paper, the sender had scribbled blasphemous biblical references and allusions to George. The messages were strikingly similar to the 'God–Satan' letters received by the Edaljis in 1892–95. Conan Doyle was sure the scribbling had been done by the same person who wrote the 'God–Satan' letters. The envelope was postmarked 'Long Beach California'. The letter-writer gave his name as 'Lewis' and his address as 'The Ark'. Conan Doyle immediately wrote to the head of police at Long Beach hoping to trace whether there was a Frank Sharp from Cannock living in a place called 'The Ark'. He was convinced that the packet had been sent by Royden's elder brother, Frank, who now lived in the United States.

The newspaper cutting with its wild scribblings convinced him that he was on the right track. He waited patiently for an answer from Long Beach police.

Meanwhile, Royden Sharp was keeping both Conan Doyle and Anson busy. He had been telling local villagers that he was working for the police, and even produced some letters from the police to prove his case. To another villager he said that he had been hired at a certain price a week to keep abreast of George's movements. Conan Doyle received the news from his informers and promptly passed it on to Anson. 'I have no doubt that it is absolutely false but in that case it will help you to gauge the man's character, since he undoubtedly spread the report,' said Conan Doyle.[6]

It seemed everybody in Great Wyrley had been stirred up by Conan Doyle's articles and the events of three years before were very much the topic of conversation. The fact that the cattle-killings had continued added to the fervour in the village. Conan Doyle was in regular touch with his sources locally and wrote nearly every day to Anson with further tips.

Mr Williams, a tobacconist at Cannock, gave Conan Doyle further information about Hart. He said that Hart used to employ a workhouse boy named Jimmy as a helper in his slaughterhouse in 1903. Jimmy heard his master say, 'If we can't do any more horses we can [set] fire [to the hay]rick, and clear them that way.' Conan Doyle thought it would be a good idea for the police to find Jimmy and see if he had further information. A day after Green's horse was killed, Hart was also supposed to have said, 'I taught the chap how to do it, but a pretty mess he has made.'

Information on Hart could also be obtained from Mr Wynne of Clovelly, Cheslyn Hay. Wynne had told Conan Doyle that Hart's name was often mentioned by Green as being a member of a gang during the killings of 1903. Green and Hart were frequently together at this time. Another name mentioned by Conan Doyle was J. V. Greensill of Cheslyn Hay who seemed to enjoy Hart's confidence. 'All this is, I admit, very vague but I send it for what it's worth,' he wrote.[7]

However, while Conan Doyle was writing to Anson in all earnestness, the police chief was doing his own spadework. Anson wrote to all the people concerned who had supplied information to Conan Doyle. He wrote to Beaumont, Arrowsmith and Greatorex.

Anson asked Greatorex for copies of Royden's handwriting. He also wanted to see all the anonymous letters that he had in his possession as there would be a very large number 'which could by no possibility have been written by Royden Sharp, but Sir Conan

Doyle has not seen them.'[8] Anson desperately wanted to prove Conan Doyle's theories wrong.

Undaunted, Conan Doyle carried on. He had learnt from Mr Mellor, a retired butcher, who had employed Royden as an apprentice, that he had inflicted cruel atrocities on the animals. Mellor had given this information to Inspector Campbell at the time of George's arrest, but it had not been followed up.

Meanwhile Beaumont had information that Sharp had recently been absent from home for two nights and even his mother did not know where he was. 'I venture to suggest that if Mrs Sharp were herself interviewed results might come of it as I have reason to believe that she lives in terror of her son,'[9] Conan Doyle wrote to Anson.

The letters and information did not make the slightest difference to Anson, leaving Conan Doyle frustrated. He shot off yet another letter to the police chief:

'My information about Sharp,' he said curtly, 'comes from seven or eight people, some of whom are unknown to others. It is supplemented by a careful comparison of dates and of handwriting so that I do not feel that it can be so easily set aside.'[10]

The more information Conan Doyle supplied, the more it put Anson's back up.

The police chief was thoroughly disapproving of the articles that Conan Doyle had written in the newspaper. Though Conan Doyle had not named Royden Sharp, it did not take long for locals to surmise who he was referring to. Reporters had started arriving in Great Wyrley again and were walking around and chatting with the villagers. Some had even reached the Sharp house and were watching it.

Anson decided it was time for action. He left his salubrious surroundings in Stafford to visit the modest working-class home of the Sharp family in Cannock. Watched by curious locals, the police chief entered the house. The news spread through the village like a flash and there was speculation about whether young Sharp was going to be arrested. But Anson had no intention of arresting anyone. He spoke to Royden and his mother and asked for the addresses of Royden's brother Herbert and his sister Beatrice. He was, in fact, looking for sufficient proof to clear Royden Sharp.

Herbert Sharp lived in Bristol and was surprised to receive a letter from the chief constable of Staffordshire police. Anson tried to win Herbert's confidence saying that Conan Doyle's theories in the newspaper articles were 'ridiculous nonsense'.

'Everyone knows that your brother is pointed to: the newspaper correspondents knew all about it the first day and they were here, and probably before that,' wrote Anson, adding that he was 'perfectly satisfied that the charges are absolutely baseless'.[11]

He advised Herbert to consult a solicitor as the charges were 'very near slander'. He also wanted to see any letters that Herbert may have received recently from Conan Doyle. He offered to pay Herbert's train fare from Bristol to Cannock if he would come down to see him. He said he was obliged to investigate the accusations made by Conan Doyle. 'Your brother is stated to have had a horse fleam (a sort of lancet) in his possession. If he has got *anything* of that sort will you get it from him and bring it with you. He has told people that he is in the employ of the police, which I don't much like,'[12] wrote Anson.

Meanwhile, the Staffordshire police arrested a young Wyrley butcher called Hollis Morgan, for allegedly killing a horse on the night of 26 August, and for the maiming of two horses in the same month. After downing far too many pints in the public house, Morgan had declared that George Edalji was innocent of killing the horses, and that he would kill a horse to prove it. Morgan was one of Shapurji's parishioners and a regular church attendee. Even the vicar did not believe that he could have done it. Neither did Conan Doyle, who urged Anson to investigate if Morgan had any allies, as it was not possible for him to kill two horses in different fields at the same time.

Conan Doyle was becoming a thorn on Anson's side. No police action seemed to be good enough for him. Anson had just finished fuming over some of his letters when another one arrived giving him further detailed information.

The name of the porter who had carried Royden's bags in November 1903 at Cannock station was A. Beenham Drayman, and he lived near the Baptist chapel in Cannock. He had noticed that the bags were marked for Rotherham. Five letters were sent from Rotherham in 1903. These were the letters signed G. H. Darby, who called himself the 'Captain of the Wyrley Gang'. The letters were with the Home Office, and were said to be rude and apparently in a disguised hand. It was clear that they were written by a local as they referred to Cannock as a district not a town, something only a local could have known. Mr Greatorex had no knowledge of Sharp being at Rotherham.

Moreover, when Mrs Greatorex saw the 'Martin Molton' letters, she apparently exclaimed, 'Why it is Royden's handwriting.'

Conan Doyle asked Anson to check with Greatorex about the lancet comment made by Royden, about his maniacal laughter and whether Royden's mother had ever expressed her concerns about her son to him. Vouching for Greatorex, with whom he had had a long correspondence, he described him as an 'absolutely honest man, and as I know, a very unwilling witness against Sharp, who is, in a sense, his ward.'[13]

Knowing that Anson was not receptive to his ideas, Conan Doyle had just one request: that he keep him under observation at present. He gave Anson further information:

'Three months ago he was seen at early morning climbing the garden railings to get into his home. So I am informed by one who saw him. Why should an innocent man come & go in such a way?'[14]

Conan Doyle had requested his informers, Arrowsmith and Beaumont, to write to Royden Sharp, so that they could have samples of his handwriting. Consequently, he had in his possession two signed letters sent by Royden, which were in completely different hands. It convinced Conan Doyle that Royden could change his handwriting.

Anson did not want to be taught policing by Conan Doyle. He had been examining the letters and postcards given to him by Greatorex and was convinced that the 1903 letters and earlier were not written by Royden Sharp. He did admit, however, that some of them during George's trial could have been written by Royden. A large number of people in Wyrley and the surrounding areas had started writing anonymous letters. It had become a game for many. He told Greatorex: 'there was nothing in those letters to make the writers liable to prosecution so far as I can recall them. They were not letters to be treated seriously.'[15]

One of the letters had alleged that Greatorex's sons, Wilfred and Anthony, were in school with George and that he hated them like poison. Anson asked Greatorex if there was any truth in the statement that George Edalji was at school with his sons. 'Wilfred was, as I know, at Walsall but I don't think I asked you about the other sons. Perhaps you would not mind letting me know where they were educated and also their present ages.'[16]

Like two players on a chessboard, Anson and Conan Doyle made their moves, the former secretive and determined to get the upper hand, while the latter played his cards openly and provided information and sources.

There were wedding invitations to be sent out, flowers to be organised and the honeymoon booked, but the groom-to-be was deep in the Edalji case. Jean found herself having to do most of the preparations with the help of her family. Woodie was invaluable as always, organising everything from train and hotel reservations to the casks of champagne. 'The Ma'am' too was keeping a keen eye on all the details.

Conan Doyle was in regular touch with his Baker Street Irregulars in the quest for the truth. In a telling letter on 12 September, less than a week before his wedding, he asked Arrowsmith to tell Beaumont that things were going better and that they were 'certainly right in playing up to the police at the present'.[17]

Never mind the subordinates but go for Capt Anson. He is stupid and prejudiced but would not, I think, connive at absolute injustice. I am plying him hard and so is Mr Greatorex who had an interview of 3½ hours with him the other day. We will win him yet. His letters have altered much in tone, as you will see from enclosed. So my advice is to keep up our hearts & pile in all the information we can, caring nothing for personal snubs or slights. I think we [will] win.

Yours faithfully, ACD.

In another letter to Arrowsmith, he wrote:

I enclose Captain Anson's latest. It will make amusing reading when we have proved our point.

I simply replied that my case was too strong to be put aside so easily and did not depend upon any one person. Return when read. ACD.[18]

～✦～

Meanwhile, the atmosphere at Great Wyrley was that of an overheated cauldron. The killings continued in all their brutality, anonymous letters were flying around and nearly everyone was writing to Conan Doyle about Royden Sharp. The locals had become investigators themselves. The killings had stopped briefly when Farrington was arrested in March 1904, but they had started again with renewed vigour shortly after George's release from prison. On 19 August 1907 a mare had been slashed and on 26 August two horses had been killed in different fields. Now Hollis Morgan had been arrested, but the villagers were not convinced. The Darby letters continued. It was clear to the villagers that the police, once again, had the wrong man. George himself was staying clear of Great Wyrley, so that he could not be accused of any of the killings.

Beaumont was up for a bit of local sleuthing. He had always had his suspicions about Royden Sharp and was eager to help both Conan Doyle and Anson on the case. His milk rounds were a useful time to pick up the village gossip and some leads. He was told by an official at the S. S. Waterwork Company that one of their employees had seen Royden arriving in Cannock early on the morning that Harrison's horses were found dead. Royden came off the 7 a.m. train and called at the Railway Hotel for a drink. Beaumont informed Anson of what he had heard.[19]

Anson replied to Beaumont inviting him to meet him on 19 September at his offices in Stafford offering to pay all travel expenses. He conceded it was a 'most peculiar thing' for Sharp to return early morning to his house, and that he would like to have the 'most accurate verification of this point'.[20] He asked Beaumont to bring with him any letters that he had or which had aroused his suspicions.

Beaumont had a store of stories for Anson. He told the chief constable that Royden was known for his 'journeyings abroad at night'. He had also been reliably told by a young edge-tool manufacturer on his way to work at 6 a.m. that he had seen Royden walking through the River Hill field towards Mill Green, Cannock.

He was soaking wet, apparently having been out all night. It was clear he was avoiding the main road and was walking through the fields from Wyrley to his home in Cannock. Beaumont also had information that Royden and his mother were soon going to leave the district. This news had apparently reached Beaumont's ears from Royden's uncle who was a councillor in Hull and who had told a friend. Beaumont suggested that Royden should be watched.[21]

Beaumont's story did not impress Anson who asked him for 'real evidence'. 'Many statements have been made as to Sharp's absences at night, but when investigated they have so far proved to be mere hearsay: Nothing but absolute proof by someone who really knows is of any real value. Who can speak to Mrs Sharp not knowing where her son was?' said Anson.[22]

Challenged to name his sources, Beaumont supplied the same: two respectable tradesmen had told him that Royden had been out for two nights and his mother did not know he had returned at breakfast time on Tuesday morning. Beaumont traced the source to a man named Will Foster, who worked in an office on Mill Street. He had seen Royden Sharp on Tuesday morning and saw him call at the Railway Inn for a drink.

The young man who had seen Royden in the fields was George Stringer, a resident of Wolverhampton Road, Cannock. Satisfied with his detection, Beaumont wrote to Anson that there would never be an arrest unless the miscreant was caught red-handed. He also challenged Anson: 'I would like to say if you question the truth of any statement I have made in the past either to Inspector Campbell or to Sir Conan Doyle I am prepared to undergo the strictest scrutiny with regard to the same.'[23]

Meanwhile, Arrowsmith's shop assistant had seen Royden climbing down his own railings early in the morning. He conveyed the information to Conan Doyle, who also heard from Greatorex that Royden had told a friend that he disappeared after bedtime, was out all night and returned by the seven o'clock Cannock train from Walsall. All eyes on the village seemed to be watching Royden Sharp. Conan Doyle conveyed this information to Anson, and added that he 'had no doubt as to Sharp being the author of the Martin Molton letters'. In a small inscription at the bottom of the page, he added: 'I shall be absent for some time.'[24]

Conan Doyle was due to marry Jean Leckie in four days. No matter how pressing the Edalji case was, he would have to give it a rest for a while. His future wife had been more than patient, but now he owed her his full attention.

⌒⌒

Hollis Morgan, the butcher who had been arrested for killing the horses on 26 August, was released from jail after the prosecutor said that certain examinations had been made and the general results were indecisive. There was nothing on which the jury could convict and the police were withdrawing the charge against Morgan. Moreover there was evidence that he was away in Wolverhampton on the night of the killing. His landlady had the key of the house and his bicycle was locked up.

Lord Hatherton announced in court: 'Morgan you are discharged. You have brought it upon yourself by your own foolish statements.'[25]

Morgan then left the court and was cheered by a large crowd outside, with many people shaking hands with him as he left.

It left one question still open. Who had killed the horses on 26 August? The residents of Great Wyrley were filled with a sense of unease. Many were nervously watching Royden Sharp. He came and went in the night and was seen alone in the fields at unlikely times. No explanations were offered and Anson seemed to be turning a blind eye. The village of fear waited for news of more killings.

# 19

## *The Baker Street Irregulars*

On 18 September 1907, Sir Arthur Conan Doyle, forty-eight, married Jean Leckie. The wedding was held at St Margaret's Church, Westminster at 1.45 p.m. The venue had not been disclosed to the public and only a few friends and family were informed. The bride looked radiant in a white silk gown embroidered with Spanish lace and pearls on silver tissue. Conan Doyle wore coat and tails with a white waistcoat and a large gardenia in his buttonhole. His brother and close confidant, Innes Doyle, was the best man. Arthur had often written to Innes about his relationship with Jean before Touie's death. He had waited years to be able to take Jean to the altar.

Conducting the wedding was Cyril Angell, husband of his youngest sister, Bryan Mary Doyle or 'Dodo' as she was called. Angell was a Church of England priest from Westmorland in north-west England. The bride's train was carried by Dodo's five-year-old son, dressed as a pageboy. Conan Doyle's mother, Mary, the 'Ma'am', was present, along with his daughter, Mary, eighteen, and son Arthur, fifteen. The reception was held in the Whitehall Rooms, Hotel Metropole at 2.45 pm. Conan Doyle was in a buoyant mood as the couple left for the reception. As Jean tried to climb the red-carpeted stairs at the hotel, she got caught in the long train of her gown. Her husband simply lifted her up and carried her, to cheers from his friends and family. Inside, the 250 guests enjoyed champagne, caviar and smoked salmon. The room was decorated with tall palms and white flowers.

The shining stars of London's literary scene were present: friends and fellow authors Jerome K. Jerome, Bram Stoker, J. M. Barrie and Max Pemberton. Conan Doyle's defence of George Edalji had made him a hero. His friends from the publishing world were all there to share his special day, including George Newnes, owner of the *Strand Magazine* and *Westminster Gazette* and Herbert Greenhough Smith, editor of the *Strand Magazine*, where the Sherlock Holmes stories were regularly published. Everyone raised a toast to the health and happiness of the newly-weds. Mary Doyle looked proud and happy for her son and his beautiful bride. Standing among the celebrity guests and the family was the shy and awkward figure of George Edalji. He presented the couple with the complete works of Shakespeare and Tennyson and stammered out his congratulations when his turn came.[1] Conan Doyle recorded later that 'there was no guest whom I was prouder to see'.[2]

Jean's parents had a house in Crowborough in Sussex. Knowing that his new wife was very close to her parents, Arthur bought a house near them named Windlesham. In 1907, after ten years at Undershaw, the house he had bought for his first wife, Touie, Conan Doyle moved out, taking his books, papers and belongings to his new home in Sussex, and a new life.

He took Jean on a long European honeymoon. All the years of waiting and all the heartbreak and sorrow were firmly behind them. They waved goodbye to their family and sailed across the Channel, starting their holiday on 21 September at the Hotel Regina in Paris. From there they travelled through the cities of Berlin, Dresden, Venice, Rome, Naples, Athens, Smyrna and Constantinople, immersing themselves in the culture and history of the continent. Conan Doyle had left instructions with his trusted assistant, Woodie, to forward all mail to him. Throughout the honeymoon, there would be one set of urgent correspondence that he would carry on with: that relating to the George Edalji case.

Letters from Anson were coming thick and fast to Windlesham, the new Conan Doyle residence, and Woodie was redirecting them to their owner. Barely a few days into his honeymoon, Conan Doyle wrote to Anson from the Hotel Bellevue in Dresden.

He informed the police chief that he had had the advantage of seeing a number of the specimens of the persecution letters of 1892–95 and outlined his theory that they were written by three people: a boy and two grown men living in the same house.

Conan Doyle said he had obtained signed letters by all the Sharp brothers. While Walter Sharp's writing corresponded closely to one set, Royden's corresponded to the boy's handwriting. Frank Sharp's writing was like the third, but Walter's was in places quite identical. It was impossible for him to have any doubt that the brothers, who lived at that time at Halton's, not far from the vicarage, were the conspirators.

The headmaster of Walsall had received threatening letters (of which Conan Doyle had seen a copy). The letter in a boyish hand was received after Sharp had been expelled from the school for forgery in 1893. Conan Doyle stated that the last 'Martin Molton' letter he had received alluded to the headmaster of Walsall by his name, Mr Aldis, and reviled him exactly as the earlier letters did. Thus, apart from the style of the handwriting, the internal evidence showed that the boy persecutor of 1893 and 'Martin Molton' were the same. Royden Sharp's script corresponded with both, and he was the man who had cause to hate the headmaster.

Anson was not convinced. He wrote to Conan Doyle that he would look into his 'assumption' that Frank and Royden Sharp had written the anonymous letters.

Conan Doyle and Jean carried on their travels through Europe and moved from Dresden to Venice. Sailing over the Grand Canal under the clear Venetian sky, the couple were enjoying their quiet getaway. As they checked in to the luxurious Royal Hotel Danieli, a former palace, with its views of the church of San Giorgio Maggiore over the lagoon, Conan Doyle was handed his mail again. One of the enclosures was a reply he had been impatiently waiting for. It was postmarked Long Beach California.

The brief letter buoyed his spirits. It was from Geo W. Young, the city marshal of Long Beach, California and was the confirmation that he was so eagerly looking for. It said: 'Frank Sharp did at one time room at a house in the city called the "Ark".'[3] The police chief informed him that he had now moved to Santa Ana, Orange County, California and was working for the Pacific Electric Railway Co, on the construction department. He could be contacted through his foreman, Mr Grieve.

Conan Doyle was overjoyed. He had finally nailed it. Thousands of miles away from Wyrley, he had uncovered Frank Sharp. Here was the final proof of everything that he had asserted: Frank Sharp had written the 'God-Satan' letters of 1892–95 and was now living in the US. It had taken over five months for the California police to investigate and get back to him, but it had been worth the wait.

The city marshal was a great fan of Conan Doyle and was clearly delighted to be helping the famous author.

Conan Doyle could not contain his excitement. Jean would just have to wait a while to see the sights of Venice. He wrote immediately to the Home Office saying he had made a major breakthrough in the Edalji case and that he had found the person who wrote the anonymous letters of 1892–95.

In the letter to the Home Office, Conan Doyle explained his 'final proof':

You are aware that I put the letters down as the work of three brothers, Frank, Wallie and Royden Sharp, of whom the first was a peculiar religious monomaniac who wrote as 'God-Satan', and the last was a schoolboy of 13 years of age. Both the writing and internal contents convinced me that this was so, though I was not fortunate enough to have my view officially adopted.

Some four months ago a sheet of a newspaper was sent to me from a town in California, scribbled all round with strange religious blasphemies, with allusions to Edalji worked in. Both the style and the writing seemed to me to be that of 'God Satan'. A religious reference on a card was attached to the paper, and in the corner of the card the words 'The Ark'. I was at once prepared to stake my whole case upon the fact that this was the work of Frank Sharp, whose own people declare that he is dead. I wrote to the postmaster, waited two months and then wrote again to the head of Police. I enclose his reply. My question simply was whether a man named Frank Sharp formerly of Cannock lived there, and if he was connected with 'The Ark'.

It must be clear to you now how sound my reasoning has been; how else could I give a name to this anonymous writer out of the 80 million people in the States?[4]

Stanley Blackwell was amazed to read the latest letter sent by Conan Doyle. The minister at the Home Office was used to receiving these letters on the Edalji case, but this one was different. Conan Doyle was confident he had solved it. He had found an F. Sharp from Cannock in California, and he was stating that it was the same man who wrote the 'God-Satan' letters. Blackwell looked closely at the enclosures. Woodie had sent him the original newspaper with its scribblings and blasphemous writings and references to George Edalji. He was not sure he agreed that the handwriting matched that of the 'God-Satan' letters, but he had to admit it was a remarkable coincidence.

Anson had to be informed. Blackwell wanted to be certain of the facts. He sent a copy of the letter to Anson and asked him to make discreet enquiries. He suggested that Anson write to the city marshall at Long Beach and also get a member of the Sharp family to write to the Frank Sharp in the US. It was possible, after all, that F. Sharp had discussed the case with 'Lewis' who had then sent the letter and newspaper to George. 'But even so, the coincidence taken in consideration with the God-Satan letters is striking and difficult to get over,' Blackwell told Anson.[5]

Blackwell asked Anson to make sure his case was watertight. He asked him to get a physical description of F. Sharp in the US to see if it matched Royden's brother. He also advised the utmost discretion: 'One cannot be too careful in dealing with C.D. as you know,' he said. 'If he successfully proved "God-Satan" was Frank Sharp, it would electrify the great B.P. [British Public] with whom we have to reckon'.

Anson thought little of Conan Doyle's letter forwarded to him by the Home Office. He underlined the first paragraph and on the margins he inserted two large exclamation marks. He also underlined the words 'final proof' and put an exclamation mark next to it.[6]

Conan Doyle, too, wrote separately to Anson informing him of his new discovery.

'I claim therefore that this final proof that Frank Sharp wrote the God-Satan letters enables us to say with equal certainty that Royden Sharp was both the coarse boy of 1893 and "Martin Molton" of 1907,' he wrote.[7]

The latest correspondence from Conan Doyle both annoyed and perplexed Anson. Surely it was not possible that Frank Sharp had moved to California and had written the original letters. Anson firmly believed that the Sharps were innocent. He immediately cabled the chief of police at Long Beach.

'Is there any person named Lewis at The Ark. Is there any connection with Frank Sharp same address. Please ask if sent a paper to Edalji last March.'[8]

The letter written to George Edalji on the newspaper cutting had been signed by 'Lewis'.

The city marshal replied by telegram:

'Lewis at Ark religious fanatic. Letter Following. No connection Sharp.'[9]

It was exactly the reply Anson had wanted.

A detailed letter from Geo Young to Anson confirmed the details about 'Lewis the Light', a religious fanatic. He informed Anson: 'Frank Sharp has no connection with him that we know of.'[10] Anson was delighted. Conan Doyle's theories were crumbling. The case would be dead before he returned from his honeymoon, he thought.

Unaware of this development, Arthur and Jean were still travelling through Europe. The newly-weds moved from Venice to Rome, enjoying the grand architecture of the Italian capital. However, Edalji and the battle with Anson and the Home Office were never far from Conan Doyle's mind. He waited eagerly for his mail which was forwarded on a daily basis from Windlesham by Woodie. The post he received did not always leave him in a good mood, however, especially if it was from Anson.

Sitting at his desk at the Grand Hotel in Rome, the author fired off a letter to Anson, still arguing about the disguised handwriting of Royden Sharp. 'Your letter of October 5 reached me here. I was unable to understand it.'[11]

Conan Doyle asserted once again that Royden was disguising his writing. 'Of course, you do not find this in his ordinary writing otherwise it would cease to be a disguise,' said Conan Doyle somewhat exasperatedly. 'There is therefore no "assumption" that

Sharp is the author of particular letters, as stated by you, but there is a strong case for it.'

The combative correspondence continued over the month of October. As Conan Doyle travelled on his honeymoon, the letters from Anson followed him.

There was a new one waiting for him when he and Jean arrived in Naples and checked into the Grand Hotel du Vesuve. Jean was half wishing that dear Woodie would stop sending the letters from the chief of Staffordshire police. Inevitably her irate husband would want to answer it immediately.

Sir, you cannot deny that my reasoning has enabled me to pick Frank Sharp out of the 80 million of America, when his own people profess not to know where he is,' raged Conan Doyle. 'To say that there is "absolutely nothing" against a man who exhibited a weapon & said it was the sort of one which did the outrages, is a statement which makes one feel rather hopeless about the use of getting evidence. I wonder what would be something if that is nothing.[12]

More angry letters were exchanged while the couple were at Naples. Anson was clearly beginning to prove a source of annoyance in the middle of Conan Doyle's honeymoon. There seemed to be no getting away from the Edalji case. For Jean, the charms of Italy were being lost with each arrival of mail from England.

However scornful Anson was of Conan Doyle's theories, he was forced to begin enquiries on the new lead. He needed to know more about 'Lewis the Light' and Frank Sharp in the USA. He was certain it would all go nowhere, but the Home Office wanted a watertight case. Unfortunately for Anson, Conan Doyle seemed to be leading this investigation, and it was Anson's lot to do the fact-checking. He mistrusted and disliked Conan Doyle's Baker Street Irregulars, Beaumont, Arrowsmith and Greatorex, particularly the former two. He decided to get in touch with the most reliable of them: Greatorex.

Anson needed to get hold of Frank Sharp's handwriting and he asked Greatorex if he could supply this. He also needed to know Royden's movements from 1900. He asked Greatorex if Royden was not 'on the sea' between the following approximate dates:

'Sep 29 1900 to 6 February 1901

March 8 1901 to 25 March 1901

April 26 1901 to 30 April 1901

May 29 1901 to 31 July 1901

August 28 1901 to 6 September 1901

And after Oct 1 1901 he does not appear to have been on the sea at all. Is there any reason to question these dates?'[13]

A few days later Anson wrote to Greatorex again asking him if he could help clear up without doubt 'whether or not Frank Sharp was at home from the middle of 1892 to the end of 1895 (i.e. *during the whole time*, or at any rate with only occasional absences)'.[14]

Greatorex sent him a sample of Frank's writing and informed him that he was home in October 1893 and after.

Beaumont was under instructions from Conan Doyle to let the chief constable know if he had any new information. Though he did not enjoy interacting with the arrogant Anson, Beaumont did his duty. He had heard that Royden was going to London on 7 October and that he had sold anything that was of value in his garden. Given that Royden Sharp's house and district were under close observation, he informed Anson: 'It is significant to me that all is very quiet both as regards letters & maiming. This is exactly what happened in 1903 when he was watched for six weeks or more. As they have sold their garden stuff I expect we shall soon neither see nor hear any more of them in this district and I presume a good job too.'[15]

Anson replied by return post to Beaumont:

I find Royden Sharp is at home; was there any serious reason to think he had gone to London yesterday? I do not think it is possible that he did go. I am much puzzled to account for the mistakes, which are made as to his train journeys. Is it possible that there is someone very much like him who is mistaken for him?[16]

He told Beaumont that it was unfair to accuse a man without proof.

The somewhat stern letter from Anson put Beaumont on the back foot immediately, and he wrote back to Anson apologising if he had gone beyond his duty as a citizen in forwarding information to him. The news that Royden Sharp was going to London on the first train on Monday morning had come from Royden himself who told it to 'a gentleman whose word is absolutely above suspicion,' said Beaumont.[17]

He was beginning to get defensive. He had provided information as an honest citizen, and ended up being chastised. He informed Anson that he had no wish to be suspicious of an individual without a cause. Anson clearly did not believe that Royden had gone to London. 'If a man's movements are being watched he cannot be blamed if he misleads people,' was his surprising response to Beaumont.[18]

He said the same to Arrowsmith, once again defending Sharp.

'Royden Sharp is not truthful: but very many other people are the same & I cannot feel surprised if, after the iniquitous way in which he has been painted in the newspapers as guilty of serious crimes, he should take some satisfaction in misleading people, even the police, as to his movements,' said Anson.[19]

The chief constable also challenged Arrowsmith about why he thought that the police should have arrested Harry Green after he admitted killing his horse. Arrowsmith was not a man to easily give in to Anson. He had provided information on Green to Inspector Campbell in 1903, but nothing had come of it.

Arrowsmith now gave Anson the full details:

Green had previously worked at a chemist's shop two doors from him, and he knew him well. On the morning that his horse was killed, Green went to Cannock police station and informed them. The police offered a £50 reward.

However, that night, Green came to Arrowsmith's shop in great excitement to escape questioning by the police. Arrowsmith felt he had something to say and he took down all the information, which he duly handed over to the police. Green was called in to the police station and questioned. At first he denied it, and then he signed a confession that he had killed his horse. He told Arrowsmith that night that the police were not going to prosecute him and he was leaving for South Africa as soon as he could. Arrowsmith recalled that Green told him: 'When I do one, my pals will do one to get me out of it.'

Meanwhile, a man named Burton came to meet Arrowsmith. Burton lived in Cheltenham, but had at one time been very close to John Hart (the butcher) and his friends. Burton told Arrowsmith that Hart was definitely mixed up in the case. When the G. H. Darby letters appeared, Burton became uneasy, as 'Darby' was the nickname used by Hart and his pals when they spoke to him. Thinking that he could inadvertently get mixed up in this, he tried to find out some more. Burton noticed that several of the G. H. Darby letters came from places where he had seen Hart the day before. Yet when he asked Hart about being at these places, he denied it. Burton agreed to see Superintendent Bishop and Inspector Campbell, but he came away angry and disappointed as the police told him that they did not want to know who the culprit was, as they were satisfied at having arrested Edalji.

Burton told Arrowsmith that he had been past Hart's slaughter-house the night before Stanley's horse was killed in Landywood on 3 November. He had overheard Hart talking to a companion in an excited manner, saying, 'I told the young B— Green when to do it & I meant to stand by him & I have done so.'

On the Sunday night before Edalji's trial commenced at Stafford, Anson took Green secretly down to his pantry and went through the whole case with him to try and find any connection between him and Edalji. Green emphatically repudiated it.

'And yet if the papers reported the case correctly the prosecuting counsel said "Green killed his horse to shield a lifelong friend" which was absolutely untrue. Was Green then in league with anyone else? I suggest he was,' added Arrowsmith.

To Arrowsmith, the inference was obvious.

'If Green killed his horse and Hart killed Stanley's to shield Green, then as the police had let Green go they could not have Hart without involving themselves as the feeling ran very high against letting Green go.'

Arrowsmith said that the butcher with whom Royden was apprenticed had told Campbell about his cruel manner, but it was ignored. He said he would not be silenced any more.

'Twice this year it has been stated in this shop that if I will stick to *them* I shall be well paid but I have principles and shall carry them out. I beg to suggest that you arrest Mr S before Sir Arthur returns and will help you to carry it through and you will have done a great good in the community,' said Arrowsmith.[20]

His defiant letter and the challenges he threw at the Staffordshire police displeased Anson.

'I do not for a moment believe your statement that you have been offered money to act for the police,'[21] Anson wrote back. He suggested that Arrowsmith was mixing up fact with some fanciful thinking and could not be relied upon. To the irritation of Arrowsmith, Anson now praised Beaumont and said he had given him information which constituted proper grounds for an enquiry.'I have not the least doubt of his good faith nor of his good intentions,' he said.[22]

The chief of police had successfully divided the opposition. Arrowsmith had no choice but to wait for the return of Sir Arthur Conan Doyle. He was determined not to let the matter rest. The village of Great Wyrley was still heaving with tension. Nothing it seems had changed since the fateful summer of 1903. Royden Sharp and John Hart were still roaming free.

# 20

# Frank Sharp

In late October, Anson received a lengthy letter from Royden's sister, Beatrice Sharp, who lived in Llandudno in Wales. He had written to her for information about her brother Frank. He wanted to know where Frank worked and when he left the country. Anson was determined to build a complete profile of the Sharp family. Three of the Sharp brothers were on the radar of Conan Doyle, while Anson believed them to be innocent.

Beatrice provided the details about her brothers.

Frank Sharp was the eldest of the brothers. He was born on 1 January 1869. He had lived the first ten or twelve years of his life at the Shrubbery, Hednesford. About 1882 or 1883, their father moved to The Mount, Hednesford, close to the Old Hednesford Co.'s Pits near the Cross Keys Inn. Frank was educated firstly at Board Schools Five Ways. He then went to a small private school at Cannock. Beatrice did not think Frank had gone to Walsall Grammar School. If he did, it would have been in 1884, and his name would be recorded there.

In October 1884, he left Hednesford to become an engineer's apprentice, with Harvey & Co., Hayle, Cornwall, where he stayed until 1890. He was in charge of the company's exhibit at the Crystal Palace Exhibition in 1890.

About 1890 or 1891 he went out to India as a mine manager. Beatrice could not remember the name of the firm or address of his mine or bungalow, but Harvey & Co. would know this. She believed that they supplied the machinery and ore crushers for this mine, and that they had something to do with his appointment.

In 1892 he had a severe attack of fever in India and was ordered home. Beatrice said she had cables related to this illness which could confirm the dates. He returned to The Mount, Hednesford and remained there during his convalescence. Around November 1892, he went to Beira, Africa, as an engineer. The family did not remember the address of the firm or his address. Beatrice suggested that if Anson wanted the Beira dates, he could get them from an ex-girlfriend of Frank's. They were nearly engaged, and had corresponded while her brother was in Beira and for some time on his return. She did not know why the relationship ended.

In March or April 1894, Frank returned to The Mount, Hednesford. Their father had died on 21 December 1893. Frank helped their mother settle into Hatherton House, Hatherton in June 1894. Sometime in the autumn of 1894, he went to Cardigan to manage Bridgend Foundry, owned by the Sharps' sister, Laura Kelly. She was then just widowed and was now Mrs Burge. He lived there in Fishguard in Pembrokeshire until the end of 1898 (probably October). About this date he went to Cliftonville, Cannock, residing there with their mother until September or October of 1899.

Shortly after, he left for Mexico and was last heard of by his mother at Christmas 1902.

A letter was received from him by his friend Tom Garland, a chemist in Cannock, in July 1904. Nothing had been heard of him since.

Beatrice enclosed the letter Frank had written to Tom. In it Frank said that he had not heard from his family for over twelve months despite writing to them. He hoped to hear back from Tom and know 'if they all are dead or alive'.[1] Frank wrote that for the last eighteen months he had travelled around all of Mexico in search of a climate that would suit him. The south gave him fever and dysentery and when he was in the north he had a cough and chest trouble. He had struck a medium in the state of Guanajuato where he now lived. He described his days in the city and asked Tom to see his mother and give his message. His mail could be sent to him c/o the British Consul, Mexico, Mexico City. 'I may be travelling and letters very often follow me around for weeks,' he wrote.

Beatrice said she did not know why Frank had not received their letters. They had written regularly to him.

I may say that Frank never once set his foot in Wyrley or the neighbourhood, & did not even know that such people as the Edaljis existed. The name Edalji was never heard in our house until the 1903 or 1904 outrages when in common with everyone else the case may have been discussed by any or all of us.[2]

The second brother, Herbert Sharp, was born in December 1870. He had gone to the same school as Frank until 1884 after which he went to Walsall School for a short time. He then went to Harvey & Co. in Hayle to join Frank as an engineering student in 1885. He remained with Harvey & Co. until 1891. He then worked with Pethwick Bros Contractors for about six months at Blagdon, Somerset. On leaving them, he went as engineer on a Mediterranean boat for twelve or eighteen months. He returned home on the death of their father and remained at Hatherton until about March 1895. He then went to Mexico and was in the employ of the United Mexican Mines Ltd, Great Winchester Street, London. He returned in February 1897, and visited their sister Laura in Cardigan. He became engaged and was married in June 1897. He left Cardigan with his wife for Mexico and returned to England early in 1901, going on to buy a house in Cardigan. He settled his wife there and turned back alone to Mexico where he stayed until about June 1902 when he returned to Cardigan and to his wife. He moved to Reading in 1903.

Herbert then had an appointment in Egypt with the Nile Valley Company in Egypt as an engineer and was there until April 1905. He came home to Reading on leave and went back to the same mine in Egypt before returning to Cannock in March 1906. He was living with his mother at Cliftonville until June 1907.

Their third brother, Walter Sharp (deceased), was born in 1876. Early days were spent at The Mount, Hednesford. He was educated at the Board School and Walsall Grammar School, which he left in 1893.

He was articled to Mr Sopwith, general manager of Cannock Chase Collieries, Chase Town, as a mining engineer student. He lived in lodgings at Chase Town and remained there until 1898. He went to manage Bridgend Foundry for their sister for about twelve months. In 1899, he was sub-manager of Atherton Collieries near Manchester. He stayed there for about fifteen months and left to take a post under the Champion Chanelling Co. 7 Craven Street, off the Strand in central London. His solicitor, H. F. Simpson, 4 Chapel

Walks, Manchester, would have all the dates of his movements which were uncertain as he was travelling abroad for the coal-channelling company. All letters were addressed c/o Mr Simpson who forwarded them until September 1904 when Walter became manager of the Durban Navigation Collieries, Damhauser, Natal, where he remained until his death in November 1906. Mr Sopwith could give full information as to his conduct at the Cannock Chase Colliery, said Beatrice.

Beatrice said she had also written to Wallie's solicitor and friend, Mr Simpson, for particulars on his movements.

'Frank, Herbert & Wallie had very little connection with Cannock,' said Beatrice. 'As for the Wyrley business I do not think anyone of the family heard of it until the 1903 outrages.'

Beatrice said that the elder siblings had never lived in Cannock. When her mother moved there, the family consisted of Royden, their niece Olive and for a short time, their sister, Mrs Robinson. Mrs Robinson left shortly after to be a nurse.

'The more I think over the thing the more am I amazed,' said Beatrice, who was shocked that her brothers were suspected of harassing the Edalji family. 'How could any person, on such slender links make a claim of suspicion against our boys. We have had less to do with Cannock & Wyrley than probably anyone in the district.'[3]

Beatrice had been in touch with her mother to ask for particulars, but she had learnt little. Her mother mixed up her four boys hopelessly, had been very worried lately, and being deaf made it even more difficult. She was over seventy years of age.

Anson immediately set to work with the information supplied by Beatrice. He wrote to Mr Sopwith, the general manager of the Cannock Chase Collieries, asking for information about the Sharps. He sent Sopwith a copy of Conan Doyle's statement on Royden Sharp and asked him to confirm whether Peter Sharp, their father, who worked at the old Hednesford Pit of the Cannock Chase Collieries, and was now dead, was indeed 'known to be a drunkard'.[4]

'Many or most of the statements are wild nonsense,' said Anson. 'But I should be greatly obliged if you would tell me what you can of the Sharp family and reading the case of Sir Conan Doyle,' said Anson.

Meanwhile, Beatrice was doing her best to help Anson. She wrote to him that he should perhaps check Frank's dates for return from India with his bank in Rugeley. It was near the Shrewsbury Arms Hotel and Mr Pratt was the manager there. Frank had made an arrangement with his firm that his monthly salary would be paid into the bank when he was in India and Beira. Their father, Peter, would then take charge of this (Mr Pratt was well acquainted with him) and he sent Frank a monthly or quarterly allowance back to India. Frank did not need much there as he was in the hill country and had no need of cash. The account could have been in Peter's name and the records would be there for when money was paid in and drawn out. Perhaps the name of the firm could also be found through the bank.

She informed Anson that Frank had become a freemason before going to India. He probably joined the Cannock Lodge of which their father was a member. Their father thought it would help him abroad. Beatrice herself left the house in 1884 and became a nurse and therefore knew little of her brother's movements as her own work was very absorbing. She was satisfied if she heard from him occasionally. 'I know so little of what happened at home,' she said.[5]

Beatrice was grateful to Anson for his advice about the family leaving the neighbourhood. Her mother, however, did not want to leave and felt that as 'Royden *positively* had nothing to do with the outrages or letters, no harm could come out of it.'

'We, who have seen more of the world, have proved that harm does come out of nothing,' said Beatrice. She informed Anson that she had implored her mother to leave, and if she did not want to herself, to at least send Royden away. Her sister, Mrs Robinson, was also trying to persuade her to leave. 'I am afraid we shall lose patience and they will have to fight things out for themselves.'

Beatrice was confident that if the person in Long Beach California was Frank, he would definitely reply as he had nothing to hide.

The letters from Anson and the fact that her brother was being watched by neighbours and the press, troubled Beatrice. She wrote again to Anson saying she had begged her mother to send Royden away '*at once*' and she had agreed. She was going to ask an uncle of theirs, who had a tobacco and cigar manufacturing unit in Hull to ask if he could find work for Royden in his factory for the time being. If nothing worked out, she said she would go personally to Cannock with her sister, Mrs Robinson, and perhaps their united efforts would move their mother. 'I shall put things very strongly to her hoping to frighten her.'[6]

The letters between Beatrice and Anson reveal that he was well aware of the Sharp family's efforts to get Royden away. He had clearly feigned surprise when he was informed by Beaumont that Frank and his mother planned to move and had sold their garden furniture. Anson was playing a double game.

Meanwhile, he had traced the company in London that had employed Frank and found the information he was looking for: Frank was employed from the end of 1890 till March 1893 by a company called the New Davala Moyar Gold Mining Company in Wayanad, South India (present-day Kerala). As the greater number of the 'God-Satan' letters were written towards the end of 1892 and in the first two or three months of 1893, it was clear that Frank could have had nothing to do with them. Anson wrote to Mrs E. A. Robinson, Frank's sister. 'I have long ago satisfied myself that Royden could not have written any of them. So there only remains Walter for Sir A. Doyle to accuse of the whole lot; so far he has only indicated him as being concerned in the "persecution" without specifying exactly in what way.'

He also informed Beatrice that he was convinced that Royden had not written the letters. 'No doubt other points will be raised when Sir A. C. Doyle comes home, probably Walter will be accused of doing the writing as he has already been mentioned as having been mixed up in the "persecution" of the Edaljis.'

Anson had seen Mrs Sharp, their mother, who had come to see him that day and said she would arrange for Royden to go away for a time. The police chief was glad to hear that: 'I am not creating an imaginary danger, but, if another maiming case occurred nothing would be easier than for evilly disposed persons to do what might seem to throw the strongest suspicion on Royden.'

Anson was feeling triumphant. He had gone out of his way and conducted the investigation himself to steer the blame from Frank and Royden Sharp. Unlike the Edalji case, where he was all too ready to believe the reports from Upton or Campbell about Edalji, and had never once visited the vicarage, or spoken to Shapurji and his wife, he was working methodically on the Sharps. He had personally visited their house, written letters to the entire Sharp family, the police in California and to Conan Doyle's informers in Great Wyrley: Arrowsmith, Greatorex and Beaumont. He himself was advising Royden to leave the village so he could not be accused of any future maiming. Yet, when George Edalji had said he did not want bail so that the next maiming would not be blamed on him, it was used against him in the trial to prove that he was part of a 'gang'. Whereas Edalji's pleas of innocence had been ignored, Anson was working differently when it came to the Sharps.

Meanwhile, there was further news coming out from California. The Edalji case had become a global investigation following Conan Doyle's intervention. The police chief, Geo Young, wrote to Anson with more details about Lewis the Light and the Frank Sharp in California. Lewis, who lived in The Ark, made a living by scouring the daily papers and other periodicals for names of people who were in the public eye or in trouble. He then cut out the piece and filling it with a lot of biblical references sent it to the person named and demanded they send him money. If they did, he would pray for them and if they didn't, he would see that they were damned.[7]

His true name was Lewis Burgess Greenslade, born at Witheridge, North Devon, England. He was five feet four and half inches in height and weighed 116 pounds. He was fifty-five and a half years old, had brown eyes, a grey beard and was missing the top part of his thumb, which had been removed as a punishment for committing a felony.

Before leaving England, Lewis had got into some sort of religious trouble and Sir Henry Knight of London would know all about him if they wanted to look him up. The police chief enclosed a copy of Lewis's handwriting, written in the presence of Detective Phillips.

The 'Ark' was a cheap boarding house and not a religious place. Lewis said he had read in the papers that Edalji was found guilty of mistreating some horses and that Arthur Conan Doyle was interested in the case and he had therefore sent the letter to him.

Young also sent a description of Frank Sharp. He was English, aged about thirty-eight, and his height was five foot seven inches. He had a brown moustache, grey eyes and a florid complexion from working on the railways laying tracks. He was a foreman. Sharp's address was care of A. Grieve, 744 Chestnut Avenue, Long Beach, California. The police chief thought he did not know Lewis.

Anson was satisfied that the letter and newspaper cutting had not been posted by Frank Sharp, and therefore he could not be the person who wrote the 'God–Satan' letters. The police chief was having a good day. He had also received another letter from Beatrice Sharp which had made him smile in triumph. It said the 'Frank Sharp' in the US was not her brother. Conan Doyle's case was rapidly unravelling and Anson was delighted.

Beatrice had written to the 'Frank Sharp' in the US, and he had replied to her very courteously saying that he was a Welshman who had been living there for some time and was very sorry to have raised false hopes of her brother being alive. He was delighted to know that Conan Doyle had been on the wrong track this time, but had to admit that it was a real coincidence that there was a Frank Sharp living in The Ark, the address from which the letter had been sent to Edalji.

It was an uncanny coincidence, and Anson knew that it would not be easy to take away the credit from Conan Doyle for having traced a Frank Sharp in the United States. To establish his case with Conan Doyle and the Home Office, he needed absolute confirmation of the same. He wrote to Geo Young at Long Beach police station saying it was necessary to clear the doubts placed in the case by Arthur Conan Doyle.

> I find that Sir A. C. Doyle is still not satisfied that the 'Frank Sharp' who he is seeking is not the person who was lodging at 'The Ark', nor is he satisfied that Frank Sharp did not have anything to do with Lewis and the communications sent by the letter … It is very particularly desirable to clear this matter up if possible. Can you very kindly let me know as nearly as can be ascertained the date when Frank Sharp left The Ark? This at any rate might throw some light on the question.[8]

Anson had also discovered that Royden had been at a school in Lincolnshire between 1892 and 1893. He had also been informed by a veterinary surgeon that the wounds inflicted on the horse could not have been caused by a fleam such as the one shown by Royden to Mrs Greatorex. He was delighted that he was unpicking Conan Doyle's theories. The author was expected back in England around the first week of November and the police chief could not wait to confront him with his mistakes. A warm glow of satisfaction was filling Anson. He would prove yet that policing was based on facts, and could not be handled by the creator of crime fiction.

He wanted the paperwork ready before Conan Doyle's return. Within a week, Anson had built his case. He wrote triumphantly to Greatorex that he had received a letter from Mr Layton, the headmaster of Upwell school, confirming that Royden had studied there. Since Frank Sharp was in India and Royden at Upwell, it was not possible for them to have written the letters together – as there were often two different handwritings on the same paper. Nor could they have – pushed them under the door, or thrown them into the garden at the vicarage at Great Wyrley.

> I consider that Sir A. Doyle has behaved with most unpardonable recklessness in making this charge, without any evidence whatever. It was anyhow open to him to ascertain, with your help, where these two were at the time in question, before he accused them of this misconduct.

Anson was ready to ambush Conan Doyle.

He informed Beaumont of the latest developments and received a reply acknowledging that mistakes had been made. However, Beaumont pointed out that Frank Sharp of Cannock had gone to work in Wales after he left school. He was a good draughtsman and worked in a colliery district and his employers had told Conan Doyle that he was 'drunken, reckless and immoral'.[9]

Beaumont, too, was struck by the many coincidences that had occurred. 'It begins to appear that many coincidences of this kind have in some degree led us astray. However it is only right to acknowledge mistakes of this kind and I hope Sir A. C. Doyle if he knows of it has already done so, for we cannot hope to get redress for one person by inflicting wrongs upon another ...'[10]

Anson then told Beaumont something that would startle him. He said that he had another reason for 'feeling *certain*' about the authorship of at least one of the 1903 Greatorex letters. It was far more than similarity of handwriting. 'I think a man who served in this force away from Cannock has found some pleasure and perhaps a little profit in making statements which will only mislead those who receive them: he was a man who wanted a promotion and did not get it.'[11]

Little is known of the person that Anson was referring to. If Anson had a hunch that someone in the police department was the author of at least some of the anonymous letters, why did he not pursue it? It was incredible that the chief of Staffordshire police simply looked away, and allowed George Edalji to take the blame.

Conan Doyle returned to England with his new bride after their long honeymoon. They had both enjoyed their travels and each other's company. Jean was intelligent and witty and challenged Conan Doyle. She was the perfect companion. He would later look back on his years with her and say: 'There are some things which one feels so intimately to be able to express, and I can only say that the years have passed without one shadow coming to mar even for a moment the sunshine of my Indian summer which now deepens into a golden autumn. She and my three younger children with the kindly sympathy of my two elder ones have made my home an ideally happy one.'[12]

He had been informed about the true identity of the F. Sharp in California, but was not fully convinced that he was not the same man as the one from Cannock. At any rate it was an amazing coincidence that there could have been an F. Sharp residing in The Ark from where a letter was sent to George Edalji.

There was also some good news on arrival.[13] The Law Society, at the prompting of Sir George Lewis, had readmitted George to the solicitors' roll. They had clearly decided that he was not capable of any dishonourable conduct. George was now free to practise. He had started working in a law firm in London. Conan Doyle felt a sense of quiet satisfaction at this result. George had been vindicated. He would never return to Birmingham or his house in Great Wyrley, but at least he could work again and regain his dignity. He had become an international celebrity.

Back in Windlesham, Conan Doyle continued his quest to prove George's complete innocence. He sent some of the 1903 letters to a French expert to examine them and give his opinion about whether they could have been written by George. A man of honour, Conan Doyle updated both Beaumont and Arrowsmith about his latest moves.

Meanwhile Anson continued to vent his anger with Conan Doyle on the hapless Beaumont. When Beaumont suggested that he had heard that the headmaster of Walsall had suspected Royden Sharp of stealing the school key and placing it at the vicarage door in 1892, Anson immediately blamed Conan Doyle for misleading him. 'Sir A. C. Doyle is very much to blame for his reckless habit of stating as facts matters which are only hearsay & not even first-hand hearsay,' he railed.[14]

The original copy of his letter has paragraphs deleted and other paragraphs written over, as Anson angrily made his case against Conan Doyle to Beaumont, concluding furiously that he had one of the postcards in his possession and 'it was no more written by Royden Sharp than by you or me, I have no doubt whatever as to the writer'. It is not clear who Anson was convinced was the writer: was it George Edalji, the discontented police officer, or a third unknown person?

Anson also referred to evidence he had obtained from Horace, George's younger brother. Horace had apparently told a friend that George had a habit of writing anonymous letters. The friend had informed the police. Anson wrote to Beaumont:

I have known of it all along ... it was one chief reason for the certainty which existed in my own mind: but Horace was very anxious to keep out of the case, naturally & so his evidence has scarcely been made any use of. Sir A. Doyle knows it, & of course nothing can explain it away. A public inquiry would have suited me far better than the hole in the corner sort of business, which has taken place & would have given me a chance of expressing a great many falsehoods.

There were too many unanswered questions, and Beaumont was completely confused.

The New Year had begun and the Edalji case was still burning. Conan Doyle was still demanding compensation for George. Letters were flying between Anson and the Home Office, between Anson and Conan Doyle and between Anson and Arrowsmith, Beaumont and Greatorex. Everyone was angry. George, meanwhile, had quietly resumed work as a lawyer, building a new set of clients. His certificates and framed medals lined his wall again. His fame was both a setback and an advantage. He was still campaigning for his compensation, but he had left Conan Doyle to continue the fight. At any rate, he was grateful he could at least resume his work. It had been four years since he had worked as a solicitor.

However, George missed his old life at the vicarage. He had not seen his family for months. He missed his conversations with his father and the outings he took with his sister Maud. He missed his long walks in the countryside. London, in contrast, was a busy city with horse carriages rattling down the streets, thousands of busy commuters going to work, hawkers loudly peddling their wares and the smoke from thousands of chimneys leaving a haze at night. Life had changed completely for him since that fateful day of August 1903, but George knew he had to simply take it on the chin and move on.

Towards the end of January, Anson received a letter from F. Sharp of Santa Ana, California. It was written under the company letter-head of the Pacific Electric Railway Company, Los Angeles Inter-Urban Railway. Sharp responded to the list of queries sent by Anson.

Asked whether he had been in Long Beach in March last, Frank Sharp replied: 'No.'

He said he had been employed by the above company since 1 June 1903 and was appointed to his present position on 1 January 1907, on which date he left Long Beach to take up residence in Santa Ana.

'The following particulars ought to convince Sir A. that he is on the wrong track,' wrote Sharp. 'You state Mr Frank Sharpe (*sic*) left his home about seven years ago, well let our Sir A. Doyle strike the trail as we say in this New World.'[15]

Sharp stated that he had been employed by William Pozzi in Welshpool, Montgomeryshire, in 1884 as a warehouseman. He left Welshpool to go to South Wales about the year 1892 and worked in Ferndale probably for twelve months. He then left there to work at Treharris R.S.O. where he remained until early 1895. He then moved to Nixon's Navigation Colliery, Merthyr Vale. He attached a testimonial from Nixon's which said: 'He has always been attentive to his duties and his conduct satisfactory; T Williams, Manager.'

He left England for the US on 14 September 1899, sailing from Liverpool on the SS *Scotsman* (Dominion Line) and was wrecked on Belle Isle, on which island they remained for three days till they were picked up by the SS *Montford* (Elder Dempster Co.). They landed in Rimouski and were sent from there to Quebec. He then went to Toronto where he remained until the following March, working for F. Simpson and Sons, grocers of 736–8 Yonge Street.

Sharp attached a copy of the letter about his employment:

Mr F. Sharp has been in our employ since Jan 1. We have found him industrious, sober and honest. He leaves of his own free will to British Columbia. F. Simpson.

He then went to British Columbia, working at Canmore Fernie Extension and Union but on account of the extreme cold, he left Canada and went to Southern California on 1 November 1901 and worked for the Los Angeles Pacific Railroad until June 1903.

'I do not remember another F. Sharp in Long Beach and as regards Lewis the Light, I do not know him, but I am informed he is a harmless religious maniac,' wrote Sharp. He attached other testimonials regarding his character. He said he hoped that Anson did not think he was being boastful but it was rather to show Sir A. Doyle, who he had always admired as a novelist, that he was 'making wrong deductions this time, possibly by an overdose of cocaine. I hope he will see that an apology is due to those much to be pitied ladies as well as to myself.'

Sharp said that friends and the people mentioned in the letter would vouch that this was his handwriting. He also enclosed a photo which he had taken for the company in working clothes in November 1904. He left The Ark in December of that year.

He added a postscript.

The funny part of all this is that my name is Fred not Frank but this is a country of nicknames and I am always *Shorty* to my friends and always signing myself F. When a letter comes addressed to Frank it must be for me (in the mines) especially coming from the old country. F.S.

Anson felt he had checkmated Sir Arthur Conan Doyle. Triumphantly, he thought, there would be no compensation for George Edalji.

# 21

# *Endgame*

Ever since the creator of Sherlock Holmes decided to fight the battle on behalf of a hesitant and awkward Parsee lawyer, exposing inefficiency and prejudice on the part of the police forces of Staffordshire, Anson had been his primary opponent. The volley of letters exchanged between the two shows how acrimonious this relationship had become. Anson saw Conan Doyle as a novelist and writer of fiction, incapable of a real police investigation. He resented the fact that legions of his fans were now seeing him as a crusader for justice for Edalji. Conan Doyle, on his part, saw the police chief as stubborn, prejudiced, unhelpful and considerably rude. Anson was prepared to go all out to humiliate Conan Doyle before the Home Office.

So obsessed was the chief constable with showing up Conan Doyle, that at one stage he actually laid a trap for him. The writer had been receiving threatening anonymous letters with London postmarks. Conan Doyle was convinced that Royden Sharp was behind them and would therefore have had to be in London at the time they were posted.

In a file marked 'Confidential' Anson relates the incident.[1] Anson deliberately asked Royden to buy a ticket for London and announce his date of travel 'in the most open manner'. Royden readily obliged, letting everyone who was willing to listen know that he was going to London. Anson knew that the news would get back to Conan Doyle via Beaumont or one of his other informers.

On the day in question, the informers were on the lookout. The railway-station porter, the ticket clerk and Beaumont were all watching as Royden boarded the train from Cannock. He would have to change in Birmingham for the London train. However, unknown to everybody, when Royden reached Birmingham, the ticket was taken from him. Accompanied by a police officer, Royden went in the other direction to the far end of the county. He spent a week there visiting public houses and helping the police locate offenders and made daily reports to Anson. Beaumont reported to Conan Doyle that he had left for London. Just as Anson had predicted, 'Sir A. Doyle wrote triumphantly that this time there was clear proof that the man had been in London: obviously therefore he was the writer of the threatening letters!' Meanwhile, Anson smugly kept the London ticket in his possession. It now lies in the archives at Portsmouth Library.

Quick to point out Conan Doyle's mistake, Anson attached a copy of the letter signed 'A. Nark', received by the author at the Grand Hotel and posted in London on 17 April 1907. He wrote on the file: 'It was on "evidence" and "proof" such as he obtained in the above described instance that the great Sherlock Holmes based his accusations.'

It was not the first time Anson had laid a trap. He had done this in 1903 to ensnare George Edalji by sending him an anonymous letter to confuse him. Anson revealed that the 'Lover of Justice' letter in 1903 which had been received by George Edalji, and had so perplexed the investigators, had actually been written under his instruction by a solicitor, C. A. Loxton. By strange coincidence, George had mentioned his name during his arrest and thought that Loxton had been involved in some way with the letters, Loxton being an old rival of his. The letter was posted in Rugeley by Anson himself. George had innocently passed the letter to the police. A few days later he handed Inspector Campbell the 'Greatorex' letter which said 'none of the people think you are the right sort'. The 'Lover of Justice' letter had a similar phrase: 'The people all said it must be you because they do not think you are the right sort.' To Anson it was proof that George wrote the 'Greatorex' letter using some of the same lines from the 'Lover of Justice' letter.

He allowed Conan Doyle to fall into the same trap. Conan Doyle asserted that the handwriting in the 'Lover of Justice' letter matched that of Wallie Sharp and that the language of both letters was similar. It was another way of showing up the author. It goes to George's credit that he was convinced that it was Loxton who wrote the Greatorex letter.

After the discovery of the true identity of F. Sharp in the USA, and the details of the movement of the Sharp brothers from 1892–95, Anson felt he had won round two of the battle against Conan Doyle. But he was still seething. Despite his making the case to the Home Office, Conan Doyle still had the popular vote. Through his newspaper articles, he had got the nation on his side, and had questioned and humiliated the police. He had restored George Edalji to the roll once again, allowing him to work as a solicitor. His anger against the popular author festered deeply. He made elaborate notes on every point raised by Conan Doyle and presented these to the Home Office as his final summing-up of the case.

One of the factors that apparently convinced Anson that George Edalji had written the letters was the fact that his brother Horace had claimed that George had the habit of writing anonymous letters. After George's arrest, Horace told his friend and neighbour Christopher Hatton that he believed that it was George who wrote the letters of 1892–95. Christopher told him to tell his parents immediately. Horace had always had a difficult relationship with his family. George and Maud were close, while he was isolated. His parents were full of praise for George, who was the brilliant one. He had won prizes in school and university and practised as a solicitor. In contrast, Horace never went to university and was a junior clerk in the civil service. He was hesitant about telling his parents, but apparently decided to do so, on Christopher's advice. Summoning up his courage, Horace went to the vicarage, but seated in the living room was Yelverton, and he could not speak up. He then decided to write to his mother and father.

His letter was not well received. Charlotte responded with a thirteen-page letter, asking why Horace had not spoken out in 1895 when the incidents occurred. Overnight Horace became *persona non grata* with his family. Though he attended one day of the pre-trial hearings, he did not attend the trial itself. It was George's parents and his sister Maud who stood by him attending every day of the proceedings. Horace wrote a letter to his friend Christopher giving the details and, consequently, an anonymous letter was sent to George's defence counsel, Vachell (either by Horace or by Christopher), giving the startling information that George had a habit of writing anonymous letters. Charlotte and Shapurji dismissed Horace's statement as the words of a disgruntled son and jealous younger brother. Horace did not want to be involved in the case and therefore his statement could not be produced in court. He remained confused and conflicted, however, torn between his suspicions and filial loyalty. In the letter to Christopher, Horace said he could not be certain of the truth. He even suggested that a man called Warne could have been responsible for the maimings.

In a Home Office file marked 'SECRET' is a note from Gladstone on 6 June 1907. It mentions a conversation the Home Secretary had had recently over dinner with Alfred Hazell, the MP for West Bromwich. Hazell told him that Vachell, George's solicitor, was actually convinced that Edalji had written the letters. When the trial was under way, a member of the family, probably Horace, had brought in a letter which had been found in one of George's drawers. It was brought as a specimen of George's handwriting to show that it was different from the anonymous letters. The letter was a long one of several pages. It contained several scraps of paper an inch or two in diameter. The letter was addressed to the maid at the vicarage and was full of foul 'unmentionable' language. It told her to put these scraps under the doormats and about the house. On the scraps were abusive remarks like 'Curse Edalji'. The letter had not been posted.

Vachell said he decided to suppress the letters as it would have been damaging to the case. When the 'Martin Molton' letters began in January 1907, he mentioned it to Hazell and apparently said: 'He's at it again.' Hazell, in turn, related the conversation to Gladstone at the Home Office. Hazell however said that Vachell firmly believed that George should not have been convicted based on the evidence produced in court, and that the Home Office had done the right thing by pardoning him.

The letter in the drawer remains a puzzle. It could have been just another of the letters received by George which he kept in his drawer. The vicarage had received several abusive notes written on scraps of paper in the period between 1892 and 1895. It was also questionable why the police had not removed it when they searched the house, if it had been lying in the drawer. Horace may have been prompted by jealousy to accuse George. Or he may genuinely have believed that he wrote it.

There was one person who believed Horace; it was Anson. Horace informed Christopher that George was short of money and in serious debt. He suggested that George had carried out the killings for money. He mentioned that he had been sent a bankruptcy petition and that George had made a trip to London around the time.

When things came to a head after the Home Office committee report, Anson wrote to Hatton requesting him to tell Horace to reveal what he knew about the letter-writing. Anson said that it would be far better if Horace told Conan Doyle himself, so that the latter could draw his own conclusions.

> If C.D. troubles me personally with his news about the letter-writing I shall tell him to ask Edalji and family to state to him candidly what Horace told him ... Anyhow I would rather the information came to Conan Doyle from Horace Edalji & not from me. But it has got to come from one of us.[2]

All Anson's anger was directed at Conan Doyle, who had stirred everything up.

'Is C.D. quite mad?' he asked.[3]

'Is he an utter fool as well as a knave?' he wrote to Stanley Blackwell at the Home Office and suggested that there were 'Popes and Emperors in Lunatic Asylums, so why not Sherlock Holmes!'[4]

In a letter to the Home Office he stated that Sir A. Doyle was 'consistently inaccurate' and questioned his methods. With reference to the letters from California he said: 'Sir A. Doyle ignored Lewis' name altogether and jumped to the conclusion that Frank Sharp was the writer, just as he had already (now, admittedly, in error) jumped to the conclusion that Frank Sharp wrote the God-Satan letters.

'The man in the US was named Frederick Sharp ... and had "no more to do with the Edalji case than has the President of the United States".'[5]

It was, said Anson, as the jury believed, George Edalji who had written the Greatorex letters.

Over the years, Anson remained obsessed with the case. His files contain the detailed, typed-up 51-point rebuttal of Conan Doyle's allegations.

Titled 'Notes on Sir A. C. Doyle's "Statement" of accusation against Royden Sharp', he presented his arguments.[6]

He stated that Conan Doyle had given a wrong account of the weapon Royden had shown to his aunt. Apparently, Mrs Greatorex was not sure that it was a 'horse lancet'. What she had seen was actually a large pocket knife with several blades, one of the blades being a veterinary fleam, as roughly sketched by Conan Doyle. Anson stated further that Mr Forsyth, the veterinary surgeon would testify that a fleam could not have caused some of the wounds.

He also denigrated Conan Doyle's description of Royden as having 'criminal tendencies' saying that he had got into trouble at the age of eleven or twelve for setting fire to a rick but it did not justify 'Doyle's sweeping statement'.

The 'forgery' in school was no more than a bogus letter that Royden had brought in once to excuse his absence from school, nor was he expelled from school. 'The boy was "removed by his father",' said Anson. 'Royden Sharp was a lazy, idle boy at school, but this does not convict him of killing horses.'

Anson supported Royden again and said that even if he went to Liverpool to become an apprentice on a sailing ship, it was unthinkable that he had gone to Blackpool to post a letter containing a hoaxing advertisement which he was not clever enough to have composed. Moreover, Anson said that the character shown on his discharge notes were uniformly 'very good'. Conan Doyle himself had said he had communicated with the captain of the ship who had given Sharp a good character. His four years' apprenticeship record was 'sober, diligent and attentive to his duties'.

He also claimed that there was nothing that suggested that the Sharps had a hatred for the Edaljis, as many people in the village received these letters. He said the writing began in 1889 when Royden was a child.

'Does not Doyle understand that all these people (Greatorex included) lived at Hednesford and that Sharp lived at Cannock and some distance away? The Sharp and Greatorex families would not have the same immediate friends as they were not close and lived about two miles apart. It was not true to suggest as Doyle had done that Sharp and his family were the only people who could know exactly the same circle,' said Anson.

He noted that Doyle identified the 'Lover of Justice' letter as having been written by Wallie Sharp. In fact, Anson knew that this could not possibly be true, as he himself had planted the 'Lover of Justice' letter.

At a later date, Royden Sharp went to prison on a larceny charge. During this period, the Darby letters continued: 'therefore I suppose even Doyle would admit that Sharp could not have been Darby,' said Anson.

'What a tangled web he weaves!' he said about Conan Doyle. The author, he said, had suggested that Royden had gone to Rotherham and posted a letter, but actually the letter in question was posted from Walsall. Neither was it Royden Sharp and his two friends who allegedly threatened a young girl and her mother, Mrs Handley, when they were on their way from Great Wyrley station. Anson thought the incident was just a practical joke and that there was no 'terror in the district'.

> Doyle got people to write to him [Royden], in sham friendliness, to get his writing: I saw these things, and of course instructed the man to take no notice. Sharp does not live with a pen in his hand, like Doyle. And I should think very seldom indeed puts pen to paper: Doyle I suppose can hardly understand such a possibility.

Anson saw no significance in the wording of one of the letters which was 'I am as Sharp as Sharp can be' and described it instead as 'merely Sherlock Holmes varnish'.

Given that Anson himself had allowed the prosecution of George on flimsy and circumstantial evidence, it was ironical that he would declaim against Conan Doyle: 'A man must be stark mad to really believe that the "evidence" so far adduced could in any way be sufficient for a prosecution, let alone a conviction.'

In another statement to the commission on the Edalji case, Anson said that Conan Doyle needed to be exposed for his inaccuracies as his accusations of inaction against the police were very serious.

'The public has not yet learnt to appreciate Sir Arthur Doyle's statements at their true value: ... and therefore mere silence is not, I consider, a sufficient and satisfying answer to the imputations made by him against the good faith of the police in this matter,' said Anson.[7]

The Home Office did no such thing. Although they remained firm on not giving any compensation to George, they did not want to make a public spectacle of humiliating Conan Doyle. His crusade slowed down over the next few years but did not stop.

In August 1911, a schoolboy called George Archer-Shee was paid substantial compensation by the Admiralty in a widely reported case. The Admiralty had unjustly charged him with stealing a postal order belonging to a fellow student and expelled him from the government school that he attended. The case was brought before the House of Commons and the Secretary to the Admiralty admitted the wrong done to the youth and appointed a committee for compensation. His father claimed £10,000 but the committee awarded him £7,000.

Shapurji wrote a letter to the *Daily Telegraph* bringing up the case for compensation again. He recalled that the commission appointed by the Home Secretary to report on the case of his son George Edalji had admitted that the charge of horse-maiming was wrong but they did not repay the heavy expenses that he was compelled to incur:

If Mr Archer-Shee's was a case in which compensation to the amount of £7,000 was to be made, my son's was a case in which a greater compensation ought to have been made. Mr Arthur-Shee was not even formally indicted but was simply sent home. My son was put in prison, kept with felons, robbed of his liberty and ruined in his professional business; and for defending him and for appealing to the Home Secretary for him I was driven to ruinous expenses; yet neither the late Home Secretary not the present one has done anything to compensate my son or to repay the heavy expenses which I was compelled to incur.

Mr Archer-Shee's father is a squire, and therefore £7000 is paid to him. My son cannot claim a squire as his father, therefore the Home Office and the government can disregard his case. Is this justice? Is this Liberalism?[8]

Conan Doyle immediately followed up the letter. Writing from Berlin, he thanked the *Daily Telegraph* for always giving generous space to those who pleaded the cause of the 'ill-used Edalji'.

He said he had been campaigning for years to get this matter set right but had almost abandoned the task in despair in the face of the obstinacy of the officials and the callousness of the public. He said he had approached the new Home Secretary (Winston Churchill) about the matter, but was met by the 'chose jugée' (the case is closed) attitude that had excited Britain's national indignation against France during the Dreyfus case.

'At the same time, I have such confidence in Mr Winston Churchill's clearness of vision and sense of justice that I am convinced that if the undenied and undeniable facts were laid before him he would instantly see how untenable is his position, and contrive that justice be done.'[9]

Apprehensive that the new Home Secretary, who was a friend of Conan Doyle's, would reopen the case, Anson continued to write to the Home Office and to Conan Doyle. In his last two replies to Anson written in 1911, Conan Doyle's anger had reached boiling point.

'I do not as a rule answer your letters because they are uncourteous in manner & as unreasonable in matter that I do not think they deserve an answer. If I answer this one at some length it is rather in the hope of bringing to an end a correspondence which is a waste of time and energy,' he wrote.

When I had convinced myself of the innocence of Edalji, I set myself to procure his pardon, and this, which was my only object, I successfully accomplished, though to the deep disgrace of British administration he has been given no compensation for the grievous wrong which he had suffered.

In the course of proving Edalji innocent I came across indications of another man's guilt. This I laid before the Home Office as I conceived it to be my duty to do. I did not lay it before the Staffordshire police because they had been so involved in the original scandal that I thought it should go before an independent authority. It was admittedly not a complete case, but it was a case which might well have been the foundation for a thorough independent investigation. It included a number of assertions as to facts, calligraphy etc, every one of which I believe to be absolutely accurate, save for coincidence (which was not in the least vital to the case) of there being two men of the same name in California.

I have changed no opinion since, nor have I seen any reason in any letter you have sent me to do so. My opinions were not based on one or two witnesses, but as my Home Office statement showed upon a number fortified by the opinions of experts on handwriting. *I have no doubt at all that the Martin Molton letters came from the source indicated.*

When Arrowsmith says that I tried to trace the man's movements on the day a letter was posted in London it is quite true. What then? The result of my enquiry was that he could not have posted it himself. There is nothing wonderful in this, or unusual in the use of an intermediary. It in no way disproves my case, as you appear to imagine.[10]

Incensed by the letter, Anson replied:

You complain my letters are uncourteous in manner. Let me remind you of one or two things. Beginning to write to me with an assumption of friendliness, on the pretence that you were *about to make* an investigation of the Edalji case, when you had in fact already made up your mind on the subject and had probably written most of the matter which you afterwards sub-edited and published in the Daily Telegraph, you got what you could out of me and then did your best (though this amounted to little enough) to turn it to my disadvantage. You had not even the decency to return to me documents which I had lent to you, when I asked you to send them back. That I had treated you in a perfectly courteous manner you at that time freely acknowledged.

Later on, finding that the Home Office authorities were, after some little experience of your methods, not as ready as at first they had been to accept your statements and assurances as being genuine, you descended so low as to attempt to discredit me with the Home Secretary by making a lying accusation of a peculiarly offensive and objectionable nature against me. Fortunately, I had your letters and mine to prove your falsehood. Then, finding that this proceeding had not answered your purpose, you were not ashamed to try and screen yourself with the flimsy excuse that the poor miserable wretch Churton Collins had put the accusation into your head.[11]

The issue that Anson was so angrily referring to was about the sleeping arrangements between Shapurji and George at the vicarage, and the statement that Anson had made that he presumed the vicar had 'good reason' for getting the boy to sleep with him.

Anson claimed he had meant that Shapurji locked the door to prevent George from getting out for his night-time activities. Conan Doyle took it as a suggestion from the police chief of sodomy by the vicar. Given that this was suggested in the anonymous letters as well, Conan Doyle felt it was a rumour that was being circulated in the village. He referred the matter to the Home Office in a meeting he had with Gladstone, Blackwell and Chalmers, the Undersecretary of State, saying Anson had accused Shapurji of 'sodomitical practices' with his son George. He said that his friend John Churton Collins (a professor at Birmingham University) knew there were rumours in Great Wyrley about the vicar's alleged sodomy.

On receiving a letter from Blackwell about this, a furious Anson had accused Conan Doyle of 'abominable lies'.

Conan Doyle was not prepared to listen to Anson deride his friend Churton Collins:

Your letter is a series of inaccuracies mixed up with a good deal of rudeness, but so far as it all regards myself, I can disregard such nonsense. When however you describe the late Professor Churton Collins, a man whose boots you are not worthy to blacken, as a 'miserable wretch' you only degrade yourself.

It was clear he did not want any more to do with Anson and his rantings.

Instead he brought up the matter of Anson's rude letter with the Home Secretary. Churchill's office assured him that a strong letter was being sent to Anson. For Conan Doyle, it was time to cut off Anson completely.

On 9 March, Anson received a letter from Lewis & Lewis, solicitors to Conan Doyle. It curtly informed him: 'Sir Arthur Conan

Doyle has requested us to write to you asking that you will not at any future date address him personally but that if you have any communication to make in connection with the case you will address it to us on his behalf.'

The chief of Staffordshire police would not go quietly. In a letter to the Home Office, he said that he had stated four years ago that Sir A. Doyle's allegation was an 'abominable falsehood', and so it was no different that he had accused him of 'lying'. He added: 'And I shall have as much pleasure in using the same word as often as may be necessary until he has apologised to me.

'This matter is a personal one between Sir A Doyle and myself.'[12]

It was clear that Anson would carry the grudge against Conan Doyle all his life.

# 22

## *Aftermath*

The years passed by in London and Great Wyrley, George working in his solicitor's office in Southwark, his walls once again decorated with his certificates and medals, his father – older and frailer – still conducting the Sunday service at Great Wyrley, baptising children and burying the dead. Horace, who had been cut off by the family, married Annie Magee of Corsham, Wiltshire, in 1907. The wedding took place in Glasgow. As a final rejection of the Edalji family and his Parsee roots, he took his wife's surname, Magee, in 1911 and buried his past. He later moved to Ireland with his wife.

The killing of horses continued sporadically over the years till 1935, as did the G. H. Darby letters, threatening policemen, prison governors and even Anson himself. Journalists would often turn up at the vicarage to ask Shapurji's opinion on the killings or letters. Commenting about a spurt of letters and some fresh mutilations in 1912, George said that his main concern was the 'ludicrous' efforts of the police over the last nine years. He told the journalists that the police should get rid of the notion that anyone whose name they were unable to spell or pronounce was a foreigner, or that foreigners were most likely to commit such ferocious crimes.[1] But the Great Wyrley killings were gradually fading from people's memories.

In 1913, Shapurji received an anonymous letter in which the writer said obscene things about him and demanded that he pay him £5 which he should send to the Liverpool GPO. Shapurji sent the letter to the police chief in Liverpool and requested that if anybody called for a letter at the Liverpool post office (which he, Shapurji, would send addressed to a G. Robinson), the person should be arrested.

The Liverpool police chief sent Anson a copy of the anonymous letter and Shapurji's letter to them.

Anson dismissed the letter and immediately said it had probably been written by George. He said that George, who he described as being 'niggerish in appearance', may have gone to Liverpool with his 'dumpy' sister Maud to meet debt collectors and posted it from there. The offensive letter lies in the files in the National Archives.

'It is quite possible that Edalji's sister, who is I believe a dumpy little thing slightly after his own pattern but not nearly so niggerish in appearance, may have been with him. If any proof of this should at any time be obtained it would be more than interesting to me as showing that she is in league with him, and this would explain a good deal of past history,' wrote Anson.[2]

Anson's contempt for the Edaljis was in sharp contrast to his attitude to the Sharps. His opinion of Royden Sharp did not change even when he received a report from Superintendent W. M. Grove at Cannock police station in September 1913 that Wilfred Greatorex had called in at the police station and said that Royden Sharp had been drinking heavily and threatening to kill his mother and sister. Greatorex had said that he was certain that Royden was mad and that he was afraid of him. He had also stolen money and silver spoons belonging to his mother.

On 1 September, Royden's mother and his sister, Mrs Robinson, came to the police station and took out a warrant for theft against Royden, who was arrested. Mrs Robinson said she was sure that he had a revolver and a large dagger but the police could not find it. They found a large hunting knife, 'very blunt and rather rusty' hidden in a drawer in the linen press, and some cartridges in his bedroom. Royden pleaded guilty, and was remanded in custody. On 8 September he was presented in court and charged with stealing three silver spoons and two pounds and given a sentence for six months' hard labour.[3]

Conan Doyle and Jean Leckie had three children and life was a whirl of family gatherings, travelling, writing and socialising. There was also the case of Oscar Slater. In 1912, it was the second real-life case that Conan Doyle took on after that of George Edalji.

On the evening of 21 December 1908, an elderly lady, Miss Marion Gilchrist, eighty-two, was found murdered in her flat in Glasgow. Her head had been smashed and a gold crescent brooch stolen. The police were told by a fifteen-year-old eyewitness, that she had seen a man running out of the close which led to Miss Gilchrist's street just after 7 p.m. wearing a Donegal hat and light coat. He was dark, clean-shaven and his nose was slightly twisted towards the right side. Oscar Slater, a thirty-nine-year-old German Jew, who had visited a pawn shop to sell a brooch, was reported to the police. The physical description of the man in the hat matched that of Slater. The police soon realised that the brooch in question that had been pawned by Slater was not Miss Gilchrist's brooch. It had been pawned long before the murder took place. However, all the facts were covered up at the trial and Slater was made a scapegoat.

He was arrested, tried, found guilty and sentenced to death. However, his lawyer organised a petition signed by 20,000 people that the evidence was circumstantial, and the death sentence was commuted to life imprisonment. The case interested Conan Doyle who published *The Case of Oscar Slater* in 1912 calling for a full reprieve for the accused. Once again, Conan Doyle rose to the defence of an innocent prisoner and set out his arguments with forensic precision, fighting for the release of the man held in Peterhead prison. Unlike with George Edalji, he did not go to the scene of the crime or make his own investigations. He merely pointed out the flaws at the trial. Slater may have been a gambler and a man of disrepute, but he was not the murderer. But the attitude against Germans was hardening and soon events in Europe would overtake Conan Doyle and Slater.

On 4 August 1914 as Big Ben struck 11 p.m., Britain entered the Great War against Germany. The next four years would see the railway stations packed with young men setting off for the front, some mere teenagers, charged up with the idea of fighting for king and country. Within months the trains would be full of injured soldiers returning home, an army of walking dead, shell-shocked and changed for ever.

Conan Doyle, fifty-five at the time, knew he was too old to serve at the front line but was determined to do something. Immediately, he began to organise a Volunteer Reserve company in Crowborough. Writing in his memoirs, he later described himself as 'old Bill, the very last line of defence'.

One day in 1915, he stood in his garden with Jean and heard a deep throbbing sound. The sound rose and fell. Both of them realised that it was the rumble of artillery fire that was floating from the trenches in Flanders, just over a hundred miles away across the Channel. 'I find it very hard to do nothing,' he wrote to his mother. The family was out at the front line – Captain Malcolm Leckie, Jean's favourite brother, and his brother, Innes, now Lieutenant Colonel Innes Doyle. Woodie, now Major Woods, was also in France. Arthur wrote to the War Office, offering his service as a doctor on the front. He knew he was old, and had not practised as a doctor for a while, but he could help with the wounded. The War Office politely refused.

At the beginning of September, Kingsley, his son, joined the Royal Army Medical Corps. Soon the news of the deaths started arriving in Windlesham. In late December, a distraught Jean heard of the death of Malcolm Leckie, killed at Mons. He was posthumously awarded the DSO. Conan Doyle's sister, Lottie, lost her husband. On the mantelpiece in his study, Conan Doyle put up the photos of the family who had gone to war. It was soon to become a memorial site with decorations that they had received. He spent the rest of the war giving lectures and writing a history of the war.

In London, George Edalji watched as the young men went to fight in the trenches. He was thirty-eight years old and his eyesight made him unfit for service. He continued to work in Southwark taking up a small number of cases.

One and a half million Indian soldiers volunteered for the First World War and went to fight in the freezing, muddy trenches of France and Flanders. Many of the injured were brought to England, to be treated in hospitals in Brighton, Brockenhurst and New Milton. Those who recovered were taken for sightseeing tours to the capital, and Londoners experienced for the first time the presence of a large number of turbaned soldiers. But there remained the fear that lonely white women would mix with them, and consequently they were banned from visiting them in hospital. Nor were the Indians allowed to go around unescorted or without passes. English nurses were also not allowed to tend wounded Indians, leading to accusations from the soldiers that they were thought good enough to fight and die for England, but not good enough to be treated by English nurses.[4]

The war had brought changes in Great Wyrley and the surrounding villages. Training camps were set up in Cannock Chase for British and New Zealand servicemen. Rows of barracks were built over the fields in Cannock Chase and the rumble of guns and artillery training could be heard in Brockton Camp and Rugeley Camp. Prisoners of war were also brought to camps in the area. Charlotte threw herself into community work, was active with the local Red Cross Society of Cheslyn Hay and helped raise money for the Soldiers and Sailors Fund.

Shapurji, who was rapidly losing his eyesight, consoled the families grieving for their lost ones. With the war claiming more lives, memorial services and prayers for the dead became regular in St Mark's Church. By 1916, the frail and blind Shapurji could not even fill the parish register, relying on the church wardens to do so. Maud would often guide her father up the pulpit steps where he continued to preach till the end. His final vestry meeting was in Easter 1918 at which he appointed a church warden. A week later he suffered a cerebral haemorrhage. Five weeks later, on 23 May, Shapurji Edalji died at the vicarage, his wife and daughter by his side.

George came up from London, distraught at the death of his father. Till the end, his father had continued to fight for compensation for him. Horace, the estranged son, joined the family in mourning. Briefly, the family were united again in grief at the vicarage. The villagers attended the funeral and paid their respects to the Parsee from India whose life had been defined by struggle and duty and who was finally buried in a churchyard thousands of miles from the place he was born. The *Cannock Chase Courier* described him as a 'faithful and devoted pastor'. He had served as vicar for forty-two years.

A few months after the death of Shapurji, the war was over. The names of the dead and those who had served were commemorated on a memorial in Great Wyrley. Two hundred and eighty-six young men from Great Wyrley had gone to war. The village had lost twenty-five of them. The memorial which stands on Walsall Road has some familiar names: five members of the Farrington family are mentioned, including a T. Farrington (Thomas Farrington, the uncouth miner who was arrested in 1904). There were also two members of the landowning Hatton family including a C. Hatton (possibly Christopher), friend and confidant of Horace. Listed on the plaque is one member of the Greensill family (the man who was close to John Hart the butcher), and a Whitehouse (the insurance agent, who had last seen George enter the vicarage at 9.30 p.m. on the night of 17 August 1903). Lastly, there was a T. H. Morgan (possibly Thomas Hollis Morgan, the man wrongly arrested for killing two horses in 1907). All of them had survived.

His father's funeral was the occasion of George's last visit to Great Wyrley. Charlotte moved out of the vicarage with Maud after an emotional farewell from her parishioners who gave her a wallet and £30 as a farewell gift.[5] They moved to Coalbrookdale, a village in the Ironbridge Gorge in Shropshire, to live with her sister Mary Sancta. However, Mary Sancta, who was older than Charlotte, died within a few months. The funeral took place in their childhood church of Ketley, where the sisters had been baptised and where their father had been the vicar. Horace travelled from Ireland again for the funeral, his second meeting with his family in a few months. The tragedies had not healed the relationship, however. Mary Sancta had left her all her money to Charlotte, her 'favourite nephew' George and niece Maud. George and Maud received £1,404 18s 4d to be divided between them.[6] Horace remained an outsider.

Maud looked after Charlotte for the next few years, becoming chief carer to her as she had been to her father. However, when Charlotte's health deteriorated, she moved her to a care home in Shrewsbury. In March 1924, after a life devoted to her late husband and family, and dedicated to the service of the poor, Charlotte died. It was time for the three siblings to be united again as they said their final goodbye to their mother. Horace came with his wife, and once again there was a marked tension in the air: Charlotte had left all her money to George and Maud (£2,814 5s) and cut him from her will.[7] Charlotte was buried at St Mary's in Ketley next to her parents and her sister. It was the church in which she had married Shapurji all those years ago.

The death of Charlotte was the final break from the past for the Edaljis. Maud lived for a while at the house in Coalbrookdale but then moved to Welwyn Garden City, so she was within commuting distance from her brother in London. Neither sibling ever married.

And what of Anson, the man who had vowed to get 'penal servitude' for George Edalji when he was a mere teenager, and who had gone head to head with Sir Arthur Conan Doyle over the Edalji affair?

Over the years, he had festered over the Edalji case and his clash with Sir Arthur Conan Doyle. It was obvious, that despite making mistakes, Conan Doyle had had the moral victory. He had managed to get a free pardon for George and made him an international celebrity. The Staffordshire police had not come out of the whole business looking good.

In a final bid to set the record straight, Anson wrote a detailed report of the Edalji affair, with particular reference to the points raised by Conan Doyle. He enjoyed pointing out the mistakes made by the great writer and stressed that actual police work was different from writing fiction. The statement was marked 'For Police Information' and was clearly meant to go into the official records. He warned of the great damage that would result from the 'general adoption of Sherlock Holmes methods'.

Anson cleared Horace of any suspicion, saying 'I may say at once that no shadow of suspicion has ever existed against him ... I am satisfied that the brother Horace Edalji has always deservedly borne the character of an honourable and upright Englishman: he never came into this case at all ... except with regard to an incident of his having accidentally put on his brother's coat and finding in it a document which caused him to warn his brother against what he was doing.'[8]

He dismissed Conan Doyle's suggestion that the motive was 'colour hatred' as it was too much work to be done for that reason and because letters were also sent to others in the village. Anson further dismissed the theory of 'persecution' as having an 'Eastern flavour' and declared that there was not the faintest connection to be discovered on this ground.

A note in the Home Office files reveals that Anson had been ready to go into the witness box during the trial, but Disturnal thought that if it was revealed that the police were forging letters, it would go against him. Anson, had after all, deliberately sent an anonymous letter to George Edalji.

As a result the real authorship of the 'Lover of Justice' letter was never disclosed to the general public. Neither George nor Conan Doyle knew that Anson was behind it. At the trial the jury were made to believe that George had written it.

Anson continued in service with the Staffordshire police. He was honoured with a CBE in 1925 and retired as chief constable in 1929. He was made a KCB in 1937 and died ten years later.

He may well have been scornful of Conan Doyle, but it is clear that he did not employ the meticulous methods of investigation that he later used to trace the background details of the Sharp family. When Inspector Campbell accused George Edalji of the killings and letter-writing, he did not once visit Shapurji and Charlotte at the vicarage, nor did he follow his own rules – that he laid out so strenuously in the case of Royden Sharp – to ensure that a man was innocent until proven guilty. It was clear that Anson and his team had decided that George was guilty and went about collecting 'evidence' to prove their point. The lackadaisical method used by the police was evident even to the layman. At every stage, the police and the counsel for the prosecution distorted and misrepresented facts. The jury was blatantly misled.

Anson's attitude to George Edalji was in complete contrast to his dealing with Royden Sharp. In George's case he was actually setting up traps – sending him an anonymous letter that had been written under his orders. In Royden's case he was protective, repeatedly telling the family that they should leave the area. He went to the extent of wilfully misleading Arthur Conan Doyle just so that he could embarrass him before the Home Office. He never had a good word for the vicar, who had worked tirelessly in the community. The only person he could exonerate was Horace Edalji as his account fitted in with Anson's theory about George. When he described Horace as an 'honourable and upright Englishman' it was clear that he did not think that the Asian Vicar of Great Wyrley, or his studious son with the bulging eyes and 'niggerish' colouring, were honourable or upright. So scornful was he of George's plea of suffering from severe myopia that he told the Home Office that he actually saw better at night, as his eyes glowed in the dark like a cat. On no account was George considered an 'Englishman'. Anson wrote his version in the police files, hoping to ridicule Conan

Doyle, but he unintentionally showed up his own prejudice in the case.

Maud was convinced that Anson's antagonism towards her family stemmed from racial prejudice. 'Captain Anson seemed to have a prejudice against us because our skins were darker than other people's – I always feel that colour prejudice had a good deal to do with the Chief Constable's attitude,' she wrote in a detailed letter to Hesketh Pearson, biographer of Arthur Conan Doyle, in 1956.[9]

The famous author, too, had not been without fault. Despite his meticulous investigations into Royden Sharp and his family, he had not checked the dates that the brothers, Frank and Wallie, lived in the area. Afterwards, he was triumphantly proved wrong on these by Anson. If Conan Doyle had simply written to Beatrice Sharp, there would have been no confusion. Perhaps it would be fair to say that he suffered in a way from the same problem as Anson: once his mind was made up about the culprit, he chose to find information that suited the case. By linking Royden Sharp to the 1892 letters, and insisting that he was the one who wrote the Greatorex, Martin Molton and other letters, he inadvertently weakened his own case. It could well be that Royden – a habitual troublemaker – may have got involved from 1903 after he returned to Great Wyrley.

Conan Doyle himself remained convinced that Royden was the killer and the author of the letters. He wrote in his memoirs: 'The mistake that I made … was that having got on the track of the miscreant I let the police and Home Office know my results before they were absolutely completed.'[10] He believed there was a strong prima facie case, but it needed the cooperation of the authorities to 'ram it home'. That cooperation, he said, was wanting.

Meanwhile, Conan Doyle had some more professional satisfaction with the Oscar Slater case. He had taken up his cause in 1912, but the war had taken over, and Slater remained in jail. In 1925, Slater smuggled a letter out of prison. It was an appeal to Conan Doyle to help him. He had been impressed with Conan Doyle's intervention in the Edalji case and asked if he might once again help to prevent a miscarriage of justice. Conan Doyle renewed his call for the release of Slater, personally contributing towards his legal fees. Once again he picked flaws in the case, though he did not personally investigate it, as he had done with George. Slater was eventually released in 1928 and received £6,000 compensation. Conan Doyle met him in the courtroom and shook his hand. However, unlike George, who enjoyed Conan Doyle's friendship and support through his life, Slater did not win over his benefactor. They fell out when Conan Doyle asked Slater to refund those who had contributed their personal money towards his defence after he had won compensation. Slater refused, and Conan Doyle would have nothing more to do with him.

Conan Doyle continued to ask for compensation for George. But his plea fell on deaf ears. He wrote in his memoirs that he, too, had received letters threatening to kill him, making him sure that the people he was dealing with were insane as well as criminal. However, the Home Office did not care, and he mentally began to class them as insane too.

> The sad fact is that the officialdom in England stands solid together, and that when you are forced to attack it, you need not expect justice, but rather that you are up against an un-avowed Trade Union the members of which are not going to act the blackleg to each other, and which subordinates the public interest to a false idea of loyalty.

The tribal loyalties of the establishment had always irked Conan Doyle and it did so more than ever over the Edalji case.

During the post-war years, Conan Doyle travelled incessantly, drawing large crowds to his lectures in Europe, Australia and the US. The writing continued as usual, a two-volume book on spiritualism, and *The Case-Book of Sherlock Holmes*. His study in Windlesham in Crowborough still had the photographs on the mantelpiece of the family members lost in the war. His son Kingsley had died in October 1918, just a few days before Armistice Day. His brother, Innes, had died of pneumonia in France in 1919 even as he was returning after the fighting. Woodie, thankfully, had survived and was back as his secretary.

Arthur had become weak, but he continued to write. He was working on a Regency tale when the end came. On 7 July 1930, he was short of breath and needed oxygen. He saw the sunrise through the open windows of his bedroom and asked his family to help him to a chair. There, seated near the window in his dressing gown, surrounded by his three children, Denis, Adrian and Lena Jean, he held Jean's hand and closed his eyes for the final time.

He was buried in the grounds of Windlesham, near the garden hut where he had often worked through the summer days writing his stories and essays.

George read the news of Conan Doyle's death in the papers. He now wore specially made glasses, and looked different from the bulgy-eyed awkward young man who had been arrested in his office in Birmingham and who had written desperately to the author he admired so much. His hair was grey, his look sober. Optometry had progressed and his eyesight could at last be partially corrected. He picked up his pen to write a condolence letter to Jean. Another chapter of his life had come to a close.

⌒⌒

The years went by for the Edalji family. George moved in to live with Maud in the mid thirties, commuting daily from the house in Brockett Street, Welwyn Garden City, to his office in London.

The maiming of cattle and the Darby letters continued.

In 1934, after another series of cattle-killings, George wrote an article in the *Daily Express*. It was subtitled 'By the man who was wrongly imprisoned' and carried a picture of an older George seated in his office.

'The story of these maimings of horses and cattle will no doubt seem to the present generation more like a wild thriller than a description of events that happened in an English village,' wrote George. 'Older people will remember the widespread sensation which the "Terror that walks by night" as he was called, created at the time.'[11]

In 1935, a man called Enoch Knowles was convicted at the Staffordshire Assizes for sending menacing letters through the post. Anson's successor, Colonel H. P. Hunter, believed that Knowles was the writer of the anonymous and pseudonymous letters which had begun thirty years ago when the cattle-maiming commenced in 1903. From 1907, he had signed himself as 'Captain Darby' of the Wyrley gang. However, it was doubtful whether Knowles killed the horses and cows.

Minutes from a Home Office meeting record that the ministry thought that Knowles could have been the author of the letters ascribed to George Edalji. However they felt that the Edalji case was 'very old history' and since they could not definitely prove that Knowles was responsible, and Edalji had been cleared of the conviction and was not 'apparently in straitened circumstances' it seemed 'useless to reopen his case'.[12]

The Darby letters stopped after the arrest of Knowles. They had started when George was in prison, so he was never accused of writing them. Whether the same person wrote the 'Greatorex' letters, the anonymous letters in 1903, and finally the 'Martin Molton' letters was never confirmed.

The people of Great Wyrley never really had closure as to who had killed the horses and cattle in 1903. Could it have been John Hart the butcher or Farrington (who was arrested later)? Or could it have been Royden Sharp as Conan Doyle thought? He had after all returned to the area from 1903 and the police had found a large hunting knife in his house years later. He had been arrested for theft and was clearly violent and disturbed. Conan Doyle was convinced that the killings of 1903 and 1907 were of a different nature from the later ones. He was also convinced that it was the job of two men, since two horses were killed on one night in two different fields in 1907. Could these have been done by Royden in collusion with someone else?

The Edaljis never got confirmation about who wrote the threatening letters of 1892–95 and later. On her deathbed in 1905, Elizabeth Foster swore to her husband that she had not written them. Was it a disgruntled police officer, as Anson had suspected? He had never followed the trail. Or was it someone totally different?

In 1893, Shapurji had sent details to the police about people who may be involved in writing the letters. He named a James Morgan, an insurance agent, who wrote for certain newspapers. He lived with his sister in Upper Landywood in Great Wyrley. He was a man of talent and education, but had fallen on hard times. He was reputed to be able to write in different styles of handwriting. Hearing the rumours flying about him, Morgan called at the vicarage and showed Shapurji a book containing specimens of his different styles of handwriting.

He denied he was the author of the letters. Shapurji dictated a few lines to him and noticed that he wrote in a 'laboured fashion as if he wanted to make his handwriting as different as possible from that of the letters'.[13]

Others on Shapurji's watchlist included:

Holmes, a clerk at the office of Whitehouse & Sons, edge-tool makers, Bridgtown, who had had a quarrel with Brookes.

Albert Mears, a clerk at the same office, who was some time ago, often ordered off the premises by Brookes for getting his boy to steal tobacco.

George Greensill, a clerk at the office of J. P. Gardner (clerk to the justices, Cannock) who was said to have composed a public apology in the name of George Edalji and Fred Brookes.

Daniel Cotton, organist at Wyrley Church until Easter 1891. He left because Shapurji would not allow him to turn Fred Brookes out of the choir.

Was it the petty village rivalries that led to the vicious and threatening letters? No one would know.

In addition, there were:

Harry Stanton and Mrs Stanton and their sons, relations of Elizabeth Foster.

Elizabeth Foster (who had allegedly written the original letters in 1888) was also a suspect. Her two brothers William Foster and Jabez Foster lived at Cannock. The Fosters and Stantons were relations. Since one of the avowed objects of the letter was avenging the wrong supposed to have been done to Elizabeth Foster, could they have been involved?

Shapurji had given all the names to Sergeant Upton, who had not followed up any of the leads.

In 1914, G. A. Atkinson, a reporter for the *Evening Standard* wrote the book *G. H. Darby, Captain of the Wyrley Gang: An Investigation*. It had a preface by Conan Doyle and Anson. Atkinson tried to organise meetings with the Home Office in 1915 saying he had some information he would like to share, but the Home Office dismissed him as someone who simply wanted to make some money. No other suspect was ever investigated.

During the Second World War, George received the news that his office had been bombed and everything destroyed. Among the wreckage lay his prized bronze medal and certificates that he had always so proudly displayed on his wall.[14] He worked from another office in Argyle Square till 1951. His eyesight was deteriorating gradually, and like his father before him he was soon almost blind. Maud looked after him as she had looked after Shapurji. The siblings kept to themselves and not many neighbours were aware of the past notoriety of Maud's elder brother. In due course they received news about their estranged brother Horace. On 11 June 1952, he had died of leukaemia in a nursing home in Dublin. He was buried in the city under the name of Horace Edward Magee.

On 17 June 1953, after over five decades of strife, George passed away from a coronary thrombosis, his sister Maud by his side. He was seventy-seven.

Two years after his death, Maud received a call from London. It was from a council employee who had been excavating the rubble near George's bombed-out office in Southwark. He had found George's bronze Law Society medal and recognised his name inscribed on the back. He contacted Maud and returned the prized medal to her.[15]

Maud continued to write to the Home Office for compensation. Her last letter to Major Lloyd George, Home Secretary, was on 25 March 1956, in which she once again demanded compensation for the expenses and humiliation the family had suffered. Maud asked why a public inquiry had not been held and if the Home Office was aware that the Home Secretary at the time, Herbert Gladstone, had insisted on a private inquiry. She wanted to know if they were aware that one of the three members of the committee, Sir A. de Rutzer, was a cousin of Captain Anson, and that Sir Reginald Hardy's wife was a cousin of Gladstone. What hope was there for justice being done under such circumstances? she asked. Maud also enquired what secret information Anson had given to the Home Office, which the Home Office refused to divulge. 'Was it right or fair for Captain Anson to give secret information behind my brother's back?' she asked. Over half a century after the events, Maud's letters sounded almost desperate. One could sense that the trauma had never gone away. Perhaps Maud was living her final days in extreme poverty and desperately needed the money. But by then the Home Office was not interested in the George Edalji case any more. They informed her that there was no justification for reopening the matter at this date. Maud died in 1961. The last member of the Edalji family was buried after a simple funeral. She left a legacy for the upkeep of her parents' graves, but no instructions for the maintenance of her own grave and that of her brother.[16]

George Edalji never received compensation. The mystery of the Wyrley Ripper remained unsolved. The case was soon forgotten.

# Epilogue

It was one of the hottest days in July in the summer of 2019 when I found myself in the Hatfield Hyde Cemetery in Welwyn Garden City. Before me lay five acres of land covered with more than 4,000 graves and memorials. The cemetery had been opened in 1924, and the graves were a collection of old and new. Shiny granite headstones inscribed to loved ones sat next to old graves with worn-down headstones. Plastic flowers, candles and fresh flowers dotted the different graves. Some were well tended, others barely visible over the ground. There were a few Commonwealth War Graves, their stone distinct from the others, the inscriptions recalling lives that had been lost in the Second World War.

I had a rough map of the site where George was buried (it showed a single square marked 'B' near a rose garden), but there were no signposts and no way of telling where 'Plot B' was. Nor could I see a rose garden. There was no office onsite and no gardeners at work. I realised I would have to comb the whole graveyard searching for George's grave. My nineteen-year-old niece was with me, and we decided to do this together in an organised manner, going methodically through the plots. We were looking for old graves and untended ones: no one would have visited George's grave after Maud died. We were also looking for Maud's grave. Surely, she would be buried next to her brother?

Two hours later, we were still there, back where we had started. The afternoon sun was beating down relentlessly on us. I looked again at the slip of handwritten paper for any clues. Listed in the register of burials were the briefest details: George Edalji was entry number 1,691. Various columns mentioned his name, age, address and date of burial (20 June 1953). The service had been performed by Rev. K. Mitchell. The space labelled 'description and situation of grave space' was unhelpfully blank. I noticed another small entry – C 234 – it was the number of the grave.

For a brief moment, there was hope. Surely, if they were numbered, this could be easy. But few of the graves had numbers on them. I found an 'A', and a 'B', quite far apart and not in any particular order. Finally we noticed a 'C'.

'It has to be here,' I told my niece. 'We've got to look again.' We had spent nearly another hour combing the same area, going round in circles. No sign of George Edalji. Not one of the graves had his name on it.

We were ready to leave, when I looked at the area for one last time. Two graves had sunk into the grass. There was one small plot which just had grass. There may have been a grave there once. Could it have been here? my niece asked. I had no idea.

My eyes travelled along the graves again. We were definitely standing in Plot C. This was where George was buried. I simply had to find him. My eye rested on one grave, which was completely covered with bramble and ivy. In sheer desperation, I knelt by its side and started pulling at the ivy and weeds. There was a small headstone. The roots had gone into the stone and buried it. I kept pulling, removing the overgrowth. Finally I could see some carving. It was barely visible. With a piece of tissue I scrubbed the mud and dirt. Slowly, from the depths, emerged one word – THOMPSON. Suddenly, I felt a rush of adrenaline. I cleaned the word next to it, my niece now helping me. Another word – EDWARD.

'It's got to be him,' I shouted in excitement. 'His full name was GEORGE EDWARD THOMPSON EDALJI'. To a passer-by, we would have looked like two crazy women, frantically pulling at the weeds on a grave and scrubbing it. Luckily, there was no one to watch us. The cemetery was empty except for a lady sitting quietly in the distance. We carried on, our expectation heightened. The sun was burning my back. And then, from the corner of the stone, in the lightest of inscriptions, I read the word 'GEORGE'. My niece went to the other end of the line and uncovered 'EDALJI'. It felt like magic.

We did high-fives and momentarily collapsed on the grass. It had taken nearly four hours in the sweltering heat, but we had found George Edalji.

I went back to fetch a bottle of water, and anything I could find in the car boot: a sponge, more tissues/ hand sanitiser. I was determined to uncover the headstone of this sad and lonely man who had lived such a traumatic life, never fully redeemed. And, here he lay in a grave that could barely be traced. It was as if George Edalji was going to remain a mystery as much in death as in life. As I sat there cleaning his grave, I reflected on George's troubled life.

And then, slowly, the words on his gravestone emerged:

GEORGE EDWARD THOMPSON EDALJI
ELDEST SON OF REV SHAPURJI EDALJI
VICAR OF WYRLEY, STAFFS
DIED JUNE 17 1953, AGED 77
THE STRIFE IS OVER, THE BATTLE DONE
ALSO MAUD, SISTER OF GEORGE
PASSED ON DECEMBER 4 1961

Maud had been buried with her beloved brother. The single line from the sixteenth-century hymn defined George's life. Ironically, it was an Easter hymn: '*The strife is o'er, the battle done / The victory of life is won / The song of triumph has begun / Alleluia! Alleluia!*' Once again my mind travelled back to the photo of the family taken on Easter Day on the steps of the vicarage. They would have sung the hymn at the service conducted by Reverend Shapurji Edalji all those years ago. George's troubles would have begun soon after.

Maud's inscription on his grave was poignant; his strife was truly over. The remarkable life of the unremarkable George Edalji would end far away from the home of his ancestors in India and the village in Staffordshire where he was born. An obscure grave and a small inscription would be all that was left of the family story.

His case was considered one of the famous miscarriages of British justice, yet it is ironic that few today have heard of it. Sir Arthur Conan Doyle's 'J'Accuse' aimed at the British establishment caused a sensation at the time, but George Edalji did not go down in the history books as Alfred Dreyfus did. He was given a free pardon, but was never compensated. His whole life – and those of his family – was spent campaigning for justice. But the gates were firmly slammed shut, and the powers that be collectively pulled up the drawbridge. In five decades, through two World Wars and the end of Empire, George received nothing. At the end, he died in semi-poverty with his lonely and inconsolable sister by his side. The frayed net curtains at the window hid the story of a human tragedy.

He, however, left a legacy for the future, for others who may have been denied justice. His case led to the Criminal Appeal Act of 1907 and eventually the setting up of the Criminal Appeal Court. Perhaps, that would be the single contribution of George Edward Thompson Edalji, the son of an immigrant, born in England, but always a foreigner.

# Notes and References

ABBREVIATIONS

| | |
|---|---|
| ACD | Arthur Conan Doyle |
| PL | Portsmouth Library |
| TNA | The National Archives |
| HO | Home Office |
| SR | Staffordshire Records Office |
| BRL | Birmingham Reference Library |

INTRODUCTION

1 Arthur Conan Doyle, *Memories and Adventures*, Oxford University Press, Oxford, 1989 (1924), p. 217.

2 Sarvepalli Gopal (ed.), 'Jawaharlal Nehru to Motilal Nehru, 18 January 1907, London', in *Selected Works of Jawaharlal Nehru*, Series 1, Vol. 1, Nehru Memorial Fund, Delhi, 1972, p. 36.

3 Shrabani Basu, *Victoria & Abdul: The True Story of the Queen's Closest Confidant*, The History Press, Stroud, 2010.

4 Conan Doyle, *Memories and Adventures*, p. 215.

5 David Lammy, 'The Lammy Review', 8 September 2017. Available at https://www.gov.uk/government/publications/lammy-review-final-report.

PROLOGUE

1 *Illustrated London News*, October 1903.

2 George Edalji, 'My Own Story', *Pearson's Weekly*, 7 February 1907, TNA, HO 144/988/112737.

1  A BAPTISM IN BOMBAY

1 Shapurji was not certain of his year of birth and said it could be 1841 or 1842.

2  Now in Pakistan.

3  On 26 November 2008, terrorists would come on a boat to Apollo Bunder, walk under the Gateway of India and attack the Taj Hotel.

4  Christian converts in India at this time connected with the Protestant Missions numbered around 120,000. It was nearly equal to the number of Zoroastrians in India, Persia and other parts of the world during the same period.

5  John Wilson, *The Star of Bethlehem and the Magi from the East*, William Whyte, Edinburgh, 1857, p. 9.

6  Ibid., p. 132.

7  Charlotte Edalji to Sir George Lewis, 25 January 1904, Edalji files, BRL, 370797.

8  *Northampton Mercury*, 12 December 1868.

9  Ibid.

10 Roger Oldfield, *Outrage*, Vanguard Press, Cambridge, 2010, pp. 187–9.

11 Shrabani Basu, *Curry: The Story of Britain's Favourite Dish*, Sutton Publishing, Stroud, 2003 (1999), p. 128.

### 2 GREAT WYRLEY

1  Roger Oldfield, quoting from the Great Wyrley Parish register 1845–1886, SRO, D1215, in *Outrage*, Vanguard Press, Cambridge, 2010, p. 231.

2  Ibid.

3  Arthur Conan Doyle, *Memories and Adventures*, Oxford University Press, Oxford, 1989 (1924), p. 216.

4  Shompa Lahiri, *Indians in Britain: Anglo-Indian Encounters, Race and Identity, 1880–1930*, Routledge, Abingdon, 2013 (2000), p. 5.

5  Panikos Panayi, *Immigrants, Ethnicity & Racism in Britain 1815–1945*, Manchester University Press, Manchester, 1994, p. 38.

6  Chamion Caballero and Peter J. Aspinall, *Mixed Race Britain in the Twentieth Century*, Palgrave Macmillan, London, 2018, p. 2.

7  Shrabani Basu (ed.), *Re-Imagine: India-UK Cultural Relations in the 21st Century*, Bloomsbury India (British Council project), Delhi, 2014, pp. 1–4.

8  Charles Dickens, 'The Noble Savage', in *Household Words*, 11 June 1853.

9  David Olusoga, *Black and British: A Forgotten History*, Pan Macmillan, London, 2016, p. 412.

10 Gordon Weaver, *Conan Doyle and the Parson's Son*, Vanguard Press, Cambridge, 2006, p. 18.

### 3 LETTERS

1  *Gloucestershire Echo*, 15 January 1889.

2 Ibid.

3 Arthur Conan Doyle, *Memories and Adventures*, Oxford University Press, Oxford, 1989 (1924), p. 13.

4 Ibid., p. 25.

5 Ibid., p. 25.

6 Ibid., p. 26.

7 'The Original of Sherlock Holmes', Dr Harold Emery Jones, *Colliers*, 9 January 1904.

8 Andrew Lycett, *Conan Doyle: The Man who Created Sherlock Holmes*, Weidenfeld & Nicolson, London, 2007, p. 118.

9 *Birmingham Daily Post*, 20 January 1893.

10 Ibid.

11 S. Edalji, letter to *The Times*, 14 August 1895.

12 George Edalji, 'My Own Story', *Pearson's Weekly*, 7 February 1907, TNA, HO 144/988/112737.

## 4 A KEY AT THE DOORSTEP

1 A report by Upton to Anson, 19 December 1892, PL, ACD6/1/3/1.

2 Maud to Home Secretary Lloyd George, 8 February 1956, TNA, HO 45/24635.

3 A report by Upton to Anson, 19 December 1892, PL, ACD6/1/3/4.

4 George Edalji, 'My Own Story', *Pearson's Weekly*, 7 February 1907, TNA, HO 144/988/112737.

5 Ibid.

6 Andrew Lycett, *Conan Doyle: The Man Who Created Sherlock Holmes*, Weidenfeld & Nicolson, London, 2007, p. 149.

7 Ibid., p. 150.

8 Lord Salisbury in *The Times*, 1 December 1888.

9 Dinyar Pheroze Patel, 'The Grand Old Man: Dadabhai Naoroji and the Evolution of the Demand for Indian Self-Government', PhD dissertation, Harvard University, 2015. Available at https://dash.harvard.edu/handle/1/17467241.

10 *Funny Folks*, 15 December 1888.

11 *Punch*, 23 July 1892, p.33.

12 Fred Wynne to ACD, PL, ACD/6/7.

13 Fred Wynne to ACD, TNA, HO 144/988.

14 ACD's 'Statement of the Case Against Royden Sharp', May 1907, PL, ACD/6/7.

15 *Lichfield Mercury*, 3 and 10 March 1893.

## 5 THE VICARAGE UNDER SIEGE

1 *Case Submitted to Secretary of State for Home in the matter of George Edalji*, n.d. possibly February 1904, Edalji files, SRO, A3/A/1/6.
2 Ibid.
3 Ibid.
4 *Lichfield Mercury*, 31 March 1893.
5 Gregory B. Lee, quoting from the *Liverpool Review*, 9/1 (January 1934) p. 12 in 'Dirty, Diseased and Demented: The Irish, the Chinese, and Racist Representation', *Journal of Global Cultural Studies, December 2017*. Available at http://journals.openedition.org/transtexts/1011; DOI.
6 Ibid.
7 Andrew Lycett, *Conan Doyle: The Man Who Created Sherlock Holmes*, Weidenfeld & Nicolson, London, 2007, p. 185.
8 Maud to Lloyd George, 8 February 1956, TNA, HO 45/24635.
9 Lycett, *Conan Doyle*, p. 197.

## 6 A PERIOD OF SILENCE

1 George Edalji, 'My Own Story', *Pearson's Weekly*, 7 February 1907, TNA, HO 144/988/112737.
2 Arthur Conan Doyle, 'The Case for Mr Edalji', *Daily Telegraph*, 11 January 1907.
3 *Cannock Chase Courier*, 26 January 1901.
4 Shrabani Basu, *Victoria & Abdul: The True Story of the Queen's Closest Confidant*, The History Press, Stroud, 2010, p. 183.
5 George Edalji to Stone, 29 December 1902, Edalji files, BRL, 370797.

## 7 THE KILLING FIELDS

1 *Daily Mail*, (n.d.) June 1903, quoted in *Pearson's Weekly*, 7 February 1907, TNA, HO 144/988/112737.
2 Letter to ACD from a 'well-wisher', 23 May 1907, TNA, HO 144/989.
3 *Case Submitted to Secretary of State for Home in the Matter of George Ernest Thompson Edalji*, petition submitted to the Home Secretary, n.d. possibly February 1904, Edalji files, SRO, A3/A/1/6.
4 George Edalji, 'My Own Story', *Pearson's Weekly*, 7 February 1907, TNA, HO 144/988/112737.
5 Ibid.

## 8 A PUBLIC SPECTACLE

1 George Edalji, 'My Own Story', *Pearson's Weekly*, 7 February 1907, TNA, HO 144/988/112737.

2  Ibid.
3  Ibid.

## 9 A TRIAL IN STAFFORDSHIRE

1  *Lichfield Mercury*, 4 September 1903.
2  *Sunderland Daily Echo*, 5 September 1903.
3  Shapurji Edalji, *A Miscarriage of Justice: The Case of George Edalji*, United Press Association, London, 1905, p. 8.
4  Internal Home Office note: M. D. Chalmers to Staffordshire court official with instructions about Yelverton's application for the names of the jury, 13 Nov 1903, Edalji files, SRO, 112/737/7.
5  Ruth Paley, ed., *Justice in Eighteenth-Century Hackney: The Justicing Notebook of Henry Norris and the Hackney Petty Sessions Book*, vol. 28, London Record Society, 1991, item 218. Available at https://www.british-history.ac.uk/london-record-soc/vol28/pp. 32–46.
6  Chamion Caballero, 'Inter-Raciality in Early Twentieth Century Britain: Challenging Traditional Conceptualists Through Accounts of "Ordinariness"', in *Genealogy*, 17 April 2019, 3(2), 2019, Vol 21. Available at https://www.mdpi.com/2313-5778/3/2/21.
7  Chamion Caballero and Peter J. Aspinall, *Mixed Race Britain in the Twentieth Century*, Palgrave Macmillan, London, 2018, p. 99.
8  George Edalji, 'My Own Story', *Pearson's Weekly*, 7 February 1907, TNA, HO 144/988/112737.
9  *Staffordshire Advertiser*, 23 October 1903.
10  *Case Submitted to Secretary of State for Home in the Matter of George Edward Thompson Edalji*, petition to Home Office, n.d., possibly February 1904, Edalji files, SRO, A3/A/1/6.
11  *Lichfield Mercury*, 23 October 1903.
12  Ibid.

## 10 THE CASE FOR THE DEFENCE

1  Case Files of George Edalji, SRO, A3/A/1/6.
2  Ibid.
3  *Lichfield Mercury*, 23 October 1903.

## 11 PRISONS AND CAMPAIGNS

1  *Wolverhampton Express & Star*, 26 October 1903.
2  Case Files of George Edalji, SRO, A3/A/1/6.
3  A. D. Denning to Charlotte Edalji, 31 October 1903, PL, ACD/6/7.
4  Statement from Henry Sutton, Ludlow, 31 October 1903, PL, ACD/6/7.

5 Statement by S. Macgregor Grier, 3 November 1903, PL, ACD/6/7.

6 *Lichfield Mercury*, 26 August 1904.

7 Charlotte Edalji to Sir George Lewis, 25 January 1904, Edalji files, BRL, 370797.

8 Mary Sancta to George Lewis, 27 January 1904, Edalji files, BRL, 370797.

9 Edalji files, SRO, A3/A/1/6.

10 Internal letter, Home Office, SRO, 112/737/7.

11 *Lichfield Mercury*, 8 January 1904.

12 *Walsall Advertiser*, 21 November 1903.

13 *Manchester Courier*, 27 August 1904.

14 Edward Evershed, Hon. Sec., Birmingham Law Society, to R. D. Yelverton, 3 November 1903, Edalji files, BRL, 370797.

15 Petition from George Edalji to Home Secretary, 27 February 1904, Lewes Prison, TNA, HO 144/988.

16 Anson to M. D. Chalmers, Undersecretary of State, 12 December 1904, TNA, HO 144/990.

17 *Walsall Advertiser*, 25 March 1905.

18 Ibid., 28 January 1905.

19 Ibid., 21 October 1905.

20 *Truth*, 12 January 1905.

21 Shapurji Edalji, *A Miscarriage of Justice: The Case of George Edalji*, United Press Association, London, 1905, Preface.

22 *Lichfield Mercury*, 13 October 1905.

23 Jabez Spencer Balfour, *My Prison Life*, Chapman & Hall, London, 1907, pp. 67–8.

24 Gordon Weaver, *Conan Doyle and the Parson's Son*, Vanguard Press, Cambridge, p. 206.

25 *Lichfield Mercury*, 12 October 1906.

26 *Herald*, 20 October 1906.

27 Edalji to Anson, 21 December 1906, PL, ACD/6/7.

28 The Sherlock Holmes museum in London still gets letters addressed to Holmes from all around the world to help solve crimes and personal problems. These are kept on display at the museum, at 221b Baker Street, London NW1 6XE.

### 12 A MEETING WITH GEORGE

1 Arthur Conan Doyle, *Memories and Adventures*, Oxford University Press, Oxford, 1989 (1924), p. 215.

2 Ibid., p. 222.

3  John Dickson Carr, *The Life of Arthur Conan Doyle*, Carroll & Graf Publishers, New York, 2003 (1949), p. 158.
4  *Umpire*, November 1906.
5  *Daily Telegraph*, 11 January 1907.

## 13  ELEMENTARY!

1  Arthur Conan Doyle, *Memories and Adventures*, Oxford University Press, Oxford, 1989 (1924), p. 218.
2  Anson to ACD, December 1906, TNA, HO 144/989.
3  Ibid.
4  The account of the letters of 1888 and 1892–95 was published in *Truth* magazine in 1905, but Arthur Conan Doyle's article had a far larger reach.
5  Letter in the *Daily Telegraph*, 17 January 1907.
6  'The case of George Edalji: A Question for Ophthalmologists', letter in the *British Medical Journal*, 13 January 1907.
7  *Aberdeen Daily Journal*, 17 January 1907.
8  Letters from ophthalmologists submitted by ACD to Home Office, January 1907, TNA, HO 144/990/112737.

## 14  MARTIN MOLTON

1  Anson to Macnaghten, 14 January 1907, TNA, HO 144/988/112737.
2  Ibid.
3  H. B. Simpson to Anson, 23 January 1907, PL, ACD/6/7.
4  *Yorkshire Post*, 15 March 1907.
5  Ibid.
6  Romer to Gladstone, 15 February 1907, TNA/HO/144/988/112737.

## 15  A FLAWED PARDON

1  Press cutting, 'Mr Edalji's Pardon', TNA, HO 144/990/112737.
2  *Nottingham Evening Post*, 18 May 1907.
3  Ibid.
4  Simpson notes on Edalji's letters, 3 February 1907, TNA, HO 144/988/112737.
5  Hansard, 28 May 1907.
6  Ibid.
7  *Daily Telegraph*, 20 May 1907.

## 16 WHO WROTE THE LETTERS?

1 ACD to Mary Doyle, 27 January 1907, quoted in Roger Oldfield, *Outrage*, Vanguard Press, Cambridge, 2010, p. 111.
2 *Daily Telegraph*, 20 May 1907.
3 Ibid., 23 May 1907.
4 Ibid., 27 May 1907.
5 PL, ACD/6/7.
6 *Daily Telegraph*, 29 May 1907.
7 Ibid., 18 July 1907.
8 Ibid., 15 July 1907.
9 Ibid., 20 July 1907.

## 17 ROYDEN SHARP

1 *The Case Against Royden Sharp*, PL, ACD/6/13/3/2.
2 Ibid.
3 Letter from a 'well-wisher' to ACD, 23 May 1907, PL, ACD/6/7.
4 *Yorkshire Evening Post*, 22 August 1907.
5 *Lincolnshire Echo*, 27 August 1907.
6 *Lincolnshire Chronicle*, 30 August 1907.
7 *Lichfield Mercury*, 30 August 1907.
8 *Memories and Adventures*, p.221.
9 *Lichfield Mercury*, 16 August 1907.

## 18 CONAN DOYLE VS ANSON

1 ACD to Anson, 29 August 1907, PL, ACD/6/7.
2 Ibid., PL, ACD/6/7.
3 ACD to Anson, 30 August 1907, PL, ACD/6/7.
4 Ibid., 31 August 1907.
5 Ibid.
6 Ibid., 4 September 1907.
7 Ibid., 5 September 1907.
8 Anson to Greatorex, 10 September 1907, PL, ACD/6/7.
9 ACD to Anson, 4 September 1907, PL, ACD/6/7.
10 Ibid., PL, ACD/6/7.
11 Anson to T. H. Sharp, 4 September 1907, PL, ACD/6/7.
12 Ibid., 6 September 1907.
13 ACD to Anson, 8 September 1907, PL, ACD/6/7.
14 Ibid., 11 September 1907, PL, ACD/6/7.
15 Anson to Greatorex, 13 September 1907, PL, ACD/6/7.

16 Ibid., 29 September 1907.
17 ACD to Arrowsmith, 12 September 1907, PL ACD/6/7.
18 ACD to Arrowsmith, n.d., PL, ACD/6/7.
19 Beaumont to Anson, 10 September 1907, PL, ACD/6/7.
20 Anson to Beaumont, 13 September 1907, PL, ACD/6/7.
21 Beaumont to Anson, 24 September 1907, PL, ACD/6/7.
22 Anson to Beaumont, 24 September 1907, PL, ACD/6/7.
23 Beaumont to Anson, 26 September 1907, PL, ACD/6/7.
24 ACD to Anson, 14 September 1907, PL, ACD/6/7.
25 *Daily Graphic*, 16 September 1907.

### 19 THE BAKER STREET IRREGULARS

1 John Dickson Carr, *The Life of Sir Arthur Conan Doyle*, Carroll & Graf Publishers, New York, 2003 (1949), p. 194.
2 Arthur Conan Doyle, *Memories and Adventures*, Oxford University Press, Oxford, 1989 (1924), p. 219.
3 Geo Young to ACD, 20 September 1907, PL, ACD/6/7.
4 ACD to Home Office, 7 October 1907, PL, ACD/6/7.
5 Blackwell to Anson, 12 October 1907, PL, ACD/6/7.
6 ACD to Home Office, 7 October 1907, PL, ACD/6/7.
7 Conan Doyle to Anson, 8 October 1907, PL, ACD/6/7.
8 Anson to G. W. Young, City Marshal, Long Beach, California, 13 October 1907, PL, ACD/6/7.
9 Young to Anson, 17 October 1907, PL, ACD/6/7.
10 Ibid., 15 October 1907.
11 ACD to Anson from Rome, 11 October 1907, PL, ACD/6/7.
12 ACD to Anson, 16 October 1907, PL, ACD/6/7.
13 Anson to Greatorex, 17 October 1907, PL, ACD/6/7.
14 Anson to Greatorex, 24 Octover 1907, PL, ACD/6/7.
15 Beaumont to Anson, 7 October 1907, PL, ACD/6/7.
16 Anson to Beaumont, 8 October 1907, PL, ACD/6/7.
17 Beaumont to Anson, 9 October 1907, PL, ACD/6/7.
18 Anson to Beaumont, 10 October 1907, PL, ACD/6/7.
19 Anson to Arrowsmith, PL, ACD/6/7.
20 Arrowsmith to Anson, 15 October 1907, PL, ACD/6/7.
21 Anson to Arrowsmith, 16 October 1907, PL, ACD/6/7.
22 Anson to Arrowsmith, 17 October 1907, PL, ACD/6/7.

### 20 FRANK SHARP

1 Frank Sharp to Tom, 27 July 1904, PL, ACD/6/7.

2   Beatrice Sharp to Anson, 28 October 1907, PL, ACD/6/7.
3   Beatrice Sharp to Anson, 28 October 1907, PL, ACD/6/7.
4   Anson to Sopwith, 26 October 1907, PL, ACD/6/7.
5   Beatrice to Anson, 3 November 1907, PL, ACD/6/7.
6   Ibid., 4 November 1907.
7   Geo Young to Anson from Long Beach California, 2 November 1907, PL, ACD/6/7.
8   Anson to Geo Young, 7 December 1907, PL, ACD/6/7.
9   Beaumont to Anson, 24 November 1907, PL, ACD/6/7.
10  Ibid., 26 November 1907.
11  Anson to Beaumont, 10 December 1907, PL, ACD/6/7.
12  Arthur Conan Doyle, *Memories and Adventures*, Oxford University Press, Oxford, 1989 (1924), p. 222.
13  *Yorkshire Evening Post*, 28 November 1907.
14  Anson to Beaumont, 27 January 1908, PL, ACD/6/8/15/3.
15  F. Sharp to Anson, 21 January 1908, Santa Ana, PL, ACD/6/8/9/1.

## 21 ENDGAME

1   'Correspondence with Sir A. Doyle', Anson's confidential report, May 1920, PL, ACD6/13/2.
2   Anson to Hatton, 3 September 1907, PL, ACD6/7/32/1.
3   Anson to Home Office, 25 January 1907, PL, ACD6/14/5/2.
4   Anson to Blackwell, 26 January 1908, PL, ACD6/6/8.
5   Anson's notes on ACD letter, 8 October 1909, PL, ACD6/14/16/25.
6   Anson's notes on Sir A. C. Doyle's Statement against Royden Sharp, PL, ACD6/13/9/1.
7   Anson report, 9 October 1907, PL, ACD6/13/5.
8   *Daily Telegraph*, 7 August 1911.
9   ACD in *the Daily Telegraph*, 10 August 1911.
10  ACD to Anson, 11 January 1911, PL, ACD6/10.
11  Anson to Beaumont, 10 December 1907, PL, ACD6/6/7.
12  Anson to Chalmers, Undersecretary of State, Home Office, 9 February 1911, PL, ACD6/10/17/3.

## 22 AFTERMATH

1   *Daily Mail*, 4 September 1912.
2   Anson to Chief Constable Smith, Liverpool, 26 September 1913, PL, ACD6/12/6/3.

3  Report by Superintendent W. Grove to Anson, 13 September 1913, PL, ACD6/12/3/1.

4  Shrabani Basu, *For King and Another Country: Indian Soldiers on the Western Front 1914–18*, Bloomsbury, London, 2015, p. 152.

5  *Cannock Chase Courier*, 13 July 1918, quoted in Roger Oldfield, *Outrage*, Vanguard Press, Cambridge, 2010, p. 282.

6  Alan Jones, *The Edaljis: A Family in Turmoil*, Cheslyn Hay & District Local History Society, 2015, p. 91.

7  Ibid, p. 91.

8  Anson report, 'For Police Information', June 1920, PL, ACD6/13/11.

9  Jones, *The Edaljis*, p. 90.

10 Arthur Conan Doyle, *Memories and Adventures*, Oxford University Press, Oxford, 1989 (1924), p. 220.

11 *Daily Express*, 7 November 1934.

12 TNA, HO 45/24635.

13 Shapurji to Anson, 22 April 1893, TNA, HO 144/990/112737.

14 Oldfield, *Outrage*, p. 292.

15 Jones, *The Edaljis*, p. 73.

16 Ibid., p. 91.

# Newspapers and periodicals

*Aberdeen Daily Journal*
*Birmingham Daily Gazette*
*Birmingham Daily Post*
*Cannock Chase Courier*
*Daily Express*
*Daily Gazette*
*Daily Graphic*
*Daily Mail*
*Daily Telegraph*
*Funny Folks*
*Genealogy*
*Gloucestershire Echo*
Hansard
*Herald*
*Household Words*
*Idler*

*Illustrated London News*
*Journal of Global Cultural Studies*
*Lichfield Mercury*
*Lincolnshire Chronicle*
*Lincolnshire Echo*
*Lippincott's Monthly Magazine*
*Manchester Courier*
*Medical Press Journal*
*Midland Express*
*Northampton Mercury*
*Nottingham Evening Post*
*Pall Mall Gazette*
*Pearson's Weekly*
*Publishing Research Quarterly*
*Punch*
*Staffordshire Advertiser*
*Strand Magazine*
*The Times*
*Truth magazine*
*Umpire*
*Walsall Advertiser*
*Westminster Gazette*
*Wolverhampton Express & Star*
*Yorkshire Evening Post*
*Yorkshire Post*

# Further Reading

Atkinson, G. A., *G. H. Darby, Captain of the Wyrley Gang: An Investigation*, T. Kirby & Sons, Walsall, 1914

Balfour, Jabez Spencer, *My Prison Life*, Chapman & Hall, London, 1907

Basu, Shrabani, *Curry: The Story of Britain's Favourite Dish*, Sutton Publishing, Stroud, 2003 (HarperCollins Publishers India, 1999)

—, *Victoria & Abdul: The Extraordinary True Story of the Queen's Closest Confidant*, The History Press, Stroud, 2010

—, *For King and Another Country: Indian Soldiers on the Western Front 1914–18*, Bloomsbury, London, 2015

— (ed.), *Re-Imagine: India-UK Cultural Relations in the 21st Century*, Bloomsbury India (British Council project), London, 2014

Caballero, Chamion and Aspinall, Peter J., *Mixed Race Britain in the Twentieth Century*, Palgrave Macmillan, London, 2018

Carr, John Dickson, *The Life of Sir Arthur Conan Doyle*, Carroll & Graf, New York, 2003 (John Murray, London, 1949)

Conan Doyle, Arthur, *Memories and Adventures*, Oxford University Press, Oxford, 1989 (Hodder & Stoughton, London, 1924)

—, *The Cases of Edalji and Slater*, Cambridge Scholars Publishing, Newcastle upon Tyne, 2009

Costello, Peter, *Conan Doyle: Detective*, Carroll & Graf, New York, 1991

Edalji, George E. T., *Railway Law for 'the Man in the Train'*, Wilson's Legal Handy Books, London, 1901

Edalji, Shapurji, *A Miscarriage of Justice: The Case of George Edalji*, United Press Association, London, 1905

Fox, Margalit, *Conan Doyle for the Defence*, Profile Books, London, 2018

Gillies, Mary Ann, 'A. P. Watt, Literary Agent', *Publishing Research Quarterly*, vol. 9, 1993, pp. 20–33. Also available at https://www.academia.edu/26848974/A_P_Watt_literary_agent

Gopal, Sarvepalli (ed.), *Selected Works of Jawaharlal Nehru*, Series 1, Vol. 1, Nehru Memorial Fund, Delhi, 1972

Jones, Adam, *The Edaljis: A Family in Turmoil*, Cheslyn Hay & District Local History Society, 2015

Lahiri, Shompa, *Indians in Britain: Anglo-Indian Encounters, Race and Identity 1880–1930*, Routledge, Abingdon, 2013 (Frank Cass, London, 2003)

Lycett, Andrew, *Conan Doyle: The Man who Created Sherlock Holmes*, Weidenfeld & Nicolson, London, 2007

Miller, Russell, *The Adventures of Arthur Conan Doyle*, Harvill Secker, London, 2008

Oldfield, Roger, *Outrage*, Vanguard Press, Cambridge, 2010

Olusoga, David, *Black and British: A Forgotten History*, Pan Macmillan, London, 2016

Panayi, Panikos, *Immigrants, Ethnicity and Racism in Britain 1815–1945*, Manchester University Press, Manchester, 1994

Patel, Dinyar Phiroze, 'The Grand Old Man: Dadabhai Naoroji and the Evolution of the Demand for Indian Self-Government', PhD dissertation, Harvard University, 2015. Accessed through DASH

Pugh, Brian W., *A Chronology of the Life of Arthur Conan Doyle*, MX Publishing, London, 2009

Ridgway, Roland, *The Bygone Days of Cheslyn Hay*, Cheslyn Hay Local History Society, 2002

Vadgama, Kusoom, *India in Britain*, Robert Royce, London, 1984

Visram, Rozina, *Asians in Britain: 400 Years of History*, Pluto Press, London, 1997

—, *Ayahs, Lascars and Princes: The Story of Indians in Britain 1700–1947*, Pluto Press, London, 1986

Weaver, Gordon, *Conan Doyle and the Parson's Son*, Vanguard Press, Cambridge, 2006

Wilson, John, *The Star of Bethlehem and the Magi from the East*, William Whyte, Edinburgh, 1856

# Acknowledgements

This book was finished over the long months of the coronavirus pandemic, and I am grateful to all those who worked in difficult circumstances to make it happen. My thanks to the NHS, the key workers, the supermarket shelf-stackers, my local pharmacist and everybody who kept us fed and cared for during this time. Without your selfless work, this book would not have been possible.

I would like to thank Alexandra Pringle, executive publisher at Bloomsbury, for believing in me and giving me the confidence to go forth and explore a dark mystery. I could have no better editor than Faiza Khan, who immediately saw the broader perspective of the book and helped me to flesh out the depths of the story. Thanks to my copy-editor, Charlotte Norman, who meticulously went through my text and removed all the gremlins, and to Sarah Ruddick, senior managing editor at Bloomsbury. My thanks also to the design team at Bloomsbury, who gave me a dream cover, and to Jonathan Ring for his patience in taking my author photo.

A book like this is almost entirely based on archival research, and I am most grateful to Michael Gunton, senior archivist at Portsmouth Library, for helping me to access the Arthur Conan Doyle files. Many thanks to the archivists at Staffordshire Records Office – Tim Groom, Liz Street and Joanna Terry – for helping to locate documents and images on the George Edalji case. Thanks also to the archivist at the William Salt Library in Stafford. I am grateful to the archivist at the Birmingham Central Library for access to the George Edalji papers.

The National Archives in Kew are always a pleasure to work in, and I am grateful to the archivists for help accessing the Home Office papers on the Edalji case.

Many thanks to the author and former schoolteacher in Great Wyrley, Roger Oldfield, who has himself written about the Edalji case, for helping me locate images. My thanks to the wonderful and enthusiastic members of the Cheslyn Hay and Great Wyrley Historical Society and its chair, Malcolm Podmore, for helping me with images and insights into local history.

For being my rock of support, I have to thank my agent, Valerie Hoskins, who read my first draft, provided useful inputs and sent the book into the publishing world.

Thanks to my daughters, Sanchita and Tanaya, the first sounding board for all my stories, my frankest critics, my helper elves and my technical team, all rolled into one. I am blessed to have them by my side.

Many thanks to my niece Meghna for accompanying me to Welwyn Garden City on one of the hottest days of 2019 and helping me search for George Edalji's grave. I could not have done this alone.

To my extended family in India – my mother, my sisters and brothers-in-law – I can only say a big thank-you for always believing in me and providing a space to recharge my batteries over the years. Sadly, my father passed away while I was researching the book. I am grateful for everything he taught me.

Thank you to my friends, who have always given me their unquestioning support in all my ventures. Our Zoom chats over the lockdown were a much-needed energy boost that kept me going.

*The Mystery of the Parsee Lawyer* is here because of all of you.

Shrabani Basu
London, October 2020

# Picture Credits

Every effort has been made to trace copyright holders and obtain permission to reproduce the images in this book. The publisher would be glad to correct any errors or omissions in future editions.

The National Archives (TNA): pp. x–xi, 50, 57, 59, 60, 62, 65, 70, 88, 141, 182, 199
arthur-conan-doyle.com: pp. 159, 172, 191

## Plates

The Cheslyn Hay History Society: 1.1, 1.2 (above), 1.8 (below), 2.6
Author's collection: 1.2 (below), 2.8 (above and below)
The National Archives (TNA): 1.3 (below), 2.4, 2.5 (above)
Staffordshire Records Office: 1.4 (above and below), 1.5 (above and below), 1.6 (above and below), 1.7, 1.8 (above)
Portsmouth History Centre: 2.1, 2.3
*Express & Star*: 2.5 (below)
Trustees of the William Salt Library, Stafford: 2.7

# A Note on the Author

Shrabani Basu is a journalist and author. Her books include *Victoria & Abdul: The Extraordinary True Story of the Queen's Closest Confidant*, now a major motion picture, *Spy Princess: The Life of Noor Inayat Khan* and *For King and Another Country: Indian Soldiers on the Western Front, 1914–18*. In 2010, she set up the Noor Inayat Khan Memorial Trust and campaigned for a memorial for the Second World War heroine, which was unveiled by Princess Anne in London in November 2012. In August 2020 she was invited by English Heritage to unveil the Blue Plaque for Noor Inayat Khan in London.

# A Note on the Type

The text of this book is set in Bembo, which was first used in 1495 by the Venetian printer Aldus Manutius for Cardinal Bembo's *De Aetna*. The original types were cut for Manutius by Francesco Griffo. Bembo was one of the types used by Claude Garamond (1480–1561) as a model for his Romain de l'Université, and so it was a forerunner of what became the standard European type for the following two centuries. Its modern form follows the original types and was designed for Monotype in 1929.